UNFETTER

Tanuja Sodhi is a reputed health coach, life coach, motivational speaker and author of *Parenting in the Age of McDonald's* and *Raising a True Winner*. She is a veteran Indian Naval officer from the first batch of women officers. She is a graduate from the Institute for Integrative Nutrition, US and Optimize, US. She has earned her master's degrees in business administration and English literature. She is also a certified fitness instructor from Reebok.

Unfetter: Heal Your Mind, Body and Spirit is the result of her burning desire to help women be their healthiest and happiest selves. It also serves as an inspiration for them to dream big, 'unfetter' their spirit and relentlessly pursue their aspirations.

Tanuja is an avid marathoner and an Ironman 70.3 triathlete. When not behind her writing desk, she can be found at the gym strengthening her muscles, running on the roads or trekking in the mountains. You can reach her at tanujasodhi.com, on Instagram @itanujasodhi and on her Facebook page 'Wellness Hub by Tanuja Sodhi'.

Praise for the book

An inspiring and pragmatic guide to wellness and mindfulness, Tanuja Sodhi brings real-life experiences of others as well as her own to this handbook. Comprehensive and practical, and backed by extensive research and simple, doable tips and strategies, *Unfetter* is a must-read for anyone seeking to realign themselves physically, mentally and emotionally.

—**Kiran Manral**, author and journalist

If you're looking for a holistic approach for augmenting your health and wellness, this book is for you! Through *Unfetter*, Tanuja has crafted a compelling guidebook with easy-to-follow yet life-altering tools for achieving excellent overall health and lasting happiness.

—**Nikhil Arora**,
Author and Managing Director, GoDaddy India

UNFETTER

HEAL YOUR MIND, BODY AND SPIRIT

Tanuja Sodhi

RUPA

Published by
Rupa Publications India Pvt. Ltd 2022
7/16, Ansari Road, Daryaganj
New Delhi 110002

Sales Centres:
Allahabad Bengaluru Chennai
Hyderabad Jaipur Kathmandu
Kolkata Mumbai

Copyright © Tanuja Sodhi 2022

The views and opinions expressed in this book are the author's own and the facts are as reported by her which have been verified to the extent possible, and the publishers are not in
any way liable for the same.

All rights reserved.
No part of this publication may be reproduced, transmitted, or stored in a retrieval system, in any form or by any means, electronic, mechanical, photocopying, recording or otherwise, without the prior permission of the publisher.

ISBN: 978-93-5520-412-7

Second impression 2022

10 9 8 7 6 5 4 3 2

The moral right of the author has been asserted.

Printed in India

This book is sold subject to the condition that it shall not, by way of trade or otherwise, be lent, resold, hired out, or otherwise circulated, without the publisher's prior consent, in any form of binding or cover other than that in which it is published.

To my mom...you were the first woman I opened my eyes to...
We have lots to catch up on.
Let's do it again in another lifetime.

Contents

Foreword by Kiran Bedi — ix

Introduction — xi

SECTION I

1. Understanding Mental, Emotional and Physical Well-Being — 3
2. Mindfulness — 13
3. Nutrition — 47
4. Physical Fitness — 84
5. Sleep — 125
6. Social Connections — 142

Inspirational Stories of Real Women — 153

SECTION II

7. Purpose of Life — 175
8. Happiness Habits — 203
9. Self-Care — 218
10. Female Hormones — 227

Inspirational Stories of Real Women — 243

Conclusion — 257
Acknowledgements — 260
Endnotes — 262

Foreword

In today's highly competitive world, a staggering number of people are unhappy. Even many successful high-achievers feel utterly unfulfilled. Stress emanating from this fast-paced modern life can manifest itself in the form of mental, emotional or physical agony. As a consequence, people try to fill the deep void in their lives through transient quick fixes such as popping pills, seeking external validation or even binge eating. *Unfetter* is Tanuja's endeavour to light up the path towards sustainable well-being and happiness by prodding you to review your lifestyle, 'go inwards', identify the root cause of your suffering, and then, arm you with numerous time-tested, holistic interventions to alleviate that suffering. The wide repertoire of tools she offers may appear deceptively simple, but have the potential to transform your life in the most positive way.

The foundational concept of the book is that personal well-being and happiness are inside jobs and we can be our own best healers if we give ourselves half a chance. The book expands on the thought that health and fulfilment are the by-products of a fine balance between the crucial domains of life, such as nutrition, exercise, relationships, vocation, self-care, mindfulness and spiritual practices. Interestingly, it even touches upon the criticality of discovering our true purpose in life in order to feel fulfilled. Tanuja emphasizes the urgent need to 'start living in alignment with our soul goals' as one of the main ingredients that can make life so much more meaningful.

Through *Unfetter*, she lays out an easy yet powerful road map to transformation by weaving together a tapestry of many life-changing routines and rituals along with step-by-step guidelines on how to use them for optimal effect. What makes the book highly relatable, credible and inspiring is the interweaving of her own life experiences and various real-life stories of ordinary yet gritty women who have overcome extraordinary challenges and risen from their own ashes like a phoenix. These stories serve as beacons of hope and courage when the going gets tough. The heady amalgam of result-oriented tools and real-life stories render true heart and soul to this book.

Kiran Bedi
Former Lieutenant Governor, Puducherry
8 March 2022

Introduction

There is freedom waiting for you, on the breezes of the sky.
And you ask, 'What if I fall?'
Oh, but my darling, 'What if you fly?'

—Erin Hanson, American artist

As the doors of the intensive care unit (ICU) swung open and she was being rushed to the operation theatre, Reema's entire life flashed before her eyes. She had just turned 38, and instead of being at the peak of her health and enjoying life, here she was, much to her own disbelief, fighting for dear life.

Reema had suffered a stroke while she was working late as usual. Of late, there had been too many late evenings and late nights spent working. After all, she was very passionate about her work. And aren't we supposed to give our 100 per cent to our jobs if we're passionate about them? Besides, she had to hustle harder this year to finally get the promotion that she had been missing for a couple of years now.

Apart from the 12-13 hours a day that she put into her professional commitments, which included commute, she spent a chunk of the remaining time in a flurry of activities, such as cooking, folding washed laundry, making to-do lists and then squeezing in some quality time to check in with her daughter if she needed help with her studies.

Although Reema juggled her professional and family life with aplomb, deep down, she always nurtured a desire to join a Zumba class, and maybe, go on a day-long trek with some of her colleagues who were regular hikers. And yes, she did want to squeeze in some time for a brisk walk every day, go on a dinner date with her husband, go for a relaxing foot massage that her colleague had raved about or meet her school friend—something she had been postponing for months now. There was a time when she wanted to enrol in classical singing classes as she had been a fairly good singer during her school and college days.

While it had been almost impossible to integrate these activities into her frantic schedule, she hoped that the chance would finally arrive after her daughter got into middle school in a year's time. She would often eat on the go, quickly grabbing breakfast as she rushed to the office, or simply order pizza for dinner if her presentations for the next day needed last-minute, late-night edits.

Unsurprisingly, around the time of her annual appraisal, Reema's stress levels had skyrocketed, with migraines and high blood pressure adding to the array of health issues she had started experiencing lately. As it were, she could only afford five hours of sleep at night, but the tension around the upcoming promotion chewed away even that paltry amount of shut-eye. She had been mulling over seeing a doctor, but where was the time?

Tears welled up in her eyes as she stared at the bright lights overhead in the operation theatre. She was scared and nervous. A feeling of deep regret and resentment started seeping through her at the realization of having done nothing yet to feed her soul.

She said a silent prayer, almost begging the powers above

to give her a second chance. She implored God desperately, explaining that she had hardly accomplished anything in her life yet. How could she leave the world feeling totally unfulfilled? How would her young daughter cope without a mother? How could she be hurtling towards the end of her life so early? It just seemed too unfair.

Suddenly, the well-meaning advice from fit and healthy well-wishers surfaced from the deep recesses of her mind. Many had warned her of the dire consequences of having unhealthy eating habits and a non-existent exercise regime. She remembered the conversation with her neighbour who had suggested yoga with pranayama—to which she had mindlessly given a polite nod, before quickly ejecting that piece of information to her brain's junk folder.

As these incidents flashed through her mind, she felt a sudden and desperate urge to start living authentically and joyously this time, if given another chance. *Was it too late now?* she wondered.

There are innumerable Reemas amidst us, moving at the same dizzying speed, unable to press the 'pause' button and reflect on what it is they're seeking to achieve in life. They don a variety of avatars—ranging from corporate leaders to busy homemakers and caretakers. Surely, this type of life is not the epitome of the health and happiness they're all seeking.

Happiness cannot be an outcome of a skewed approach, such as being successful in our careers at the cost of various other crucial areas of our lives, or juggling multiple roles incessantly as homemakers and caretakers without pausing to indulge in some self-care. While all the above may be essential elements of our roles in this world, they're individual pieces of a big puzzle called life, which is made up of happiness components, such as health (physical, emotional and mental), social connections (relationships, social life and community), nourishing food, movement (physical activity), spirituality (connecting to one's spirit, mindfulness, faith, etc.), rest and recovery (sleep and quiet time), primary work or vocation (career, household management, etc.), creativity, and learning and personal growth (via education, reading, exploring and having healthy curiosity). Overemphasizing any one or two of the above, and neglecting the rest, would topple the general balance of life. The recipe of a happy life is an amalgamation of all the above ingredients in balanced measures.

Since we're all unique beings, you may say that happiness would have different connotations for different people. I completely agree! We are all 'bio-individuals', a term coined by Joshua Rosenthal, the founder and director of the Institute for Integrative Nutrition, US. No one size fits all. So, when we think about what a happy life would generally mean, it would be a unique combination of the above elements. For someone, spirituality and nurturing relationships may be of prime importance, while for another, an emphasis on movement, food, rest and recovery may be the key factors that keep them fulfilled. But what matters the most is completing this jigsaw puzzle of happiness. This can be achieved by fitting together all the pieces which could be of different sizes but are important in their own way. Completing the jigsaw puzzle of happiness can add a unique flavour to the curry of life.

I firmly believe that the three aspects of our being—mind, body and spirit—are intimately connected and form one holistic system. This implies that if one piece of the puzzle of our life is imbalanced or goes completely missing, not only will our lives be incomplete and unfulfilling, but the insufficiency in some areas will surely have a domino effect on other domains of our life unless they are proactively addressed.

For instance, if we're sleep-deprived, it will surely cause physiological as well as psychological stress in the body over time. Stress is well-documented as being one of the primary causes of chronic inflammation, which in turn is known to be the precursor of several modern lifestyle illnesses, such as cancer, type 2 diabetes, heart disease and asthma, to name a few.

Also, poor gut health can cause mental stress, as about 95 per cent of the serotonin (the feel-good hormone) in our body is made in the gut.[1] So, when the gut is unhappy, it adversely affects our mental and emotional well-being as well.

Stress emanating from the modern life can manifest itself through psychosomatic illnesses such as poor digestion, migraine headaches, stomach cramps, hypertension, etc. If left unresolved, stress can also lead to depression, which is known to be a harbinger of lifestyle-related issues such as type 2 diabetes, osteoporosis, heart disease and Alzheimer's.

Therefore, it is critical to address our neglected areas *not* just by managing the ill-health symptoms through quick fixes (like popping a pill), but by treating the source of the imbalance. In Reema's case, treating the root cause would mean slowing down the speed of her professional life to incorporate sufficient rejuvenating sleep, a healthy diet, enhanced social interactions, adequate physical movement, regular health check-ups, certain self-care tools to manage stress on a daily basis, and very importantly, including activities that make her heart dance with joy. When all the domains of her life are balanced, her stress levels will diminish, and her whole being will start healing. This is a holistic approach where we study the multiple components of the mind and the body simultaneously since they function in tandem.

Symptoms are only the signposts for the areas of our

bodies that are in need of more attention. We needn't get petrified by the symptoms themselves, but rather interpret them as requests for help from our body. We then need to unravel the root cause of the health issues we could be facing. We also need to keep a learner's mindset where we are open and curious to uncover the source of our health issues, without holding any preconceived ideas. After all, our overall well-being is complex and multidimensional, and consists of too many variables, necessitating a process of discovery and experimentation with an open mind.

Haven't we all come across people who experience a mental and emotional breakdown after holding and internalizing a lot of stress and anxiety over a long period of time? There generally is a run-up to this mental crash. While running on the treadmill of a fast-paced life, we may have been deceiving ourselves by giving credence to misleading thoughts, such as 'I have all the time in the world to work on things that'll make my soul happy. Let me first prove myself at work and at home.' While the intention behind these priorities may be well placed, it may not be in the best interest of our health. The proverb 'You can't pour from an empty cup' is very relevant today, especially for those of us who are leading hectic lives while trying to provide for our families and loved ones. We won't be able to take care of others from a place of love and authenticity if we can't take care of our own well-being.

Another critical factor in increasing the happiness quotient of our lives is living in alignment with our soul goals or what we consider our purpose in life. I can't emphasize this point enough. It was only when I discovered and eventually felt aligned with my life's purpose that I started to feel truly fulfilled. Fanning the flames of our dreams, and then striving to make them a reality, is divine joy. In fact, I feel when we postpone living in alignment with what our soul craves, we do a disservice to our 'highest selves'. Besides, we don't really know how much time we have in this physical world. None of us has come to this planet with an 'expiry date' stamped on our bodies. And, just in case we forget, there is no 'rewind' button in life! Therefore, we need to start living more authentically from the moment we realize what matters most to our 'true selves'.

I'm no philosopher, and this book is definitely not esoteric in nature. I'm just a normal woman who, over the years, has discovered highly effective tools that lead to lasting health and happiness. I know first-hand what it feels like to speed down the highway of life without a sense of balance, direction or destination. I'm more aware now than ever that driving recklessly through life can cause injury and even empty the fuel tank of life sooner than anticipated. This can leave us stranded midway on what could have otherwise been a wonderful journey to be savoured at a gentler pace. Having spent more than half a century on this planet, I have not only experienced the good, the bad and the ugly, but also the magnificent!

Now, I wish to share some of the transformational experiences that helped me enhance the quality of my life manifold. My heart is bursting with gratitude to the Almighty, the universe and the powers above for the rich and varied experiences of my life. This book is my way of sharing a few amazing and time-tested, life-changing tools and practices that can help you balance the various important domains of life. These tools can help you live a more authentic, healthier and happier life.

While on your life's journey, be very compassionate with yourself because this adventure is not a fairy tale. At times, you will stumble, fall or fail, and this is certain. Challenges help us in our personal growth. They shouldn't be viewed as threats to our existence, but rather as opportunities to become stronger and more resilient. Remember what Christopher Columbus once said, 'You can never cross the ocean until you have the courage to lose sight of the shore.' No doubt challenges hurt, but then they also turn us into more resilient, resourceful and stronger people than we ever were.

So, learn from your falls, pick yourself up and start all over again. Don't be harsh on yourself, and acknowledge and celebrate every small step forward. Don't get overwhelmed if you fall back a bit and realize that your pace is slower than others. Listen to the inner voice that is always guiding you and trust it completely. Remind yourself that you are unique with your own special gifts to offer to the world. Comparing our journey with that of others will only cause stress. Besides, we don't know everyone else's stories of trials and tribulations. When we have unreasonably high expectations of ourselves, we fall victim to perfectionism. It is perfectionism when we want to be the very best at everything we do at the cost of several other important facets of our lives. Perfectionism leads us to beat ourselves up if we are unable to live up to these unrealistic expectations. This attitude can be a mammoth roadblock in the path to success. We need to value our humanness and imperfections.

Stress can also seize us fiercely if we start obsessing about the end result of our actions. It can, in fact, take away the joy of the process of accomplishing our goals. So many people have fallen off the track by fixating on the outcome from the moment they started their journey towards their dream. Happiness is in enjoying the process rather than worrying about the outcome. As Tal Ben-Shahar, bestselling author and positive psychology lecturer, says in his book *Happier*, 'Happiness is the experience of climbing towards the peak.'² So, we need to remember that achieving lasting happiness is about enjoying the journey (the process) towards the destination. It is neither about making it quickly to the peak of the mountain (the destination), nor about simply climbing around the mountain aimlessly (having no purpose).

My book is an endeavour to light a candle in your path through the forest of life and walk along holding your hand until you can clearly see the way ahead. It also aims to arm you with a bagful of tools that you can deploy as needed, to help you deal with the various challenges you are sure to face on this arduous, albeit exciting journey. Thereafter, it is up to you to tread the course that most resonates with you, and that leads you to your unique destination.

Inspirational Stories of Real Women

I have opened up my heart and shared my own life experiences in all their glory—dreary as well as joyous—without hiding any of my dark spots. I've also shared the awe-inspiring life stories of some brave and spirited women who went through hell, and then pulled themselves out of the inferno with great fortitude. Each of them rose like a phoenix from the ashes, stronger and more confident. It would have been easy for them to crumble and fade away into the dark recesses of a cheerless life, but that was not what they settled for. Keeping the body, mind and sprit together, they pulled through their ordeals and in fact used their sufferings as fuel for their metamorphosis. Today, they motivate other women going through tough times to get a grip on their lives.

These stories can serve as beacons of hope and courage for you when the going gets really tough. They are living testimonies of my belief that we may sink all the way to the ocean floor, but by taking a hard push from the rock bottom, we can resurface with renewed strength to face life.

These accounts are examples of steely resolve, unflinching willpower and relentless perseverance. There's nothing as empowering as reading about how someone pushed past excruciating pain, demolished fear, armoured her heart and mind, and through her sheer courage, emerged stronger. These women are examples of how we can all employ a plethora of wellness tools to heal, reboot and then rewrite our own stories because we are all stories. So, when life is savage, read these stories to inspire you not to lose hope and give up.

We can explore our past to discover ourselves better, and pick up important lessons that can help us course correct for a brighter future. We must also be willing to release events from our past that hold us back and no longer serve us. We should be willing to deconstruct our traumatic story as the first step in creating a new, empowering story. Only when we release our narrative of pain do we start the process of healing ourselves.

Persistent effort has the potential to turn our life around completely and help us discover who we really are. In most circumstances, we make self-limiting choices and settle for less than our best. We are oblivious to the huge reservoirs of inner strength deep within us, and therefore, grossly underestimate the bounds of our capabilities. The truth is that our body and mind are capable of Herculean feats when they're driven to perform at their optimum levels.

I've also shared assorted experiences from the second phase of my life, in a hope that they will inspire you to dream of a more vibrant vision for your own life, one that lies a few steps outside your comfort zone. A life without goals, dreams and aspirations is mere 'existence'. Just the way I gradually overcame my hardships, I implore you to keep fueling your aspirations with micro goals and daily incremental steps.

In recent years, I have ardently started believing that good health starts from the inside out. Health is not addressed purely through physical upkeep, as is conventionally believed. In fact, the well-being of the mind, body and spirit is the comprehensive result of various lifestyle interventions, such as mindfulness rituals, a clean and nutritious diet, optimum physical fitness, adequate sleep and fulfilling relationships. These are covered in stand-alone chapters titled 'Mindfulness' (Chapter 2), 'Nutrition' (Chapter 3), Physical Fitness (Chapter 4), Sleep (Chapter 5) and Social Connections (Chapter 6).

This book also provides some useful insights on how to discover our 'Purpose of Life' (Chapter 7) and proposes a step-by-step approach to pursuing our dreams from the start to the end.

Through *Unfetter*, I have also shared inputs on installing keystone habits and deleting undesirable ones. In the chapter 'Happiness Habits' (Chapter 8), I have outlined some exceptional routines and rituals that can help us transform our lives for the better.

Since we need self-care in our lives to become the best versions of ourselves and show up with more commitment, the book has a dedicated section on 'Self-Care' (Chapter 9) that delineates different types of tools that could be deployed in varied situations.

Last, but definitely not least, this book has a section on 'Female Hormones' (Chapter 10). This book, which is primarily for women, would have been incomplete without this section. It explains the basics about female sex hormones and equips us with the appropriate tools to rebalance them. Hormonal imbalance is a rampant issue and can wreak havoc at various stages of a woman's life if not given timely and adequate care and attention.

Each chapter in this book delves deep into a crucial aspect necessary for a flourishing life and provides tools to help you transform into a complete woman, one step at a time. Most of these interventions are extremely easy to follow, yet are packed with countless health and happiness perks.

At the end of each chapter, I've added 'Are You Up for a Challenge?' a.k.a. some assignments, to help you get started with integrating the concepts practically into your life. To get the most out of this book, I implore you to pause after each chapter and put the tools therein into practise before moving on to the next chapter. This will help you to start reaping the myriad benefits of each intervention while you're still reading the book. Besides, we are most likely to be motivated to take action while concepts are still fresh in the mind.

I also got drawn towards writing this book because I realized that many women don't have access to the right resources. Many of us may not even be aware that we are in need of some good suggestions and that numerous simple wellness tools exist that can help us address our health and happiness issues effectively. This book is replete with practical tools that can lead us to a healthy lifestyle. It lays down in detail various important pillars of fulfilling emotional, mental and physical well-being.

I have aimed the book exclusively at women because, being one myself, I have a clearer understanding of what a woman's life feels like, including her unique challenges, nutritional needs that vary in different phases of her life and the hormonal imbalances that occur during certain life events she experiences.

Every woman who dives deep into this book will find some

worthwhile takeaways to enhance her life. And as for the age of my reader, I would say that if you are young, learn these important tools early in life, and if you're 'not so young,' I would advise that you're never too old to start a new thing in life. As the English novelist George Eliot says, 'It is never too late to be what you might have been.'

I implore you to explore this book with one caveat: do not wait for the 'right time' to begin implementing the tools. Just start wherever you stand right now and with whatever resources you have at your disposal. You will be able to keep marshalling resources as you progress towards your goal. Also, if you slip on the way, which you will at times, strengthen your resolve, get back up and move ahead unabashedly towards your destination.

To sum up, my aspiration behind writing this book is to inspire women from all walks of life and all age groups to be the best they can be. I pray that these pages serve as the wind beneath your wings! And let's remember what Napoleon Bonaparte said, 'Until you spread your wings, you will have no idea how far you can fly.'

SECTION I

chapter 1

Understanding Mental, Emotional and Physical Well-Being

*Everything is within your power,
and your power is within you.*

—Janice Trachtman, author

Until three to four years ago, I didn't even give a passing thought to evaluating my mental and emotional health, although I would take regular stock of my physical health. I thought I was 'doing just fine' the way I was in life. 'Doing fine' for me meant feeling healthy and fit in physical terms, by eating a clean and wholesome diet, and exercising like a maniac (almost) every single day. I thought I had everything going for me to be happy: I had an active social life—partying regularly and dancing all night; I was an accomplished runner who was the apple of numerous eyes, had hordes of 'friends', and had a Facebook friends list running into thousands. I was envied enough by other women and was soaked in constant adulation for who I was and what I did. What more could I really want from life? Was this not the ideally gratifying life that most people could only dream of? I would often ask myself these questions.

While everything appeared to be normal and near-perfect from the outside, what I felt inside was a completely different story. I felt restless, edgy, needy for attention and completely unfulfilled. It felt like I was on an emotional roller-coaster ride almost every single day of my life. Minor criticism from random people could shove me down in the dumps, while someone's praise could instantly transport me to the moon. Essentially, anyone could make or break my spirit at the drop of a hat.

My sleep was broken due to my hyperactive brain. On the professional front, I felt my work lacked soul. In the relationship department, I took my spouse for granted. My very loving husband became a sitting duck for me to vent my bottled-up feelings through constant ranting and raving. I was a perpetual damsel in distress who couldn't handle any discomfort and expected to be the centre of the universe (at least in my home). It destabilized our married life for some time with barrages of unwarranted skirmishes. In short, joy was missing from my life.

What I wasn't able to understand then was that I was holding on to a lot of subconscious childhood pain and trauma that were dormant and unprocessed at that stage. This and my lack of self-awareness were the two major contributors to my unfulfilled self. What made matters worse was my inability to figure out why I was feeling so unsettled despite having access to all the comforts in life and enjoying great physical health.

It feels funny now to remember how I would cringe when my husband joked about my flare-ups (which were very often). He would often ask me: 'You're exercising for several hours a day to keep your body fit, but what mental exercise are you doing to calm your monkey mind?' Back then, 'exercise for the mind' (read meditation, pranayama, journaling, etc.) meant nothing more than esoteric, time-wasting mumbo jumbo to me. I found myself to be an unwilling participant in any discussion that involved meditation or deep breathing. I would end the chat on a light note by implying that I would start meditating when I reached my 70s—the age when people resort to meditation for want of anything better to do.

Finally, there came a point of no return. I just couldn't take it anymore and I crumbled in the presence of my 19-year-old son, an old soul, who has been the prime catalyst in my journey of self-discovery. Odd as it may seem, he helped me 'unpack' all my unprocessed emotions and release my painful baggage as a clinical therapist would. He also managed to convince me to dabble in simple mindfulness activities that included two to three minutes of meditation, two minutes of deep breathing, keeping journal entries (about my emotional states and blessings small and big) and reading a few books such as Thich Nhat Hanh's *Silence: The Power of Quiet in a World Full of Noise* (Rider, 2015), Eckhart Tolle's *The Power of Now: A Guide to Spiritual Enlightenment* (New World Library, 2004) and Michael A. Singer's *The Untethered Soul: The Journey Beyond Yourself* (New Harbinger Publications/Noetic Books, 2007) to help me build self-awareness. These were a few of the mindfulness tools that helped me bring a positive shift in my psyche little by little.

Things started changing dramatically from that point. In just a week, I started to notice a few positive changes within me: I was calmer, less irritable and more in control of my emotions than before. For the first time in my life thus far, the realization struck that I had too much noise and clutter in my head. It also struck me that I was emotionally fragile, that I was not truly happy inside despite being super-fit on the outside and that I felt immensely unfulfilled despite all the tangible comforts in my life. Within a month of using these interventions, I felt more centred. I became more curious about the mindfulness domain and consciously started exploring and dabbling in these tools. They no longer felt fake and forced to me.

These moments of self-awareness became an inflection point that triggered a change in my entire outlook to life. I started noticing all that was going well in my life and stopped focusing on what wasn't. Simple things that I had taken for granted started giving me immense joy: my morning cup of coffee, the lush green foliage around my house and the cool breeze in my hair when I walked. My daily mindfulness practice also helped me spruce up my relationship with my spouse as I started thinking consciously before reacting to an emotional trigger, which helped me tone down my responses. And that was just the beginning of my journey towards becoming a healthier and happier me from outside as well as inside.

Through the new-found self-awareness, what I understood was that there is a **strong mind-body connection**. When stress becomes persistent and chronic, it can lead to physical psychosomatic health issues—major or minor—such as migraine, fatigue, backache, spondylitis, skin eruptions, stomach ulcers, high blood pressure, etc. When psychological stress leads to physiological problems, they are known as psychosomatic complaints. Poor mental or emotional health over an extended period of time can lead to chronic inflammation in our bodies putting us at a high risk of chronic lifestyle illnesses and even autoimmune diseases, such as diabetes and multiple sclerosis. After all, inflammation lies at the base of most of the modern lifestyle-related illnesses, be it type 2 diabetes, asthma, rheumatoid arthritis, skin issues, certain forms of cancer, heart disease, etc.

The reverse is also true: poor physical health can adversely affect our mental and emotional health. For instance, if we suffer from chronic digestive issues or sleep deprivation, they can affect our mental and emotional health by causing stress or anxiety.

It is really astonishing to observe how our psychological and physiological health and well-being are so intimately interconnected. And our digestive health, sleep patterns and stress levels are especially interlinked. Take a look at these three health scenarios: 1) You go through a few nights of bad sleep because you are awake till the wee hours. As a consequence, you're likely to develop stress and anxiety, which may, in turn, result in you experiencing migraine headaches or skin breakouts. 2) You may be having digestion issues due to days of overindulgence in junk food. This may cause you to have stress. Thus, digestive issues, when combined with stress, can wreak havoc on your sleep. 3) You are suffering from stress and anxiety due to an unhappy event like a bitter fight with your partner. You're likely to lose sleep over it, and the lack of restful sleep and stress is a potent recipe for psychosomatic issues such as stomach ache, trapezius muscle pain and migraine.

In my own case, while I was taking good care of my nutritional needs and fitness, the stress build-up from my unresolved emotions from the past led to insomnia. Stress build-up also led to chronic inflammation in the form of severe eczema (an autoimmune disease) for more than two decades, wherein I tried everything to banish it—from modern medicine and homoeopathy, to herbal treatment, but to no avail. It finally regressed and faded away mysteriously about the same time that I started using mindfulness-based interventions. The point that I'm trying to convey is that many of us take meticulous care of our bodies through following a very clean diet and working out each day (sometimes to a point of obsession), but we may ignore the criticality of addressing our emotional and mental health as well. Overall wellness is a sum total of good mental, emotional and physical health. Total focus on some while ignoring the other areas will leave us unfulfilled.

As I mentioned earlier, various mindfulness-based interventions such as meditation, journaling and gratitude exercises helped me heal myself to a great extent, and I'm still a work-in-progress. There have been many lessons learnt, one of which is: treat your body as a holistic system, since your mind, emotions and all bodily systems, such as your gut and immunity, are interconnected. The body keeps sending signals to us if it senses an imbalance in any sphere of life. This may be due to poor food habits, a toxic relationship, an illness, lack of movement, inadequate sleep, unrewarding career, etc. Therefore, it's critical for our overall well-being to always stay tuned to what our bodies are trying to tell us. Your body is a reflection of your lifestyle. Nourish it with wholesome living, and it will reciprocate by keeping you robust in your overall health—mental, emotional as well as physical.

So, what exactly is the difference between mental, emotional and physical health? Broadly speaking, **physical health** refers to a person's overall physical condition in terms of normal functioning, soundness of the body and freedom from illnesses. Physical health is just one dimension of total well-being. Examples of physical illnesses are diabetes, heart disease, high blood pressure, etc.

Mental health refers to behaviours that relate to a person's mind or brain and their ability to process information and experiences. Mental illnesses could be in the form of depression, dementia, bipolar disorder, schizophrenia, etc.

Emotional health, on the other hand, refers to the matters of the heart such as the ability to process, express or manage emotions based on the information assimilated by the mind. Emotional eating disorders, mood swings and social withdrawal are some of the instances of poor emotional health.

While there's a subtle difference between mental and emotional health, they're often used synonymously since they're closely intertwined.

Talking about these three states of health, whenever we are mentally, emotionally or physically fatigued due to our circumstances, we become a dull shadow of our true selves. We need to take the bull of adversities by its horns rather than fritter away our lives wallowing in self-pity, suffering in silence and accepting it as our fate. If we don't gather inner strength and pull ourselves together with the hope of successfully surmounting any challenge, the suffering will only intensify over time. It can lead to any or a combination of the following health issues:

- Frequent mood swings ranging between anxiety, worry, aggression, apathy, frustration, irritability, sorrow, boredom and being overwhelmed
- Persistent feelings of hopelessness and pessimism
- Loss of interest in routine chores
- Inability to focus on work
- Loss of appetite
- Aversion to sex
- Social withdrawal
- Significant weight loss or weight gain in a short time period
- Chronic fatigue and sluggishness
- Sleep deprivation
- Low self-worth and excessive self-criticism, hypersensitivity to criticism by others
- Recurrent forgetfulness and difficulty in concentrating
- Lack of interest in personal appearance
- The feeling of being uninspired

- Substance abuse and/or alcoholism
- Inexplicable health complaints, such as headaches, muscle tension, increased heart rate, palpitations, dizziness, backache, digestive issues, etc.
- Suicidal tendencies in extreme cases

According to a World Health Organization (WHO) fact sheet, depressive disorders such as depression, anxiety and somatic complaints account for almost 41.9 per cent of neuropsychiatric disorders among women compared with 29.3 per cent among men.[3] Depression is twice as common among women than in men.

The most common forms of challenges that have the potential to affect our well-being could be factors such as:

- Early childhood trauma
- Loss of a loved one
- Certain medical conditions such as cancer and diabetes
- Alcoholism and drug abuse
- Hormonal imbalance
- Accidents
- Financial hardships, unfulfilled dreams, or broken relationships
- Chemical imbalances in the brain
- Poor nutrition
- Loneliness
- Body image issues leading to eating disorders
- Overly demanding professions
- Irrational fears, phobias and insecurities.

Our mental and emotional well-being is an indicator of how we feel about the various aspects of our lives on a day-to-day basis, such as our own selves, our relationships, our work, our ability to cope with difficult situations and the process that we employ to manage our emotions. Being mentally and emotionally healthy doesn't mean that we will never experience negative emotions, but rather that when we do feel emotionally stressed, we have the resilience to bounce back quickly from these setbacks. As the famous American professor Jon Kabat-Zinn says, 'You can't stop the waves, but you can learn to surf.'

The reality is that all of us will face difficulties from time to time, and for many of us, challenges may befall us unannounced, taking us by surprise. In such scenarios, the coping mechanisms we employ to build mental, emotional and physical resilience will determine how well we bounce back and regain our equanimity. The body has a natural inclination to achieve homeostasis (its normal state of balance), but it just needs a positive nudge from us to help gather momentum.

Nothing gives me more happiness than sharing some wonderful wellness tools with you that have helped me deal with my adversities from time to time. I am sharing them with the hope that you too can reach into this toolbox and choose an intervention most relevant to your situation.

Before introducing these life-changing tools, I would like to remind you that each one of us is a bio-individual with a unique body, unique mental chemistry and a unique combination of emotions. Therefore, there is a possibility that the interventions that worked for me may not work for you. So, keep an open mind, question everything, experiment extensively with the numerous holistic approaches laid out in the next few chapters and form your own opinion. I'm very certain that you will discover your own set of protocols—a combination of interventions that work for you when you need them in your life.

I've categorized these wellness tools as per the domain

they belong to and have dedicated a chapter for each category of tools so that it is easy for you to understand their benefits and to use them. The broad categories are:

- Mindfulness
- Nutrition
- Physical Fitness
- Sleep
- Social Connections

I am always reminded of the quote by the American motivational writer William Arthur Ward, 'Happiness is an inside job.' This quote is significant because only we can create happiness in our own lives. It is our responsibility—especially with the wellness toolbox at our disposal—to help ourselves navigate through life's myriad adversities. When in despair, please do remember that every cloud has a silver lining, no matter how hopeless the situation may seem. Now let's dive right into the wellness resources!

chapter 2

Mindfulness

You are the sky. Everything else—it's just the weather.

—Pema Chödrön, American-Tibetan Buddhist

In the frenzied world that we live in today, many of us suffer with restless and overworked minds buzzing with an insane amount of activity. As I mentioned in Chapter 1, before becoming a bit self-aware, my monkey mind would refuse to sit still for even a few moments. It would incessantly goad me into thinking about something that either occurred in the past or about something that may happen in the future. It was a grave challenge to still my mind, 'live' in the present moment and enjoy it long enough to give me peace and joy. It wouldn't be an exaggeration to say that I was on an incessant cortisol 'drip', stressing about either what happened in my past (far or immediate) or what would happen in my future (relating to significant and insignificant things). And this is where various mindfulness-based interventions came in to salvage my mental and emotional health.

You would have heard the word 'mindfulness' being tossed around in conversations and print ever so often, especially in the current scenario, when stress and anxiety levels are at their peak. While some of us may understand the essence of 'being mindful', others may only have a vague idea about what it essentially implies.

Simply put, mindfulness speaks of intentionally observing and being aware of what is happening within or around us 'in the present moment', without passing any judgement, good or bad. It trains our minds to reach a place of peace and calm by attempting to bring a positive shift in our thought process and belief system. Mindfulness helps us become more 'present' in our lives rather than stressing over what happened in the past or what may happen in the future.

Being mindful also helps us develop a deeper and more authentic relationship with ourselves. This is critical because the relationship we have with our own selves, sets the tone for every other relationship we have in our lives. But we need to become self-aware first in order to have a fulfilling relationship with ourselves. This is precisely what practising mindfulness helps us achieve. Mindfulness helps us become aware of our emotions and thoughts when they surface. This self-awareness then allows the emotions and thoughts to pass through us after we process them with kindness without indulging them. It is especially very helpful in the case of thoughts and emotions that have been causing us distress.

Mindfulness tools are very powerful and vital for our overall well-being because they help us regulate our internal chemistry and prod us towards self-healing. While they start by helping us release stress and anxiety (emotional and mental well-being), they can eventually help us heal our illnesses too (physical well-being) since there is an intimate connection between our mental, emotional and physical health. For instance, stress can cause psychosomatic issues such as poor sleep, weak digestion, lowered immunity and shoulder pain, as explained in the previous chapter.

When faced with stressful situations, our sympathetic nervous system takes over our brain by elevating blood pressure, accelerating our pulse, quickening our breathing and releasing stress hormones such as cortisol and adrenaline. It is our parasympathetic nervous system that puts a brake on this turn of events to transport us back to a state of relaxation. This has been called 'The Relaxation Response' by Dr Herbert Benson, the famous mind/body medicine professor from Harvard Medical School, in his book titled *The Relaxation Response*.[4] During this state of relaxation, the body moves to a state of deep rest, which can help us change our physiological and psychological responses to stress in positive ways. When the body no longer senses any threat to its well-being and feels safe, the parasympathetic nervous system takes over and the nervous system relaxes again, providing the much-needed respite from stress and anxiety.

Mindfulness rituals are not one-time wonders though. For any mindfulness approach to bear concrete results, we need to remember a few things:

- Know our 'why': Be sure of why we are using this approach, i.e. what exactly are we hoping to achieve.
- Start small: For any tool to be effective, it shouldn't appear intimidating or overwhelming. Starting small reduces internal resistance. Practising anything for two minutes daily is a lot more effective than doing it for 30 minutes once a week.
- Morning practice: Indulge in activities such as meditation, deep breathing and gratitude, preferably immediately after waking up. These can provide a positive momentum to the day by making us feel centred.
- Be consistent: Practise it regularly. Establish a daily routine for assured results. Try doing these rituals at the same time every day.

Before I delve into each of the tools in this chapter, it's very pertinent for me to clarify a point: I could have very well termed the approaches laid down in this chapter as spiritual tools rather than mindfulness tools, but I chose the term 'mindfulness' over 'spiritual' to avoid unnecessary misinterpretation of the term 'spirituality'. Many people erroneously think that spirituality and religion are the same thing and use these terms interchangeably.

To explain in a layman's terms, spirituality concerns matters of the spirit or the soul. It has to do with a sense of peace and purpose in life. It denotes an experience of connecting to something much larger than us as individuals and is more of an individual practice. Religion, on the other hand, is a specific and personalized system of organized beliefs, practices and attitudes, usually shared by a community or a group. While most religions have spirituality as part of their faith, being spiritual is *not* synonymous with being religious. One can be spiritual without being religious.

Therefore, since spirituality in essence is an experience of our spirit, all the mindfulness activities such as meditation, deep breathing and mindful eating are said to be spiritual in nature. Thus, you could use mindfulness and spirituality synonymously, if you wish to.

Next, I would like to present to you some of the most powerful mindfulness tools that have personally helped me navigate through stress, anxiety, negative self-talk, existential dilemma and a lot more. You may experiment with them and see which ones resonate with you the most, and then make a daily ritual out of them. It generally takes anywhere between three weeks to three months to form any new habit. Only when you use these tools consistently, will they start becoming effective. (More details in Chapter 8, 'Happiness Habits')

Here are some of the mindfulness tools that we can greatly benefit from, provided we work with them consistently:

1. Meditation
2. Gratitude
3. Deep breathing
4. Journaling
5. Visualization
6. Positive self-talk and affirmations or mantra chanting
7. Mindfulness in day-to-day activities
8. Forsaking perfectionism and embracing self-love

Let us look at these points in detail:

1. Meditation

Meditation is quite simply mental hygiene.

—Emma Seppälä, author of *The Happiness Track*

While the human body benefits from putting in enough movement, the mind benefits from being still. The main purpose of meditation is to quieten the mind. And when the mind becomes stiller, the body also slows down, making it possible for the body to self-regulate, start healing and reach homeostasis.

Just like regular physical exercise keeps our body fit, meditation helps in keeping the heart and brain healthy. It also helps us shed our undesirable thoughts in favour of positive ones and aids in letting go of rigid habits and unyielding attitudes in favour of beneficial ones. Meditation equips us to better deal with challenges in our daily lives. While meditation cannot make the challenges disappear, it can provide us the 'space' we need to envision potent solutions to our problems. Meditation also helps us shift from the mindset of complaining that the 'roses have thorns' to rejoicing in the discovery of 'roses amidst thorns'.

Meditation directs our awareness to the present moment, which brings peace, tranquillity and relaxation to our mind and body. It doesn't require us to forcibly push thoughts out or to coerce the mind to be quiet. While meditating, we can allow the mind to stray, observe these random thoughts with utmost compassion, allow them to drift away on their own without being judged and then redirect our mind back to the present. Every time that the mind wanders off while meditating and we are able to bring it back successfully to the present moment, we are building new neural connections in our brain. Over a period of regular practise, meditation reinforces our ability to focus on the present moment, thereby helping us mitigate stress. As per a study conducted by a Harvard-affiliated researchers' team, practising mindfulness meditation daily for eight weeks results in shrinkage of the amygdala, which is responsible for feelings of stress and anxiety.[5]

Meditation can be practised by anyone, anytime, anywhere, in any style and without any equipment. And while some perks of meditating are immediate, others may start manifesting over a period of time as we keep practising it. There are different styles of meditation available that can be matched to suit your goals and the time at your disposal.

Some of the numerous benefits of meditation are:

- Lowers stress by reducing inflammation levels and shifting our perspective[6]
- Calms the mind by reducing fears and slowing down racing thoughts
- Boosts mood by increasing hope and optimism
- Increases the feeling of gratitude for whatever we already have

- Trains the brain to strengthen willpower and self-control
- Enhances cognitive abilities such as focus, attention span, mental clarity and decision-making skills[7]
- Helps improve sleep by reducing restlessness and mental chatter
- Enhances self-image, self-esteem, self-compassion and self-love by increasing self-awareness
- Helps us feel compassion and empathy for others[8]
- Reduces symptoms of depression[9]
- Hones our intuition, sixth sense or gut feeling

Various Forms of Meditation: What is Best for Me?

There is no 'the way' of meditating; whatever method resonates with you is the best way of meditating for you. The first step is to sit and just do it. Initially, the thought of meditating itself was tough for me. What really helped me focus was listening to relaxing music with the sound of flowing water and nature on YouTube. Resorting to guided meditation really helped me at the start when it was extremely difficult to quieten my mind. I still dabble with different methods of meditation depending on my mental state when I wake up in the morning. The different forms of meditation range from breath focus on music (binaural beats, delta waves, water sounds, etc.), body scan and guided imagery, to chakra healing. You should experiment with various forms to find your own 'sweet spot'. There is a wide spread of menu of meditation techniques to choose from. Some of the most common ones include:

- Mindfulness meditation or present moment meditation
- Guided meditation
- Mantra or chanting meditation
- Body scan meditation

- Metta or loving-kindness meditation
- Transcendental meditation
- Vipassana meditation
- Zen or Zazen meditation
- Chakra meditation
- Qigong meditation

2. Gratitude

Having a sense of gratitude is to feel deep appreciation and thankfulness for what we have in our lives, instead of fretting about what is missing. For me, gratitude is the paramount and most powerful mindfulness tool that can bring about the quickest mental shift from anxiety and hopelessness to infusing mental peace and optimism. It helps my frenzied mind to pause for a moment to reflect and introspect on things I already have, things that are going right for me and the many blessings I may have taken for granted over time.

Gratitude brings about a shift in our perspective, a swift transformation from feelings of scarcity, inadequacy or resentment, to feelings of sufficiency, abundance, adequacy and contentment. As someone has aptly said, 'What you appreciate appreciates.' Gratitude is one of the quickest and surest paths to happiness and optimism. When we focus on *what we have* in our lives rather than *what's missing*, it can bring a quick shift in our perspective. Deep appreciation and thankfulness for what is good in our lives can change our outlook from negative to positive in no time at all.

Gratitude is an incredibly powerful human emotion. It promotes optimism even when the going gets tough. For me personally, gratitude exercises have been one of the quickest game changers, from losing hope during difficult times to feeling blessed due to the abundance in my life.

It was around July 2020 when I lost my biggest identity, or so I thought. From being an accomplished endurance runner who ran half and full marathons and lifted very heavy weights in the gym, I reached a state where I could not even run 50 metres without my knees and lower back screaming with pain. In fact, all my joints, including my neck, shoulders, elbows, wrists, fingers and toes would ache even with simple daily movements. As for lifting weights, I couldn't even hold a spoon without my finger joints hurting. My sleep almost disappeared. I couldn't sleep the whole night even with the aid of supplements. All I could manage was two-three hours of fragmented sleep during the day. I felt chronically fatigued throughout the day, with my focus and attention span at its lowest ever, accompanied by persistent headaches. Stress and anxiety built up from not understanding what was happening, and this wasn't helping matters, as even a complete health check-up couldn't indicate what exactly was wrong with me. I felt myself spinning into a downward spiral of stress, which I knew could eventually morph into full-fledged depression if I didn't pull myself together. I decided to research my symptoms and take corrective actions thereafter. Based on my extensive research, I concluded that I probably had systemic inflammation due to chronic sleep deprivation.

While I started working on my sleep hygiene, I added gratitude prayers to my morning rituals of meditation and deep-breathing exercises. I also started gratitude journaling before going to bed every night. Gratitude exercises made me realize that I still had so much going for me while there was so much suffering all around due to the coronavirus pandemic. I started writing at least five things that had gone well for me each day. It could be something as trivial as someone smiling at me or feeling happy after speaking to someone on the phone. While my body took some time to respond, my stress levels dropped sharply within days. From feeling like a victim, I started feeling blessed for being alive, for having my family around me, for the healthy food that I got to eat, for being able to walk and laugh, and so on. While my joints are on their way to recovery, my heart and mind are full of gratitude for this life.

While having gratitude for the Supreme Power, the Almighty, or the God, we can feel gratitude for a whole lot of other things, such as a supportive spouse, a loving child, a wonderful friend, good health, nutritious food, a material gift, comforts in life, and of course, for being alive. Counting our blessings daily is a great reminder of the abundance we enjoy in life that we tend to take for granted most of the time.

Gratitude is highly rewarding with absolutely no downside to it. When we express gratitude, our brain releases the happiness hormones, dopamine and serotonin. These hormones help rewire our emotionally drained brains to take on a positive outlook. Even scientific research supports the 'attitude of gratitude' as being universally rewarding and fulfilling.[10]

Benefits of practising gratitude	**Ways in which gratitude can be expressed**
It gives us the ability to savour life's myriad gifts with enhanced awareness	Maintaining a gratitude journal
It provides us with an optimistic outlook, putting us in a positive frame of mind and reducing anxiety and stress	Calling up someone to say 'Thank You!'
It increases mental resilience to challenges in life	Giving an unexpected hug to someone close

It helps strengthen existing relationships and build new ones[11]	Planning a favourite meal for our loved ones
It reduces anger and aggression considerably[12]	Writing a Thank You message/email
It starts physical healing by enhancing our psychological health[13]	Sending them flowers or a surprise token of appreciation
It makes us more forgiving, magnanimous and empathetic[14]	Using or wearing their gifts in their presence
It ensures better sleep by reducing anxiety and relaxing the mind[15]	Taking them out for a cup of coffee
It raises self-esteem or our sense of self-worth[16]	Listening attentively when they're having a tough day
It has the potential to improve immunity[17]	
It increases mental alertness and attentiveness	

How Do We Hone Our Practice of Offering Gratitude?

In our pursuit of instant gratification in today's world, we often forget to pause and appreciate things, unaware that such a simple activity can deliver tremendous benefits. A powerful way of honing our spirit of gratitude and appreciation is by answering a few questions in our journal from time to time, such as:

- What aspects of your health are still robust?
- What physical and mental abilities are working well for you?

- What big or small things made you smile today?
- What are some life experiences that made you happy recently?
- What activities in your daily routine add cheer to your life?
- What material possessions you have that make you happy?
- What is one thing that you learnt recently that can improve your life?
- What thoughtful act has someone done for you recently?
- What opportunities do you currently have that you're thankful for?
- What are you better at today than you were a few years ago?
- What relationships are you grateful for?
- How can you be thankful for the challenges you've experienced in your life? What did you learn from them?
- Which basic needs don't you have to worry about today?
- Have you had a chance to help someone recently? How did that make you feel?
- Who in your life has survived something difficult? How did their recovery and revival make you feel?

3. Deep Breathing

There is a good reason why many spiritual healers and all yoga practitioners espouse and propagate deep-breathing techniques. It's because breath is *Prana*: 'the life force energy' that sustains our mental and physical health. Our daily practice of breath-focused meditation or yogic breathing that emphasizes deep breathing, activates our parasympathetic nervous system voluntarily to stop our mind from wandering, tones down emotional reactivity and soothes our jaded nerves.[18]

It is truly amazing how quickly we can flip our mental switch from being in a state of anxiety to that of calmness, simply by changing the way we breathe. Deep breathing is one of the most effective ways of lowering stress and anxiety in the body as well as the mind. Taking deep breaths settles our nerves by sending the message to our brains to slow down our heart rate and lower blood pressure, thereby enabling us to relax physically and emotionally.

Pranayama or deep breathing is known to stimulate our vagus nerve that influences heart rate variability. It works as a great stress-management tool by bringing down our heart rates, alleviating tension headaches, unfastening knots in the chest and banishing the butterflies from our stomach that cause nervous energy. The icing on the cake is that our practice of deep breathing doesn't require a specific time or place. We can do it just about anywhere and anytime—in the kitchen while fixing a meal, while at our work desk, while waiting in the billing queue of a departmental store and so on. A few breathing exercises which are a part of my daily morning ritual include the Wim Hof method of breathing, Bhastrika pranayama (bellows breath) and Bhramari pranayama (bumblebee breath).

Breathing exercises are simple to learn. Pick any breathing technique and carry out five to 10 repetitions wherever and whenever you feel the need. Someone has beautifully explained what deep breathing really feels like: 'Deep breaths are like little love notes for your body.'

Here are a few popular deep-breathing techniques that one could experiment with:

- Diaphragmatic or belly breathing
- Box breathing or four-square breathing
- Breath focus breathing
- 4-7-8 breathing or relaxing breath
- Bhastrika pranayama or bellows breath
- Anulom Vilom pranayama or alternate nostril breathing
- Bhramari pranayama or bumblebee breathing
- Kapalbhati or skull-shining breath

As is the case with other mindfulness tools, breathing exercises too will bear the sweetest fruits when practised regularly. Breathing can be a part of guided meditation, any yogic breathing technique or just unstructured intentional deep breathing.

A regular controlled breathing practice can benefit us in the following ways:

- Alleviates stress and relaxes mind and body[19]
- Reduces chronic anxiety[20]
- Increases oxygen flow
- Helps in detoxifying the body
- Lowers elevated blood pressure
- Improves focus and attention span
- Slows down the heart rate
- Improves symptoms of depression and panic disorder[21]
- Enhances the quality of sleep[22]
- Stimulates positive thought process and improves mood
- Brings relief from post-traumatic stress disorder (PTSD)[23]
- Subdues anger and irritability[24]
- Reduces the perception of pain especially in the shoulders[25]

While many of us are aware of the therapeutic advantages of deep breathing, what we may be less aware of is how to breathe right. Several maladies such as asthma, sinus infections and psoriasis could successfully be reduced or even reversed by modifying the way we inhale and exhale. As explained by James Nestor in his book *Breath: The New Science of a Lost Art* (Riverhead Books, 2020), mouth breathing can lead to nagging fatigue, irritability, anxiety, foul breath and stomach aches. Nose breathing, on the other hand, not only increases our endurance and general well-being, it also naturally warms, filters and humidifies the air we breathe. Besides, we need to breathe slower and longer rather than faster and deeper as many of us do.

French psychiatrist and bestselling author Christophe André beautifully puts it: 'Breathing is like solar energy for powering relaxation: it's a way to regulate emotions that is free, always accessible, inexhaustible and easy to use.'[26]

4. Journaling

Journaling is a practice of self-expression that involves maintaining a diary or a journal to examine our thoughts and feelings related to ourselves, other people or events in our lives. Because a journal record is a mirror to our feelings and thoughts, it is very therapeutic for our mental as well as emotional health. It allows us to let our thoughts and feelings about a stressful event flow freely without restraint, while letting us be vulnerable without the fear of being judged.

Our journal can be our closest confidante. It means that we don't need to suppress any feelings inside us simply because we can't share them with someone else. We can pour all our frustrations, fears, resentment, insecurities, sorrows, worries and everything that overwhelms us onto the pages of journals, pages that won't evaluate us. Since the journal is only for our eyes and no one else, we can be honest and fearless about sharing how we feel. Remember, there is no wrong way of journaling.

The famous holocaust survivor Anne Frank had journaled, 'I can shake off everything as I write; my sorrows disappear, my courage is reborn.'

Using any one of the below-mentioned methods of journaling can lead to several benefits for our mental and emotional health:

- Gratitude journal
- Food and exercise journal
- Brain dump journal
- Emotional release journal
- Bullet or personal planning journal
- Travel journal
- Dream journal
- Creativity journal

Advantages of Journaling

- It helps shift thought patterns from negative to positive;
- It helps release stress and brighten up our mood;[27]
- By shifting thought patterns, it can help diffuse feelings such as fear, guilt, anger, despair and low self-esteem;
- It brings about self-awareness through self-analysis;
- It helps in self-compassion and enhancing self-worth;
- A consistent habit of journaling can improve our short-term memory;
- It is a very robust tool to unleash our creative side;
- It's a great accountability tool that can help us identify unhealthy thought patterns, inept habits and behaviours, and then, work towards eliminating them;

- It has also been shown to alleviate physical issues like migraine headaches, asthma and rheumatoid arthritis;[28]
- It can help individuals recover from addictions by helping them document the challenges and triumphs, and become accountable to themselves.[29]

Here are a few useful tips before you get started on your journey of journaling:

- Find a comfortable place to write, a place that is soothing and free from distractions.
- Always date and time your entries.
- Capture any thoughts that float in your mind. Write freely without regard for form or a specific structure.
- Write honestly to reap maximum benefit. Our journal should be a true representation of who we are. Write without judging your thoughts.
- Try making journaling a daily habit, just like brushing your teeth and eating food.
- Try to use a pen and a notebook rather than digital technology as the process of physically writing down your thoughts has its inherent benefits.
- It is advisable to journal first thing in the morning, when the mind is fresh, or the last thing before sleeping, as you would have the entire day's events to reflect upon.
- It is advisable to keep your journal private. Only then will you be radically honest.
- You should always carry your journal whenever you travel.

5. Visualization

Visualization is a mindfulness exercise that entails conjuring up a mental image of what we desire, and then focusing on each of these images slowly, positively and frame-by-frame in the manner that we want events to unfurl in real life. Simply put, visualization is the exercise where we imagine and create the outcomes that we desire.

Visualization basically works by activating our mind at the 'creative subconscious' level. When we visualize, our thoughts produce the same mental instructions as physical actions since our subconscious mind cannot differentiate between our current reality and our imagination.[30] It feels as if what we are imagining has already been accomplished. Our brain then starts compiling creative inputs related to our desire and gathers all the resources at our disposal needed to accomplish this desire. Equipped with these inputs and resources, our brain motivates us, arms us with confidence, and propels us to actively accomplish our goal.

We all possess this amazing power of visualization, but unfortunately, are oblivious of its existence and potential. The images that we conjure in our minds affect a lot of cognitive processes of the brain, such as attention, perception, planning, motor control and memory. High achievers and peak performers such as American swimmer Michael Phelps, talk-show host Oprah Winfrey, professional golfer Tiger Woods and professional boxer Muhammad Ali have resorted extensively to this form of visualization or 'mental rehearsal' to enhance their performances and to manifest their dreams.

It is difficult to put into words how much I have benefitted from the visualization exercises, especially during my Ironman 70.3 triathlon preparation phase. To give readers a little background on what this sport is all about:

Ironman 70.3 entails 1.9 kilometres of open-water swimming (sea or lake), followed by 90 kilometres of cycling and 21 kilometres of running (half marathon), in quick succession, where all the three activities have to be completed within a total cut-off time of eight hours and 30 minutes. In 2017, I picked up the courage to dream of completing an Ironman 70.3 triathlon scheduled for February 2018 in Sri Lanka.

Until the time I decided to participate in this humongous event, my cycling skills were very rudimentary. I had never cycled during my childhood, and it wasn't until 2015 that I bought my first bicycle. At that point, I even had to take lessons on how to mount the bike correctly and balance it. I had absolutely no idea how to ride the bike in an aerodynamic position or how to drink water from a bottle whilst on the move and balancing the cycle with one hand. I had never worn cleated shoes for fear of falling. These are the essentials for good cycling speed in a sporting event of this magnitude. My pool swimming was decent, but I had never swum in the open sea. The only saving grace was that I was reasonably good at running. Equipped with this set of skills, I started my training for Ironman 70.3 in the middle of 2017.

In December 2017, merely two months before the big event, I twisted my ankle and fractured two little toes of my left foot. Running, which had been my biggest strength, had to be abruptly stopped for a while. But since the event was around the corner, in desperation, I reattempted to run by taping up three of my toes together and then cutting out holes over the toe area in my shoes so that they didn't hurt from friction when I ran. However, this amateur attempt cost me another foot injury. I developed tendonitis as a result of modifying my running gait to take the pressure off my injured toes.

While I had issues with my cycling and swimming, I took solace in the fact that my swimming was going strong. But this was not to be! The time had come when I had to practise sea swimming because I had to swim in the open sea off the Sri Lankan coast for my final event. I joined a sea swimming group in Mumbai and went for my first open-water swim. The moment I jumped off the boat into the sea, I felt very nauseous and disoriented. On the three occasions that I attempted this, I would feel sick and even throw up. I soon realized that I was seasick. Medical check-ups confirmed that I suffered from benign paroxysmal positional vertigo (BPPV), which causes motion sickness and seasickness.

Therefore, with about three weeks remaining for my big event, I still had issues with running and swimming. Cycling anyway was never my strong point. The excitement of attempting the big event quickly subsided. I felt extremely disheartened with no motivation to train anymore. Completing Ironman 70.3 began to look like a distant dream. I started wallowing in self-pity and cursing my fate. I had two choices at that point: to quit or just go ahead and attempt, knowing well that I wasn't in a good spot.

After feeling dejected for a couple of days, I just pulled myself together. I decided to give it my best shot. Having read about the powers of visualization and positive self-talk, I put all my faith into various mindfulness-based interventions, and started a daily practice of gratitude journaling, affirming and visualizing myself completing the event successfully. I kept training to the best of my ability with faith in the Powers above and with renewed hope.

As part of my visualization practice, I imagined my entire race from start to finish several times as a run-up to the race day. I would imagine myself swimming peacefully without any fear of nausea, in perfect rhythm, and finishing the swim in good time. Similarly, I envisioned myself cycling smoothly and running with a steady and strong rhythm, and then visualized myself completing the event by crossing the finish line extremely elated. I finally imagined myself being a finisher of the beautiful Ironman 70.3 medal, with the whole world congratulating me as 'Ironman Tanuja Sodhi'.

On the race day, I felt an uncanny calmness with absolutely no fear. With a leap of faith, I started the race by swimming, ignoring the signals that my brain was trying to send to my body about the turbulent sea. I kept moving forward with just one thought: that of completing my swim within the cut-off time. To my elation, I did complete it in decent time. This boosted my confidence to a great extent, and with this renewed self-trust, I started my cycling leg. My confidence level got a further boost when I completed it within time, despite a speed that seemed slower than what I had planned. By now, my body was screaming with exhaustion, but my mind was resolved to push through the running phase. All the mental and physical training of the last few months came to fruition, as I powered my way through the run despite fatigue and injury, and was overjoyed (an understatement!) to cross the finish line with some time to spare. Just as I had visualized so many times, the Ironman 70.3 medal was placed around my neck and I was congratulated as 'Ironman Tanuja Sodhi'!

This incident cemented my faith in the power of visualization and it has worked for me many times thereafter, in situations big and small.

The Power of Visualization: How Does it Work?

Visualization is most effective if practised regularly. So, repeat the process often for achieving the best results. Visualization basically works in four simple steps:

1. **Believe**: Believe that you can do it regardless of what anyone says or where you are in life.
2. **Quantify**: You need to specify exactly what you want, and make it measurable. Write it on paper if you can. It's the blueprint for your mental imagery.
3. **Imagine**: Think about exactly what your life would look like if you had already achieved your dream. Imagining the future course of action in detail will make you feel familiar with the situation as if it has been 'attempted already'.
4. **Take action**: Since you've already set the stage for this step by believing, quantifying and imagining, you just need to roll it out now by taking small and big actions daily to take you closer to your goal.

6. Positive Self-Talk and Affirmations or Mantra Chanting

Positive Self-Talk

All of our self-talk, our internal dialogue, is a stream of affirmations. You're affirming and creating your life experiences with every word and thought.

—Louise L. Hay,
celebrated American motivational author

Self-talk or our internal dialogue is a product of our subconscious mind, our belief system, our emotions and our general outlook in life. Self-talk can either be positive or negative. Negative self-talk can make us more pessimistic and cynical, and as a result, we may develop a tendency to judge everything and everyone around us with negativity. On the other hand, positive self-talk will heighten our optimism and train our minds to see the good in every situation. Even at times, when we don't really feel too spirited, if we prevail upon ourselves to be empathetic towards us while having an internal dialogue, our negative feelings start losing steam instantly, and we eventually start feeling lighter. Remember that your mind is always listening to whatever you're saying to yourself. Your mind and body are always trying to take cues from your self-talk in order to make them your reality. So, be careful of what you say to yourself!

Positive self-talk is great for our mental and emotional well-being and is a very powerful tool as it can reduce anxiety and stress, and make us feel calm in no time. What we speak out loud is not as critical to our well-being as what we whisper to ourselves. It is very important to indulge in positive self-talk as it can condition us to shake off self-doubt, low self-image, low self-esteem, fear and many other insecurities.

It is the conscious positive self-talk over a period of a few years that helped me overcome low self-esteem, poor self-image and some irrational fears.

Positive Affirmations and Mantras

A positive affirmation or a mantra is speaking or thinking only positive phrases. When we repeat positive affirmations or mantras to ourselves loudly or in our mind, it activates the relaxation response in our brain, weeding out negative feelings.

In today's times, when we are under constant stress, we tend to harbour a lot of self-sabotaging thoughts throughout the day, consciously or unconsciously. We don't realize that these have the force to create negative experiences, like self-fulfilling prophecies. For instance, if you often say, 'I'm feeling so miserable', or 'Life sucks', you're affirming more despair into your life.

Many famous personalities have used visualization, vision

boards with pictures, and positive affirmations to enhance their performances and to manifest their dreams. However, while affirmations are a powerful tool, they are not magic pills. They need to be practised regularly to become effective. By coaching our brain to repeat and believe in positive self-talk, we can shift our thought patterns from negative to positive as these mantras are thought pattern interrupters. Chanting the 'OM' mantra a few times, when I'm feeling edgy, helps me feel relaxed and centred almost immediately.

What's more, affirmations have been validated and widely accepted by neuroscience for their effectiveness as a tool for mental and physical wellness. According to a Social Cognitive and Affective Neuroscience research study, there is MRI (magnetic resonance imaging) evidence of neural activity, suggesting that certain neural pathways increase when people practise self-affirmation exercises.[31]

Based on such empirical evidence, we can surmise that daily positive affirmations can benefit us by:

- Enhancing self-esteem and confidence
- Reducing depressive rumination, lowering anxiety and uplifting our mood[32]
- Lowering health-impairing stress
- Increasing physical activity to be fitter and healthier[33]
- Creating positive relationships
- Mitigating negative thinking
- Increasing optimistic mindset and feelings of hopefulness[34]
- Propelling us in the direction of achieving specific goals that we aspire for

Here are a few guidelines to help you practise positive affirmations or mantras effectively:

- They should be practised regularly. Repeating them several times a day is highly recommended. A good rule of thumb is to repeat an affirmation for a few minutes, about three times each day.
- They should always be practised in the present tense. For instance: 'I *am* a successful person' is an effective positive affirmation, while 'I *will be* a successful person' is not.
- Positive affirmations only include positive words. For example: 'Every cell in my body is calm and happy' is an effective positive affirmation, while 'I am *not* anxious' is not.
- Positive affirmations are practised as statements of fact and truth. For instance: 'I *have* a fit and healthy body' is an effective positive affirmation, while 'I *could have* a fit and healthy body' is not.
- Combining positive affirmations with other mindfulness exercises such as journaling and/or visualization is a powerful and compelling way of manifesting positive changes.

Here are a few examples of positive affirmations or mantras:

- I take care of my body by exercising regularly and eating healthy.
- I am very confident and completely believe in myself.
- I am the best version of myself.
- My life is filled with love and I feel blessed.
- I feel blessed as I have a loving and supportive family.
- I always choose to be happy.
- I feel very safe, strong and indestructible.
- I feel grateful to be surrounded by so many friends and well-wishers.

- I feel immense peace inside me.
- I am successful in whatever I do.

So, whenever you find yourself sliding down the spiral of negativity, rescue yourself through the manifestation of positive affirmations. Consciously seek out positive words during self-talk. Remember, the secret to the success of an affirmation is the belief that you impose in it!

7. Mindfulness through Day-to-Day Activities

For someone who may just be starting to get curious about what mindfulness means, the concept may sound a bit heavy and daunting at first due to its esoteric nature. However, mindfulness isn't really complicated even for someone trying to grasp it for the first time. It can be experienced even in the most mundane activities such as while eating a meal, taking a shower, sun-bathing, taking a walk, listening to someone speak, watching the sunrise or sunset from the window, listening intently to the chirping of the birds, listening to music, reading a book, cooking a meal or even waiting in a queue.

Let's have a look at some examples of how we can achieve mindfulness through our routine, day-to-day activities:

Mindful eating: Most of us eat hurriedly and mindlessly, as we're distracted by thoughts of daily stressors, or we're multitasking with other activities, such as watching TV, reading the newspaper, etc. If we eat our food mindfully by engaging all our senses, it will help us relax our minds immensely by bringing our attention to the 'present moment'. So, sit down. Start with a short gratitude prayer for the meal. Eat in silence. Chew very slowly. Focus on the colour of the food, the taste, flavours, aroma, temperature and the texture of every bite. Notice how it makes you feel. Stop eating when you feel full.

Mindful eating enhances pleasure and satisfaction, helps us listen to our physical hunger cues, signals us to stop eating when we're full and even aids digestion.

Mindful walking or earthing: In today's busy and highly evolved tech era, we strive to make walking more 'meaningful' by cramming it with work-related phone calls, catching up on social media, listening to podcasts, messaging, etc. This takes away the mindfulness aspect from the walk. To make it a mindfulness exercise, we must take a walk in the park or on a trail, preferably without our phones. We should notice our surroundings keenly with all our primal senses. We must observe the abundance of nature around us, touch the leaves, smell the wonderful fragrance of flowers and listen to the birds chirping. And to enhance the experience even further, we can walk barefoot on the grass or ground and feel our feet make contact with the earth. This is called grounding or earthing. Make the pace leisurely. Mindful walking will help you calm down by taking your mind off the drudgery of the daily stressors. That's because nature can soothe our frayed nerves, and even help us cope with physical and mental pain. That's the positive power of nature!

Mindful music: To add mindfulness to the way we listen to music, we must focus completely on its subtleties, such as rhythm, beat, tempo, melody, pitch and distinctness of each instrument. During these mindful music sessions, let's ensure that we don't get distracted by other activities, as this can relegate music to the background. Put on headphones if that helps us focus. Also, there are a whole lot of musical compositions to especially improve mindfulness. Music produces serotonin that relaxes the mind and reduces the perception of pain in the body.

Mindful shower: We must use all our senses to engage fully by listening to the sounds of the water as it splashes. Inhale the aroma of soap/body wash or shampoo, and luxuriate in the warm water pouring over your bare skin. Focus fully on each part of your body as you clean yourself. Close your eyes and be grateful for this experience.

8. Forsaking Perfectionism and Embracing Self-Love

Self-love may not fit the bill of being a typical mindfulness tool, but since it is critical for our overall well-being, I took the licence to talk about it along with the other foundational interventions explained hitherto.

In today's hyper competitive world, there's a lot of negativity that constantly reminds us that we are not good enough, that there's a long way to go before we could be happy with our efforts or that we are far from being perfect. We ignore valuing our 'imperfect' efforts, judge ourselves harshly and feel disappointed with ourselves whenever we end up below our own expectations or others' expectations of us. Being perfect may sound like a great trait, but in reality, perfectionism is only a delusion. It is unreal, unattainable and unsustainable.

Striving for perfection is perilous to our state of mind because it comes from a place of ego and not from love and self-compassion. Ego disapproves when we struggle, stumble, trip or fall. That's because ego fears failure, and that fear leads to massive insecurities in us. Perfectionism is a kind of 'self-abuse' that prevents us from embracing our humanness unreservedly. Holding ourselves to unrealistic expectations of ourselves and others all the time is a roadblock to success. For instance, when we don't ace a race that we expected to, we berate ourselves saying that we are not good enough. We need to understand that we cannot have control over the outcome. It is in our prime interest to put our best foot forward and enjoy the process while not obsessing about the result.

Aiming to be perfect in everything we attempt can also lead to undue comparisons with others. This, in turn, can lead to envy, jealousy, insecurities and lower self-esteem. It is unfair to compare our lives with those of others, as everyone's success story and journey is different. When we honour where we are in any moment in life, it is a true act of self-compassion and self-love. While it's a good thing to strive to improve in all our positive endeavours, accomplishing this at the cost of our mental, emotional and physical health will only thwart our progress.

When we fixate on every misstep we take, and torment ourselves about every mistake we make, we become a roadblock to our own growth. This eventually causes a lot of stress and anxiety in our lives. Being on the guard all the time in fear of failing not only causes more mental stress but also prevents us from enjoying the present moment, and from being who we really are meant to be. As a result, we constantly suffer from low self-worth and self-esteem issues. When we beat ourselves up over a perceived failure, it's the fastest road to killing our self-confidence, dwindling our motivation levels and making ourselves unhappy.

I've witnessed several people in my life strive for perfection in various areas of their lives, and when they couldn't reach there or couldn't sustain it, they crumbled and fell prey to stress and anxiety as they couldn't picture themselves as being anybody but the best in their spheres. They developed shame and poor self-esteem.

We as humans are not meant to be perfect, and it is this imperfection in us that makes life authentic and beautiful. If we obsess over perfection, we're very likely to remain unfulfilled all our lives. Author Shannon L. Alder sums this idea up beautifully, 'There is no perfection, only beautiful versions of brokenness.'

It is more important and realistic to focus on progress rather than perfection. Valuing our humanness, with all our imperfections is self-love and self-compassion. Self-compassion, in fact, is a better motivator than self-criticism to bring about self-improvement. We need to remind ourselves that we're only human and *never* meant to be perfect, and therefore, allow ourselves to fail sometimes. Instead of ruminating over our 'failures', we need to capitalize on such events by ascertaining the areas in our life that need work and improvement, and then move on quickly.

Appreciating our progress (however small) and previous accomplishments in varied spheres will help us restore confidence in our ability to persevere and make progress with renewed zest. Therefore, self-love is about being kind, compassionate and understanding towards ourselves whenever we fail, make a mistake, feel inadequate or when someone else does better than us. It requires us not to be harsh, over critical or judgmental of ourselves under any circumstances. Put simply, it is about treating ourselves empathetically and in the same manner as we would treat a dear friend when she errs or stumbles.

Anureet Sethi, a Mumbai-based experienced clinical psychologist and founder of Trijog, an organization working on mental healthcare and holistic wellness, explained to me in an interview: 'There's a common query: if we are loving ourselves, are we becoming selfish? The answer is no. Because self-love is not about being selfish, it's about self-care. We have to start with thinking about sanity for ourselves. Only then we can extend sanity to others.'

I have personally suffered from harsh self-criticism for a long time. It has been a very negative place. An experience of childhood abuse made it tough for me to love myself unconditionally until I became aware of it recently. I've come a long way because I don't judge myself any longer when I'm unable to 'achieve'. For instance, I stopped running after a debilitating issue with my joints in the middle of 2020. Having been an accomplished marathoner for more than a decade, it could have been a devastating experience. But unlike earlier reactions to similar situations, it didn't faze me or bring down my self-worth. I was able to be kind to myself, understand the humanness of the situation and accept my vulnerability wholeheartedly. If I were the earlier version of myself, I would've crumbled with shame, denial and constant worry about what others think of me—'the achiever'—in my current state.

How Can We Develop Self-Love?

Here is a seven-step process that will enable us to develop self-love:

Step 1: The moment you feel self-criticism build up inside you, recognize it, acknowledge it, and then, accept it earnestly.

Step 2: Analyse the underlying emotions that you're feeling towards yourself, such as anger, irritation, frustration, guilt, low self-worth, dejection, etc.

Step 3: Try to look at the situation from another perspective rather than viewing it rigidly in black or white. It will help if you tell yourself that everybody messes up at times, and that having bad days is a universal human experience.

Step 4: Remind yourself of all your previous accomplishments, positive attributes and successful efforts, to offset the negativity.

Step 5: Think about what you could do that would help you be kind to yourself. If you feel that your behaviour, performance or words hurt you, build a coping plan for yourself to work on, so that a similar experience can be avoided by acting in a different way the next time. Then, forgive yourself and move past it.

Step 6: Use positive self-talk to motivate yourself on a regular basis rather than beating yourself up. Our internal dialogue literally changes our brain chemistry, and the most crucial conversations in life are the ones we have with ourselves. Positive self-talk can give us hope and bolster our mental and emotional well-being.

Step 7: Practise mindfulness tools such as meditation, gratitude, positive affirmations and journaling. They will help us become aware of our negative emotions immediately, and then help us release them effectively.

Are You Up for a Challenge?

Follow this laid-down routine every day for at least three weeks. By then, this should become a habit. Congratulations! You're on your way to becoming happier. Even if you stumble, practise self-love, forgive yourself and start the routine again till it becomes a habit.

Task 1: Meditation

Practise the following two to five minute body scan meditation:

- Find a quiet place wherever you are.
- Sit upright, comfortable and relaxed. Stand if you can't sit.
- Close your eyes.

- Take a few deep and conscious breaths.
- Bring all your attention to your body.
- As you scan your body, notice if any part is tensed, tight or sensitive. Soften it, relax it and breathe deeply into it.
- Begin with the left toes, sole, heel and then move to the right foot. Then, notice your left shin, calf, knee, thigh and then to the right leg. Move focus to the pelvis, butt, abdomen, lower back, upper back and chest. Then, notice your fingers, palms, wrists, elbows, arms, shoulders, neck and head. Finally, relax your forehead, eyelids and the facial muscles and unclench your jaw.
- Round off the session by taking a sweeping breath through your whole body, becoming aware of the body in its entirety.
- When you're ready, open your eyes.

Task 2: Journaling

Invest in a journal and before going to bed every night, write down:

- Five things/people/events that made you happy today.
- Pick a new topic daily from the section on journaling above and journal about it.

Task 3: Visualization

Think of a goal you want to accomplish in the coming year. Visualize achieving your dream from start to finish as per the steps (Believe, Quantify, Imagine and Take Action). This is how you could visualize:

- Find 10 minutes of undisturbed time, preferably on waking up.

- Sit in a comfortable position.
- Close your eyes.
- Imagine your life's dream as vividly as you can with graphic details.

Task 4: 4-7-8 breathing

- Find a comfortable place and position to sit in.
- Close your eyes.
- Part your lips. Making a *whoosh* sound, exhale completely through your mouth and empty your lungs of air.
- Close your lips and inhale through your nose into your belly for a count of four.
- Hold your breath for a count of seven.
- Exhale forcefully through your mouth for a count of eight with a *whoosh* sound.
- Repeat the cycle up to four times.

chapter 3

Nutrition

The doctor of the future will no longer treat the human frame with drugs, but will rather cure and prevent disease with nutrition.

—Thomas Edison, American inventor and businessman

Until I reached my mid-30s, I binged on junk food indiscriminately. In my childhood, I had no one fussing over me to eat nutritious food. My two siblings and I lived without a mother figure in the house, and thus, there was total lack of knowledge of nutrition in the family. Food was just a means of addressing our hunger, so that we could go about our day-to-day activities feeling fed.

This attitude of eating to feel 'not hungry' or just to deal with daily emotional stress continued until I started reading extensively on this subject while pursuing a certification in nutrition. This is when my eyes opened wide in shock. One of the most basic concepts that I learned in my academic courses was that we need a balanced diet of all major macronutrients and micronutrients for the proper growth and development of our bodies. Such a nutritious and wholesome diet during our childhood helps in building a strong foundation of health for our adulthood and old age. I realized that there had been no such foundation built for me in even the remotest sense. Ironically, my diet had generally comprised a mishmash of all the nutritiously inferior foods that I will be discussing in detail, and which I would advise you to avoid. I distinctly remember that all through these years, while on the outside I appeared healthy and slim, I suffered from multiple health issues, such as regular and severe bouts of acidity and gastric problems, stomach aches, lowered immunity that made me susceptible to fever, cold and cough, frequent mood swings, and eczema of the hands. I could never correlate these issues to my overall lifestyle, especially my poor food habits.

Armed with this newly gained knowledge and a strong belief that any day is a good day to start correcting my lifestyle, I immersed myself in learning the varied nuances of a good diet and incorporating these into my life. As a result, my eating habits improved dramatically over the years, and I started feeling a lot more responsible for my well-being. I no longer suffer from any of the lifestyle maladies that I mentioned earlier. I feel much healthier overall (mentally, emotionally and physically) at the age of 53 than I felt when I was 20 years younger. This is the outcome of an extensive 'lifestyle cleanse', with diet being only one factor out of the many others covered in this book.

I'm sure I'm not alone in my predicament of poor food choices in the past. I am also well aware of people like me who've had a difficult childhood without access to nutritious food, or the faintest idea about what a nutritious diet is. While we can't erase or amend our past, we can definitely learn from it and enhance the quality of our present and future from the moment we're equipped with the right knowledge. Therefore, in this chapter, I would like to share with you all that I learnt about a balanced diet and nutrition in all these years through my professional studies and personal experience so that you too can become healthier.

The Fundamental Concepts

Without understanding what lies at the base of good dietary hygiene, we may make repeated dietary mistakes by shooting in the dark, and end up running around aimlessly in the domain of nutrition. Before I go any further and share any dietary tools, it's important for us to understand certain foundational concepts.

1. We are all bio-individuals[35]: This means that one size does *not* fit all. We have unique bodies that come with a unique set of issues and requirements. There is no single specific diet type that will suit each of us perfectly. In fact, it might surprise you to learn that sometimes a specific diet that may have worked for you in the past, may not work for you in another phase of your life. This could be due to several reasons including changes in our age, weight, body shape, energy levels, activity levels and health status.

How do we choose a diet specific to our unique bodies? I would say that we need to experiment with different diets to figure out which of them suits our unique needs at the current stage in our life. All the innumerable diets doing the rounds have advantages as well as shortcomings. While they all may have been designed with our well-being in mind, the issue is that certain components of many of these diets may not specifically suit our individual bodies. So, examine and dabble with various diets, accept what works for you from each, and discard what doesn't. Use different dietary approaches as mere guideposts rather than obsessing over each of their components.

2. Food is medicine and food is poison: I firmly believe that a simple home-made meal can be our safest form of medicine.

A clean diet can actually save us many visits to the hospitals. Just by tweaking my diet slightly, I was able to heal myself of several health issues. Nutritious food has immense power to heal our bodies and minds. It can serve as a medicine to prevent and even cure us of many chronic illnesses. Inversely, consuming inferior foods can act as a slow poison for us, causing health issues. Therefore, we need to listen to our gut when it feels nourished with certain foods and unhappy with some others. Let us learn to recognize that every morsel we put in our mouth either supports or compromises our health; what we choose to eat can profoundly impact our overall health. The best part is that such choices are very much in our hands. Hence, we need to remember that if our diet is poor, all the world's medicines may fail to heal us, but if our diet is clean and wholesome, we may never even need medicines! By saying this, I'm not undermining the importance of seeing a doctor but rather emphasizing the point of food playing a preventative role in our health.

3. Eat real food: Foods such as vegetables, fruits, legumes, lentils, eggs, grains, spices, nuts and seeds are all real foods filled with several macronutrients and micronutrients. Packaged and processed foods (described later in the chapter) cannot nourish our body the way real foods can because the former undergo a lot of processing that robs them of their nutrients substantially. Even supplements cannot completely replace natural sources of nutrients available in real food. We should only use supplements to make up for any deficiencies in crucial nutrients while avoiding them as the primary source of such nutrients. Our bodies always respond best to real foods.

4. The 90:10 mindset: Despite sprucing up my diet over the years and eating generally clean on a regular basis, I've always built in a cheat day in my weekly diet. I am a firm believer in the 90:10 mindset in eating. By this, I mean that I eat nutritious, clean food 90 per cent of the time while indulging in my favourite foods and letting go of control on the remaining 10 per cent of the time every week. This mindset helps me stay on track for the rest of the week without feeling denied. Those of us who can follow a 100 per cent clean diet all the time have my deepest admiration and standing ovation. However, a 100 per cent clean diet means perfection, and perfection is unrealistic. We are humans and I believe it's perfectly fine to embrace our vulnerabilities from time to time. If by indulging in our favourite foods once in a while, we can stay on track for the rest of the week, then why not? Eating should be a positive experience rather than being a punishment or a chore. The 90:10 mindset can prevent us from feeling deprived and falling into a negative spiral if and when we fail. It can also help us stay motivated. After all, we should eat to nourish ourselves, not to feel deprived. I agree with what New York-based nutritionist and health coach, Jessica Cording says, 'When it comes to weight loss, feeding your soul is just as important as feeding your body. Enjoying favourite foods occasionally helps you do that.'[36]

5. Look at the big picture: It is not worth obsessing over the number of calories that we consume. While being aware of our general caloric intake may be a great starting point, ironically, obsessing over the exact number of calories in each meal every single day can add a lot of stress to our lives. Eating by counting every calorie is highly unrealistic. Good health is to be understood as an equation with myriad variables in our lives, such as food, exercise, spirituality, relationships and social life. So, obsessing over the number of calories will eventually suck the joy out of life. This is the reason why people who suffer from orthorexia nervosa (an unhealthy fixation with healthy eating) are not really happy people. Being healthy is more about *what* we eat rather than *how much* we eat. Focus more on the quality of food, and then, control the portion sizes rather than just counting each calorie.

6. Be compassionate: As mentioned previously, we are humans with our own set of flaws and vulnerabilities. This means that we could easily slip up on our dietary habits. At such a time, we need to remember to be compassionate to ourselves. As I outlined earlier, perfectionism is unrealistic and causes anxiety due to the fear of failure. When we judge ourselves every time we fall short of our own expectations, we feel shame and guilt. It's fine to fail, fall or stumble, as it is a part of common humanity. These are to be treated as learning opportunities. Shame and guilt can leave us feeling that we're not good enough and demotivate us from continuing in our efforts to eat healthy. Be self-compassionate. Be curious. Notice why you stumbled in the first place. Ask yourself: was it due to emotional stress? Or, was it due to lack of sleep or overtraining? What else could have caused it? This self-examination will help you regain your balance, and help you deal with the root cause, without using food as your primary coping mechanism.

7. Our lifestyle choices can alter our genetic make-up: Since time immemorial, we've been aware that our genetics, or DNA, determines and defines our health to a great extent. We've also known that poor dietary habits can increase our risk of developing physical and mental illnesses that our parents and grandparents suffered from. However, many of us might not be aware that there's strong scientific evidence that our lifestyles can modify our 'gene expression' to a great extent.[37] Our diet will definitely not change the sequence of our DNA, but foods that we eat can turn on or off certain genetic markers which play a crucial role in our state of health. A positive lifestyle includes clean eating, regular physical activity and efficient stress management, among other things. This can, to a large extent, modify the risk of diseases that we may be genetically predisposed to. Some of the genetic diseases that can be modified through positive lifestyle changes include diabetes, obesity, Alzheimer's, cancer and cardiovascular diseases. I read a great quote recently that explains this concept beautifully in a single phrase, 'Your genetics load the gun, your lifestyle pulls the trigger.'[38]

We need to understand that many of the lifestyle diseases such as type 2 diabetes, obesity, metabolic syndrome, heart diseases, etc. are the consequence of either one or a combination of the following: poor eating habits, lack of adequate movement, excessive stress, unfulfilled relationships and minimal exercise. Cleansing our lifestyle in a holistic manner can help us steer clear of many of these health issues without blaming our genetics for them.

8. All calories are not equal: A calorie is not just a calorie. Some calories are 'first among equals' and their quality depends on their source. Research has shown that the possible impact of a calorie of food causing type 2 diabetes is determined by where it comes from. For instance, 750 calories from green beans are highly beneficial for health, however the same 750 calories coming from a can of sweetened soda increase the risk of diabetes by seven times![39] Dr Mark Hyman, an American physician and a bestselling author, explains that the energy-balance hypothesis of 'a calorie is just a calorie' is highly misleading. Every calorie is *not* equal.[40] Therefore, to reiterate, despite having the same number of calories, sugar is dangerous for our health whereas greens, like broccoli, are very healthy.

A Balanced Diet

Keeping the above-mentioned concepts in mind, and the awareness that a nutritious diet is one of the foundational tools to live a healthier and happier life, let's dive right into the components of a healthy diet.

Thanks to the internet and the media shouting from the digital rooftops about a balanced diet, essential nutrients and countless weight-loss diets, many of us would have a general idea that macronutrients and micronutrients make up a healthy diet. For the sake of those of us who are unaware of the components of a nutritious diet (like I didn't have a clue a few years back), here's a quick overview of the primary nutrients.

Macronutrients

Macronutrients or 'macros' form the bedrock of a balanced diet. Macros consist of carbohydrates, proteins and fats. The ideal macronutrient ratio in the diet varies for each individual based on age, gender, height, body type, activity levels and health status. Therefore, specifying fixed proportions of these macronutrients for everyone is not recommended, as one size does not fit all!

There are three major macronutrients that form our diet:

1. Proteins

Proteins are the building blocks for growth that help in strengthening and repairing muscles, building healthy bones, keeping our skin soft and glowing, helping us in managing weight by keeping us satiated, boosting our metabolism, and giving us many other benefits. While proteins are very critical to health, they should be added to our diet as per the requirements of our age, weight, health status, activity levels, fitness goals, health status, etc. Too much overall protein in the diet can stress the kidneys, while excessive animal protein can raise the total cholesterol levels in the blood.

Some excellent sources of vegetarian protein are organic soybean and its products, such as tofu, dried beans (kidney beans, chickpeas, black-eyed beans and dried peas), dairy, lentils, legumes, seeds (pumpkin, hemp, sunflower, flax and chia), grains (amaranth, buckwheat, sorghum and quinoa), green peas, Greek yoghurt, nuts (almonds and walnuts) and nut butters. Good animal sources of lean protein include eggs, fish, seafood and chicken breast.

2. Carbohydrates

Carbohydrates, or carbs as they're popularly known, are the body's primary source of fuel, and are classified into two categories: simple or refined carbs and complex carbs.

- **Simple or refined carbs**: Simple carbs are primary sources of simple sugars, such as sucrose, fructose, glucose, lactose and maltose. These are mostly refined or processed carbs that come without the all-essential fibre. They are not good for health as they tend to cause insulin spikes, and constant insulin spikes can eventually lead to lifestyle illnesses such as type 2 diabetes and obesity. Some sources of common simple carbs are white sugar, white bread, white rice, refined flour and its products such as pizzas and burgers. Sugary breakfast cereals, candies, cakes, pastries, cookies, sweetened beverages and alcohol too are sources of common simple carbs.
- **Complex carbs or starches**: These provide ample fibre or roughage to the body, and get absorbed slowly. Roughage controls blood sugar spikes and creates a

feeling of satiety. The main sources of complex carbs are whole grains, such as brown rice, whole-wheat flour, oatmeal, millets, buckwheat, amaranth, barley, quinoa, lentils and legumes, vegetables like sweet potato, green beans, peas, carrot, beetroot and spinach, and fruits like apple, pear, plum, peach, pomegranate, orange and all berries.

While simple carbs are detrimental to health, consuming complex carbs in appropriate quantities is beneficial. The fibre in complex carbs helps in digestion and keeps our stomach satiated for long hours by regulating blood sugar, among other benefits.

3. Fats

The term 'fat' has been berated so much that it has created a fallacy that all fats are fattening and bad for health. It is important for us to overcome this false notion and understand that all fats are not equal. There are good fats and there are bad fats. While we may all know what bad fats are, let us take a closer look at the good fats.

Good fats are unsaturated fatty acids omega-3 and omega-6, which when consumed in moderation, are very beneficial for our health. They lower bad cholesterol levels, thereby reducing the risk of heart disease, aiding weight loss, reducing the risk of chronic inflammation that is a cause of many other lifestyle diseases, helping nutrient absorption and lowering the risk of age-related mental decline, along with being a sustained source of energy for endurance athletes during endurance events.

Some good fat sources are olive oil, coconut oil, ghee, olives, avocado, chicken; nuts like almonds, cashews, peanuts, hazelnuts, pine nuts, walnuts and pecans; pumpkin, flax, chia, sunflower and sesame seeds; and fish such as herring, mackerel, salmon, trout and tuna.

Micronutrients

While macronutrients form the foundation of our daily nutrition, it is not possible to attain physical and mental well-being without incorporating essential micronutrients, such as vitamins and minerals, into our regular diet. While micronutrients are required only in tiny quantities, they play an indispensable role in healthy and disease-free living. Most of the essential micronutrients are important for men and women alike; however, there are some vitamins and minerals that are especially significant for a woman's well-being. These include calcium, iron, folate, vitamins B12, D and B6, and magnesium.

As stated earlier, many of us try to make up for micronutrient deficiency in our diets simply by ingesting numerous vitamin and mineral supplements on a daily basis, without trying to enhance the fundamental quality of our diet. While supplements can provide some balance in a diet that is mildly deficient in essential nutrients or that occasionally falls short on these essentials, they cannot compensate for a completely unhealthy diet.

Healthy Diet Protocols

Each one of us is unique and different dietary approaches may work for us, but there are certain general protocols that are known to work universally and serve as a common denominator. I have compiled a comprehensive list of such dietary protocols that have worked in my own life and in the lives of many of my nutrition clients. If you're someone who has been struggling with following specific diets from time to time unsuccessfully, or has been wanting to follow a diet but doesn't have the time or bandwidth to follow a structured diet, worry not. Nothing really has been lost. To lead a healthy life and maintain a healthy weight, all you need to do is integrate the following guidelines into your life:

Abandon packaged and processed foods: Packaged foods are foods that come in boxes, plastic packets, wrappers, jars, bags or tins. Many of us are pressed for time to cook fresh meals, and therefore, packaged meals become our quick-fix options. Eventually, we get hooked onto the taste and texture of these foods as they're highly addictive. Thus, starts the formation of an unhealthy habit that becomes hard to discard. Replacing natural and fresh foods with packaged or ready-to-eat foods deprives our bodies of essential nutrients, besides being responsible for a number of lifestyle diseases, which include diabetes, obesity, high cholesterol, hypertension, high risk of stroke, inflammation, digestive disorders like gastroesophageal reflux disease (GERD), arthritis, dehydration, skin eruptions and a compromised immune system, to name just a few.

Packaged foods lack essential macronutrients, micronutrients and fibre needed for a healthy body. They are also filled with toxic chemical-based ingredients, such as harmful preservatives, additives, bisphenol A (BPA), monosodium glutamate (MSG), colourants, emulsifiers, stabilizers, thickeners, genetically modified plant matter, artificial flavouring, heavy metals like aluminium, etc. To top it all, they have an excess of the sugar-sodium-trans fats triad that takes a toll on our health over time. Due to these unhealthy ingredients in these 'food-like substances', our immune system can be seriously compromised over time, leading to various lifestyle diseases.

Some of the most common packaged foods best avoided

are: potato and corn chips, nachos, frozen or heat-and-eat meals, flavoured nuts, microwave popcorn, ketchup, pre-made sauces and salad dressings, canned or packaged soups, packaged noodles, packaged breakfast cereals, aerated drinks, energy bars, flavoured yoghurt, packaged juices and cookies.

If you must eat packaged food for whatever reason, make sure the food has a maximum of five ingredients, and you recognize each of these as something that you normally use in your kitchen.

Quit sugar and minimize refined carbs: Quitting sugar is one habit that has given me the quickest and most amazing results, leading me to feel great in my body and mind. I cannot deny that I've always had a massive sweet tooth. However, I've learnt to indulge smartly rather than giving in to its demands unwittingly. I've discovered the 'sweet spot' that keeps my sweet palate satiated in an absolutely healthy way without me falling prey to sugar and the refined carbs mentioned in the carbohydrates section above. I mostly indulge in a few dried blueberries or a piece of dark chocolate (85 per cent and above) as and when my sweet cravings attack. Once in 10 days or so, I also eat a portion of my favourite dessert to keep me satiated through the next 10 days or so. However, there's nothing better than giving up refined sugar completely if one can, as it doesn't serve any healthy purpose in the body.

There are just too many health detriments of consuming sugar and other refined carbs, such as increased risk of diabetes, obesity, cancer, gut inflammation, depression, fatigue, cognitive decline, acne, etc. Remember, sugar is eight times more addictive than cocaine, as per various scientific studies.[41]

Having said this, simple carbs are fine to a certain extent as an 'elective' fuel for endurance athletes as mentioned earlier.

While fruits are also simple carbs, they are also loaded with beneficial nutrients, such as fibre, vitamins and minerals.

Eat mostly high-fibre foods: Dietary fibre is a type of complex carbohydrate. It is only found in plant sources of food. Adding a generous helping of fibre in every meal is a great way to keep our gut healthy, regulate blood sugar, stave off food cravings and create satiety quickly. Fibre aids digestion, mainly by speeding up excretion and preventing constipation. It is the most important nutrient for our digestive tract that can prevent serious illnesses, such as colon cancer and type 2 diabetes. Fibre is also very rich in prebiotics that nourish the gut flora. It is also crucial for weight management, heart health and to reduce bad cholesterol.

While fibrous foods are very filling and create satiety quickly, they actually contain fewer calories in proportion to their large volume. Some of the best fibrous sources of food are green leafy vegetables, other vegetables (cauliflower, broccoli, turnip, peas, sweet potato, green beans and carrot), fruits (berries, apple, pear, plum, peach, pomegranate, orange), whole-grains, lentils, legumes, dried beans, dried fruits (dates, figs, prunes and apricots), nuts (almonds, pistachio and walnuts), and seeds (chia, flax, pumpkin and sunflower).

One important caveat: we need to increase our water intake when we increase the fibre in our diet.

Don't drink your sugar: Sweetened beverages or 'liquid sugar' are among the most fattening foods in the modern diet. That's because sugary beverages have excess sugar content and it's very easy to over-consume sugar in a liquid form. It doesn't even give us the feeling of satiety that fibrous foods can provide. Even fruit juices are chock-a-block with sugar and are just as harmful as sweetened, soda-based drinks. These sweetened beverages are a double-edged sword, as they trigger a vicious cravings cycle for sugary foods and other simple carbs, which generally leads to binge eating and overeating. Large amounts of sugar from these foods are then turned into stubborn fat in the liver.

Many scientific studies, including one by Harvard University, have concluded that sugar-sweetened beverage intake on a regular basis is associated with an increased risk of lifestyle diseases such as obesity, type 2 diabetes, cardiovascular diseases, certain types of cancers and some autoimmune diseases.[42] Another startling research revealed that it takes an average person about 50 minutes or five miles of running to burn off 16 teaspoons of sugar that are contained in a 600ml can of a soft drink![43] So, take a moment to pause and ponder before gulping down that liquid sugar!

Add high-quality protein: We have already discussed earlier in this chapter the myriad benefits of adding protein to our daily diet. Adding lean and clean sources of protein to every meal can help us stave off cravings for unhealthy foods, while providing other great benefits for health, such as being the building blocks for bones, muscles, tissues, cartilage and skin. In fact, protein is an important component of every cell in our bodies.

Eat good fats, mostly omega-3: Fat has been demonized for ages. It's high time we understood that all fats are not evil! Good fats are critical for both physical and mental growth. To name a few of the benefits: they supply fuel for the body, help absorb certain vitamins, lower depression, generate growth hormones, reduce bad cholesterol and help brain development, among a horde of other benefits. The cherry on the cake is that good fats even help us lose unwanted fat by accelerating the fat-burning process and increasing metabolism. It's not the fats in our diet but the high-sugar and high-refined carb content that is the leading cause of obesity, insulin resistance, and a number of other illnesses that are associated with unwanted weight gain.

It's the omega-3 component of good fat that is specifically most beneficial. The omega-3 in fats reduces inflammation, lowers bone loss issues such as osteoporosis, slows down the risk of mental issues like Alzheimer's and brain trauma, and so on.

Here are some of the healthiest fat sources we can add to our diet: avocado, nuts (almond, walnut), seeds (flax, sunflower, pumpkin, sesame and chia), oils (ghee, cold-pressed coconut oil and extra virgin olive oil), Greek yoghurt, dark chocolate (85 per cent + cocoa), freshwater fish (preferably wild-caught), eggs and chicken breast.

Two caveats related to fat consumption:
1. Eat fats (even healthy ones) in moderation as fats are much higher in calories compared with carbohydrates and proteins.
2. Too much omega-6 in our diet can cause chronic inflammation in our body.[44] The quantity of consumption of omega-6 should be much lower than omega-3. Some of the omega-6 fatty acid sources that can cause inflammation are vegetable oils, such as corn oil, sunflower oil, canola oil, soybean oil and cottonseed oil.

Eliminate trans-fats: Trans-fats are the bad guys and the ones to be avoided completely. Trans-fats, also known as hydrogenated fats, are mostly made from oils through a food-processing method called partial hydrogenation. By enhancing the flavour of foods, these oils get people hooked onto unhealthy foods. Worse still, it's very easy to overindulge in them as they're present in most commercially available foods.

They're responsible for a whole lot of lifestyle illnesses as they cause chronic inflammation—a precursor to heart ailments, such as raised levels of bad cholesterol, lowered levels of good cholesterol, clogged arteries and hypertension.[45] They can even cause other issues like obesity, type 2 diabetes and dyspepsia (also known as indigestion).

These fats are found in processed foods, packaged foods and foods cooked in restaurants that use hydrogenated oils. Foods such as French fries, cakes, cookies, pastries, pizzas, burgers, doughnuts, mayonnaise and ice cream especially fall in this category.

Regulate saturated fats: Saturated fats are not as evil as trans-fats but need to be used very sparingly. They can be potentially harmful to health if consumed in excess. Overindulgence in these can increase the risk of inflammation-related illnesses, such as metabolic syndrome, dementia and cardiovascular diseases. Saturated fats are mostly found in animal-based sources of food like red meat, organ meat, poultry, full-fat dairy, whole milk, butter, cheese, cream, ice cream, lard and many salad dressings.

Load up on assorted vegetables and eat some fruit: A meal plate brimming with rainbow-coloured vegetables is not only attractive to the eyes but is also mood uplifting and promotes stellar health. A plant-based diet is the primary source of fibre that is extremely beneficial for gut health. It is also the richest source of antioxidants and phytonutrients, is rich in many minerals, is low in saturated fats and has negligible cholesterol. A plant-based diet can not only prevent the risk of ailments, such as certain cancers and diabetes, but is also known to reverse them.

However, purely plant-based diets may be deficient in certain essential nutrients, such as omega-3, and vitamins B12 and D3, and thus, need to be supplemented.

Add a rainbow colour of vegetables and fruits to your daily diet to reap maximum health benefits because different colours provide different health rewards. The richer the colour of vegetables, the higher the level of antioxidants. Add vegetables to all the meals that you can.

Fruits are a very rich source of antioxidants, flavonoids and fibre that are anti-inflammatory and possess immunity-boosting properties. However, one needs to be careful as fruits are also loaded with simple sugars. Therefore, choose and eat your fruits mindfully.

Eat mostly home-cooked food: There can be nothing better than warm, aromatic and freshly cooked home food. Food cooked with the right intention, love and awareness of all the ingredients emanates positive energy into the body and nourishes it like no restaurant or packaged food ever can.

Experimenting with various healthy cooking styles such as grilling, steaming, quick boiling, stir-frying, roasting and water sautéing will not only keep us healthy and motivated but will also make the process interesting. Explore new vegetables, and new condiments and herbs that you haven't tried yet. Try out new recipes and new ways of cooking.

Planning your menu and grocery shopping in advance for the following week can help you save a lot of effort and time, and avert the guilt of eating outside food due to unpreparedness.

Regulate portion sizes: I love noted French moralist François de la Rochefoucauld's quote that reads, 'To eat is a necessity, but to eat intelligently is an art.'

A lot of my nutrition clients would feel puzzled at their 'unexplained' weight gain even though they would eat the standard three or sometimes just two meals on most days. On investigating their meals further, I would invariably find big portion sizes as the culprit for this baffling weight gain.

Portion size is one of the main components of weight management. When we are really fond of certain foods, it's very easy to overeat. We generally tend to overindulge in high-calorie foods. Therefore, it is very important to eat mindfully and pay attention to the volume of our food. We also tend to overeat when we are distracted, such as while watching TV or checking our messages on the phone.

Here are some smart ways of exercising portion control:

- Use small cutlery and side plates for even the main meals. Food on a small plate seems to appear much more than on a dinner plate.
- Eat food mindfully, taking enough time to chew every bite.
- Put your fork, knife and spoon down after every bite while you chew your food.
- Try to skip second helpings. Wait for a few minutes before going for the second round. It takes a few minutes for the brain to convey to your stomach that you're full.
- Don't feel obliged to finish your children's leftovers.
- If eating at a restaurant where the portion sizes are big, either split the dish with others at your table or get the extra food packed.

Always read food labels: Food labels are often unabashedly misleading. It's a very common practice by many food manufacturers to mention the word 'healthy' on the food label, and yet, have numerous unhealthy ingredients added to the food.

It's especially true of sugar, because of its numerous variants and countless aliases. On a number of food labels that I have read, multiple sugar variants, such as fructose, glucose, corn syrup and maltodextrin are listed separately in small quantities. These may be found towards the end of the ingredient list. Thus, sugar may show up later in the list and that too, under four or five different aliases. This is a tactic to ensure that sugar doesn't show up as the 'first' ingredient on the list because the ingredient listed first is what the manufacturer uses in the largest quantity to make the product.

Besides sugar, there are numerous other ingredients, such as preservatives, additives, emulsifiers, stabilizers and thickeners, which are generally added to packaged foods that are really harmful to our health as mentioned earlier.

Therefore, read food labels without fail. Scan the entire ingredients list on the label. If you find any of the aforementioned ingredients on the label, it's a red flag for you to drop that food from your grocery list! Even better, avoid buying a food product with an ingredient that you can't even pronounce or don't use in your kitchen.

Don't go shopping hungry and without a list: A growling stomach is an easy target for unhealthy foods to jump into your shopping cart from the supermarket racks. Willpower is at its lowest when we're hungry. When we shop on a hungry stomach, we're very likely to be tempted to buy every attractive food package that meets our eyes. I've experienced this first-hand during my grocery runs until a few years ago. Once you fill up your kitchen cabinets with unhealthy foods, there generally is no escape from indulging in them. That's exactly why 'out of sight out of mind' makes so much sense.

Also, avoid going to a food store without a list, as yet again, you're likely to come back home with a pile of junk food. According to Paco Underhill, the author of *Why We Buy: The Science of Shopping* (Simon & Schuster, 2008), 'Two-thirds of what we buy in the supermarket we had no intention of buying.'[46] The psychology behind this is that when we don't have a list of specific items handy, we start looking at the wide range of vibrant food packages on display, and end up going on an impulsive buying spree, stacking our trollies with unhealthy foods that we didn't intend on buying. And, it's a double whammy if we leave home hungry as hunger whets impulsiveness!

Eat clean food: In today's scenario, trying to eat clean on a regular basis is not short of a Herculean task. Almost any food you lay your hands on is contaminated with harmful chemicals and toxicants. Arsenic, stimulants, growth hormones and antibiotics are fed to chickens and cattle to make them appear healthy. The 'very healthy' fish that we may be eating may have picked up contaminants such as mercury and polychlorinated biphenyls (PCBs) from the water. The grains we may be consuming from the swankiest departmental store may have genetically modified organisms (GMOs). Even most fruits and vegetables nowadays are grown with strong pesticides, herbicides, antibiotics and artificial chemicals.

All these toxins can cause serious health concerns, and sometimes even autoimmune diseases over a period of time. What's really sad is that many who would have fallen seriously ill due to these toxins may never realize that the source of their sickness lay right inside the foods that they thought to be 'healthy' all along.

Foods grown non-organically are known to cause serious health issues such as thyroid dysfunction, lower intelligence quotient (IQ) in children, hormone dysfunction, breast cancer, nerve disorders, brain tumour, low birth weight and food allergies, to name a few.

Therefore, it's very critical for us to know the source of our food. Unfortunately, most of us can't investigate our food sources as it's a cumbersome and time-consuming process. Many times, the only way to know it is through the food labels that read 'organic', 'free-range and cage-free' (for eggs), 'certified humane', 'grass-fed', and 'pasture-raised' (for animal products), etc.

While organic food is the safest and higher in antioxidants, it is also painfully expensive. Therefore, it is okay to choose natural, local and seasonal food. Fresh local food is much better than imported organic food because imported food loses its freshness due to long transportation times.

Maintain a food journal: The simple act of recording what you eat can give you a lot of insights and help you troubleshoot roadblocks in your healthy eating efforts. A food journal creates self-awareness and is a great accountability tool besides being a self-care tool.

Write your experiences with different foods when you experiment with your diet. Check-in with your mind, body and emotions on how they react to these changes. Note them all down honestly. Your journal should ideally include a diet recall for a week to be able to identify specific patterns. We need to include a weekend because many of us eat outside food on weekends.

Your journal can help you identify specific patterns in your eating habits such as overeating and skipping meals, and help you make a connection between what you ate and how it made you feel physically and psychologically. It is a visual record that can help you immensely in making progress. The insights you will gain on reviewing your journal regularly will help you identify and change undesirable food habits.

To be an effective accountability tool, your food journal should include all the specifics of your diet (for all the days that you are monitoring in your journal) along with portion sizes, home-cooked meals, outside meals, add-ons like sauces and dressings, water intake, date and timings of each meal, your emotional responses and notable physical symptoms (if any). Revisit your journal regularly to see how you have progressed in your healthy food journey. And don't forget to pat yourself for even a tiny positive shift that you were able to make in your diet. This will keep you motivated.

Clear your kitchen cabinets of all junk food: Remove all unhealthy food from your pantry. Don't buy any foods that might test your willpower by luring you at the mere sight of them. Not buying indulgent foods that I just can't resist has worked very well for me. No junk food in sight, no unhealthy temptation to succumb to.

Eat early dinner: Eating dinner early has numerous perks for the body. When you eat your last meal of the day by around 7.00 p.m.–8.00 p.m., it helps burn more fat, lower blood sugar and aid in digestion. Eating dinner two hours before bedtime will help you get much better sleep too.

Try intermittent fasting: Intermittent fasting (IF) is when we alternate between periods of eating and fasting. This could be followed in different ways. Three such approaches are as follows:
   a) Eating only during an eight-hour window and then fasting for the other 16 hours of the day; for example: have breakfast at 10.00 a.m. and dinner at 6.00 p.m. and no meals after that till 10 a.m. the next day; or

b) Fasting for one whole day in a week; or
c) Limiting food intake to 500 calories per fasting day.

Intermittent fasting with an eating window of eight hours and fasting for 16 hours (16:8) works very well for me. I have been following it for five days per week for about two years now, and it has led to great health benefits. It's definitely the easiest out of the three approaches of IF.

A caveat: if you have a health condition, or are on certain medications, do not undertake IF without the advice and guidance of your doctor. If you are pregnant or are breastfeeding, IF is not for you.

IF is very effective in weight loss as it leads to ketosis, which is a metabolic process that occurs when our body does not get enough glucose or glycogen through carbs as the primary energy source, and therefore, starts burning stored fats instead.[47]

IF is most effective if we eat healthy food and do not feast on processed food once the fasting window is over.

Stay well hydrated through the day: Water is a very essential nutrient that is often excluded from healthy diet discussions since it is not something we eat. Our bodies need water to carry out numerous bodily functions that enable us to stay healthy. It helps in weight management, transports nutrients within the body, refreshes cognitive abilities, fights fatigue, flushes out toxins, prevents constipation and mood swings, and most importantly, keeps us from getting dehydrated.

Many of us consider dehydration as a very benign health problem. Some of us may not even be aware of the symptoms of dehydration. And as a result, may end up seeking strong medical treatment for dehydration symptoms, such as headaches or constipation, while all that is required is drinking enough water. Dehydration occurs when the body loses more water than it takes in. It could be attributed to hot and sultry weather, excessive sweating, fever, diarrhoea, vomiting, certain medicines, etc. Dehydration can cause fatigue, migraine headaches, light-headedness, irritability, constipation, muscle cramps, drowsiness, exhaustion, diminished focus, disorientation, and in severe cases, can even be life-threatening.

As in the case of our diet, hydration needs are also unique to each one of us. Age, activity levels, health status, weather changes, certain medications, and the type of food we eat, are some of the factors that determine our water needs. How much water do we need per day? As a thumb rule, a normal healthy person should drink about eight glasses of water a day (including other healthy fluids). This should be increased during hot and humid weather or if you are having a lot of fibre in your diet, and during vigorous physical activities. So, learn to tune into your body's need for hydration and take those sips of water in time.

Gut Health

Did you know that our 'enteric nervous system' or 'the second brain' resides in our gastrointestinal tract (gut)? And that 95 per cent of the body's serotonin (the feel-good hormone) which influences our mood in a big way is located in the gut?

This second brain is constantly communicating with the 'brain in our head', and therefore, plays a key role in regulating physical wellness and our overall mental health. Even our day-to-day emotional well-being hugely depends on the messages from the 'brain below' to the 'brain above'. A big chunk of our emotions is influenced by our second brain in the gut. The 'butterflies' that we experience in the stomach when we feel fear or excitement, are the nervous pangs in this second brain that are indicative of our physiological stress response.

The point I'm trying to make is that our gut is much more intelligent and sensitive than we give it credit for. Besides its primary functions, such as digestion, absorption of nutrients and the excretion of waste, the gut also has a profound influence on our immune system. Inflammation in the gut has been linked to stress, anxiety and depression.[48] It is called the 'gut-brain connection'. Our diet and lifestyle impact the balance and vitality of our gut. And then, our gut health and the state of our microbiome affect our digestive health, brain chemistry, heart health, immune system, liver and skin health, mood, sleep and a lot more.

Gut health is highly dependent on the balance of numerous microbiomes or microorganisms that live inside the digestive tract. Multiple scientific studies to date have shown links between gut health and the immune system, endocrine disorders, food sensitivities and food intolerance, autoimmune diseases, skin conditions and cancer. This is how consequential our gut is!

Some of the common symptoms of impaired gut health are gas, bloating, constipation, diarrhoea, heartburn, chronic fatigue, unexplained weight gain or weight loss, poor nutrient absorption, skin conditions like eczema, food intolerances and sugar cravings.

So, what really upsets our gut?

There are several diverse factors that can lead to weakened gut health, and some of them are beyond our control. These include diet during our infancy, whether we were breastfed or not, genetics, diet during adulthood, age, certain medications (especially antibiotics) and stress levels. The mode of child delivery (normal or caesarean/C-section) also has a huge impact on our gut health, and the latter mode is known to adversely impact the gut flora.[49]

As you can see, there are some factors here that we cannot control, but there are other factors such as our diet and stress levels that are certainly in our control through eating a gut-friendly diet and ensuring proper stress management.

We can restore our gut health through certain lifestyle interventions such as:

- Managing stress through self-care habits and tools mentioned in this book
- Avoiding gut-irritating foods like alcohol, caffeine, sodas (including diet sodas), processed and packaged foods, high-sugar foods, sweetened beverages and artificial sweeteners
- Adding gut-friendly foods like prebiotics (plantain, garlic, onion, flaxseeds, chicory root and asparagus), probiotics (yoghurt, buttermilk, kimchi, carrot kanji, home-made vegetable pickles [without oil], etc.), fermented foods and plant-based fibre to our diet
- Eating slowly and chewing food thoroughly
- Eating an early dinner
- Staying hydrated as adequate water flushes out toxins from the body
- Exercising regularly
- Getting enough and good-quality sleep
- Avoiding reckless use of antibiotics, unless it is unavoidable
- Using non-toxic personal care and cleaning products
- Following an elimination diet. This is done by eliminating certain suspect foods like gluten, dairy, soy, corn, eggs, shellfish and peanuts from the diet for three continuous weeks. Then, reintroducing them one at a time, every four days, and observing how the gut reacts to them.

Kris Carr, an American author and wellness activist, has described the gut in beautiful words: 'Quite literally, your gut is the epicentre of your mental and physical health. If you want better immunity, efficient digestion, improved clarity and balance, focus on rebuilding your gut health.'[50]

So, take care of your gut, trust its 'instincts' and strengthen it!

Deconstructing Food Cravings

We are human, which means that our world is not perfect. Many times, we may eat for reasons that have nothing to do with our physiological hunger (the real hunger), but to satiate either our psychological (read emotional) hunger or to subconsciously make up for the deficiency of certain essential nutrients.

Many cravings are at a more physical level such as the ones resulting from dehydration, deficiency of an essential nutrient, hormonal imbalance, seasonal craving for hot foods in winters and vice versa, those related to occasions and festivities, etc. Most such cravings can be addressed easily. For instance, craving spicy and salty foods after an endurance activity may be a sign of dehydration and sodium loss through excessive sweating. Drinking salty lemonade could address it. I remember how intensely I craved salted buttermilk after my long runs.

However, it's the psychological or emotional cravings that we need to understand carefully and sensitively. They exist at a much deeper level and need more attention. Indulging this type of craving is often a coping mechanism for dealing with uncomfortable emotions or to fill an emotional void. These cravings could be a symptom of an unfulfilled relationship, over-exercising, loneliness, not exercising at all, being bored, low self-esteem, being stressed and anxious, the stress of a very demanding career, absence of peace of mind, resentment, lack of spirituality, etc.

Cravings are important signals from our bodies to guide us towards addressing something they are missing. If we can pause and mindfully listen to our bodies' cues, it can lead us to identifying and addressing these imbalances. We cannot deal with psychological cravings effectively by being harsh on ourselves, feeling guilty, shaming ourselves and beating ourselves up mentally. We can only address and cure these cravings through deep self-compassion and with the help of mindfulness-based interventions. Food as a coping mechanism may comfort and distract us in the moment, but eating to fill unmet emotional needs can leave us feeling more distressed than before. This vicious cycle seldom ceases until we recognize the triggers (root cause) and address them proactively.

How can we deal with food cravings?

At a more corporeal level, food cravings can be mitigated by:

- Grazing on healthy fats such as seeds and nuts
- Adding lots of fibrous plant-based foods to our diet for creating satiety
- Adding more lean protein sources to the main meals
- Keeping ourselves well hydrated at all times
- Sipping warm green tea or herbal infusions
- Indulging sweet cravings with sweet vegetables (pumpkin, sweet potato, beetroot and carrot) or with a bowl of yoghurt with fresh fruit
- Indulging in creative hobbies like painting, learning a musical instrument, dancing, etc.

At the deeper level, we can tackle cravings caused due to emotional reasons by taking the following approach:

- The first step in healing is to *acknowledge the craving*. If we ignore or resist it, it is likely to become stronger. Saying to ourselves 'It's okay to have cravings' is an empathetic start towards managing cravings.
- Then, we need to take a few moments to *process our emotions*. Identifying the exact emotion that we're experiencing is very important to take the edge off the craving. At this point, having a supportive internal dialogue (positive self-talk) can really help. Telling ourselves that we are just having a human experience, is an important step towards fostering self-love and self-worth needed to obliterate the craving.
- Next, it's important to *ask ourselves these questions* before reaching out for our comfort food: 'Am I truly hungry?', 'Could it be thirst?', 'What else could be causing this impulse to eat?' This will heighten our awareness about our real hunger and help us gauge what's going on inside us. It will also help us create a much-needed pause between the trigger (craving) and the response (gratification by eating our comfort foods). This mental pause is powerful as it can save us from needless binges by shifting our thought process in the moment. If we realize that it is just thirst in the garb of a craving, we can hydrate ourselves and quell our craving.
- If the craving continues to pester us, we can use the pause to *shift our focus* by indulging in a calming activity which can get us out of our impulse zone quickly. Some of these are taking a few deep belly breaths, sipping a herbal infusion, calling up a friend,

journaling about our feelings, stepping out for a short walk, etc.
- If the craving still persists despite distracting ourselves, then we may need to *put things into perspective*. We should reflect on the consequences of succumbing to our cravings, such as lowered energy, sluggishness, unwanted weight gain, guilt, self-loathing, etc. By then, it is likely that the craving will subside.
- While we learn to manage our cravings in the moment, it is crucial to *plan ahead* by exploring the origin of the cravings and *addressing the root cause* with curiosity and without judging ourselves. These triggers could be loneliness, rejection, low self-esteem, workplace frustrations, etc. Identifying the triggers and managing them can help us eliminate the recurrence of these food cravings in the future.
- A regular practise of certain transformative self-care tools can help us reinforce our resolve against feeding our food cravings and embark on the restorative journey of mindful eating. Some of the profound interventions are meditation, maintaining a food journal (discussed in detail below), ensuring seven–eight hours of nightly sleep, enrolling for yoga classes, doing daily breath work, exercising regularly, volunteering our time for a cause close to our heart, etc. These tools further heighten our self-awareness about the triggers behind our cravings. It then becomes easier to manage cravings from this place of self-compassion and empowerment.
- We can also learn to take control of our recurrent cravings by employing the *'if-then' algorithm* discussed in detail in Chapter 8 (Happiness Habits).
- However, if our cravings arise from more serious

triggers such as depressive thoughts, rage and grief, do not hesitate to meet *a certified clinical psychologist* as they are trained in helping us deal with such issues.

Maintaining a Food Journal

Cravings can be reduced and even annihilated with the power of questions. Journal about the cravings by asking yourself questions such as:

1. Why are you triggered to eat? (For e.g., loneliness, frustration, etc.)
2. When are you triggered to eat? (For e.g., days with time)
3. What are you triggered to eat? (For e.g., sugary foods, fried foods, etc.)
4. How do you eat? (For e.g., quickly, many times in quick succession, etc.)
5. How do you feel while you are eating and immediately after you have eaten? (For e.g., guilty, happy, etc.)
6. How you feel two hours after eating? (For e.g., bloated, sluggish, heavy, etc.)

By reviewing our journal regularly (daily, weekly and monthly), we can identify certain behavioural patterns, and awareness of these can help us manage our cravings judiciously.

When we start observing the nature of our cravings and learn to surmount them with our preferred self-care tools, the cravings will eventually diminish, losing their power over our physiology and psychology. All through this process, do remember to be compassionate with yourself and not to beat yourself up when you falter or fail. It's perfectly normal to slip one step backwards when you're taking three steps forward.

You're still making progress. So, don't lose hope, plan ahead, and start afresh!

Women and Weight Loss

There was a time when health and fitness to me meant being slender with an hourglass figure. I strove day and night to remain 'slim'. My happiness was literally conditional upon the shape I saw in the mirror and the number I saw on the weighing scale. Whenever I faltered, I 'punished' myself with three hours of running and workouts. I would be over the moon if someone complimented me over my looks and shape, and I would be crestfallen if someone commented that I had put on weight. It was this easy to tug at my emotional strings and push me up or pull me down.

With time came self-awareness, and with self-awareness, I realized that I was constantly judging myself and bringing down my self-worth. It was a sign that I lacked self-compassion and self-love. Looking back, all I can say is that it was not a happy place to be in.

Obsessive preoccupation with weight and body shape is a recipe for distress and unhappiness. Excessive exposure to incessant media focused on physical attractiveness is leading many of us to attach our self-worth to how we look. This, in turn, has led us to focus obsessively on our weight and shape. When our primary focus is on being thin or skinny at the cost of everything else in life, joy becomes elusive and we put ourselves at a high risk of toppling our physical, mental and emotional health. Physiologically, it can leave us malnourished and at risk of lowered immunity. Dr Steve Maraboli, a behavioural scientist and author, aptly endorses this view. He says, 'By choosing healthy over skinny you are choosing self-love over self-judgment. You are beautiful!'

By no means am I undermining the importance of being slim, fit and feeling good in our bodies. I'm only explaining how weight is only a small piece of the puzzle called health, and unhealthy fixation on weight alone, can adversely impact many other important areas of our lives. It is especially distressing when our weight-loss efforts are triggered by skewed, socially constructed ideas of beauty.

Now, although I may slip from time to time from my ideal weight range, I neither beat myself up nor lose my sanity over a few kilos. I have learnt smart ways of getting back on track gradually without getting overly stressed. There is no denying that it took me a few years of experimentation with different dietary approaches to reach my ideal weight range. I had to unlearn a few myths and upgrade my knowledge bank to arrive at this ideal weight range that makes me feel as healthy on the inside as on the outside.

The most important determinant in weight management is the blood sugar regulation. A low-carb diet can certainly help you become a fat-burning machine. A low-carb diet helps lose unwanted fat by stimulating our metabolism to start burning fat for fuel. Most of the diet pointers that I've shared in the 'Healthy Diet Protocols' section of this chapter (p. 57) are cues on how to effectively manage our blood sugar levels.

Here are some of the other important (non-dietary) tips that are as important in weight management as the dietary tips:

Sleep for eight hours a night: It turns out that lack of sleep and weight gain are very intimately connected. When we sleep less, ghrelin (the hunger-stimulating hormone) increases, while leptin (the fullness hormone) diminishes. This leads to constant food cravings that lead us to start indulging in untimely eating.

Manage stress efficiently: Stress leads to spikes in cortisol (the stress hormone) in our bodies which can make us crave high-calorie and unhealthy foods, such as sugar, refined carbs and inferior fats. Employing self-care tools described throughout the book can really help in reducing stress.

Move through the day: Even if structured exercise is difficult to squeeze in, add as many short walks as possible throughout the day. Every movement counts. Find 'Opportunities to Move' (OTM) every 20-25 minutes (explained in detail in Chapter 4).

The next time you scrutinize yourself in the mirror and silently cringe at the imperfections that you see, remind yourself that you're much more than just your body. And definitely much more than what the world chooses to see in you.

Are You Up for a Challenge?

Maintain a food journal for three weeks.

Here are the steps to maintain and review it:

1. You can either print a food diary from numerous options online, download a food journal app on your phone (if you don't enjoy writing) or buy a blank notebook and design your own format as per your goals.
2. Write down the date and time of eating everything every day.
3. Record your weight at the start of making notes and at the end of each week.
4. Leave extra spaces on each page to record your comments or observations about everything that you eat. Here, you may make a mention of any cravings, binges and any healthy food habits you started. You can also make note

of your feelings before and after cravings, binges and the healthy food that you started eating.
5. Make note of everything that you eat every day with the exact or approximate quantity that you consume.
6. Track your water intake in case you're looking to increase it.
7. Review the food journal at the end of each week.
8. Identify the patterns in your food journal by asking yourself some questions, such as:
   - Have I just been eating due to boredom, to overcome stress or as a result of feeling other emotions?
   - Have I been eating mindlessly while multitasking with other activities such as watching TV?
9. Plan small and realistic changes to rectify these patterns.
10. Every time you make a positive change, pat yourself to appreciate your effort. You could even highlight that entry with a star or smiley to make you feel good and to keep you motivated towards making more progress.

Follow Elimination Diet

In almost all the above-mentioned stages and life phases in a woman's life, certain foods are major offenders leading to hormonal imbalance. Eliminate the following three foods from your diet, starting with one per week, starting tomorrow.

Week 1: Sugar

This will include any preparation with refined sugar, such as sweetened hot and cold beverages, confectionery items like cakes, doughnuts, pastries, cookies and desserts, etc.

Week 2: Refined flour

This will include any preparation with refined flour including bread, pizza, burger, cookies, cakes, fried snacks, etc.

Week 3: Packaged and processed foods

Some instances of packaged foods are: packaged meals, microwave popcorn packs, packaged salted snacks, ketchup, readymade dips, packaged soups, cold-cut meats, etc.

chapter 4

Physical Fitness

Health is the gift we give ourselves every time we work out.

—Toni Sorenson, author

I wasn't always an exercise aficionado. On the contrary, I actually despised exercise. I hardly even moved much through the day. When I look back at my sedentary past, I'm definitely not proud of this phase because it was the lowest point in my life in terms of my happiness and health. My emotions were in a state of disarray, my health markers were anything but good, I had no physical strength, and I had a toddler's attention span, if you understand what I mean.

While I was first introduced to intense physical exercises during my training in the Indian Navy in my 20s, I hadn't yet fallen in love with exercising. Exercise almost felt like a punishment to me. It was a tough chore that had to be done, and my body obediently complied for fear of drawing retribution from our tough and demanding instructors. But the positive aspect was that the intense training made me realize that my body was capable of withstanding an insane amount of physical rigour, that I had a tremendous inner strength which I never knew existed and that this inner strength had never been tapped into before.

Some time in 2005, I accompanied a friend to the gym and availed a few trial sessions which I enjoyed thoroughly. I then enrolled for a three-month membership and this got me started on the path to exercising. I began slowly at first and worked on various routines and machines to see what suited me best. Over a period of time, as the benefits of exercising started having a very positive impact on me, I started putting my heart and soul into the workouts. And rest, as they say, is history. Now, I'm hooked to exercising for life. Over the years, exercise has given me much more than just a fit and toned body. It has become an intrinsic part of my being.

If I were to choose a health and happiness tool that I have used most extensively in my adult life so far, exercise wins hands down. For many years at a stretch, exercise stayed as my only go-to tool for everything—from getting fit and strong to mitigating stress, to keeping lifestyle illnesses at bay, and even to being a means of socializing. Exercise alone made me feel alive! I can say this unhesitatingly that exercise has been one of the greatest life changers for me, and has been instrumental in my metamorphosis from a timid, lazy, unfit being who perpetually felt like a 'dainty damsel in distress', into a confident, active, fit and strong woman.

My biggest learning from exercising for so many years is that a sedentary lifestyle is a breeding ground for many lifestyle illnesses and mental afflictions. Lack of physical activity is not only capable of upsetting our health cart, but can derail us mentally and emotionally too.

A sedentary lifestyle is one of the major causes of preventable death worldwide. It is a high-risk factor for health issues,[51] such as stress, anxiety, and depression,[52] cardiovascular diseases, obesity, hypertension, certain cancers,[53] type 2 diabetes, osteoporosis,[54] chronic inflammation, lower back conditions, headaches, hair and skin issues, fatigue, lowered metabolism, dementia and early death. And yet, many of us don't feel inspired enough to start working out.

Despite being aware of the tremendous benefits of exercising, many people avoid physical activity due to the presence of multiple psychological and physical barriers. It is very important for us to delve deep into these obstacles to understand where they come from, and how to overcome them.

Common Barriers to Exercising

While some of us don't exercise due to sheer laziness and lack of resolve, the most common reasons that have often been cited by my coaching clients and acquaintances over so many years are listed below. Remember, where there are problems, there will be solutions as well. So, along with the exercise barriers, I have laid down some practical solutions to overcome them. These have worked very effectively for me and a large number of my coaching clients.

Barrier 1: 'I have no time to exercise.'

Extended working hours, long commutes, family responsibilities, raising young kids, a lot of travelling and caretaking duties can compel you to push fitness to the lowest rung of your priority ladder. However, there are always ways to sneak in little bits of physical activity into your day. Every minute counts towards exercise time since any exercise is better than none.

The Solution

If you can't spare time for a longer workout session, such as an hour, here are a few ideas:

- Plan ahead in the day to look for small free-time windows. Squeeze in a quick walk, do desk exercises, take a few flights of stairs and stretch during these gaps. Try to add these small exercise portions throughout the day (at least a total of 30 minutes would be good). Use a part of your office lunch break to go for a walk or to climb stairs. Have walking meetings and walking phone calls, and stretch often whenever you realize that you have been sedentary for some time. When working on projects with tight deadlines (like I had to do in the final phase of writing this book), I often resort to walking phone calls or climbing my building stairs for a quick burst of activity. It keeps me sane and reenergized to get back to work.

- Keep a short workout plan that you can do almost anywhere—at home, before lunch at work or while travelling outstation. You could consider some short workouts, such as Tabata—which is an HIIT (high-intensity interval training)-based circuit training, sprints, bodyweight exercise circuits, jump rope, etc.
- Try to slip in about 30 minutes to one hour of exercise on weekends by taking something off the schedule that is less important, or involve the whole family in an activity, such as nature walks, bike rides, day hikes, yard work, etc.
- If it is possible to wake up even 30 minutes earlier than your usual time on some days of the week, try to fit in a workout of your choice. This could be brisk walking, jogging, running, free body-weight workout, swimming, etc.
- If you don't have time to commute to the gym, work out at home by choosing a YouTube workout video of your choice. There are numerous workout videos

- available on every type of exercise, and exercises for different body types.
- You could kit up on home-exercise props like a jump rope, resistance tube, resistance band, ankle weights, a Swiss ball, dumbbells, kettlebells, a medicine ball (also known as an exercise ball, a med ball or a fitness ball) and a loop band. Then, you can exercise whenever you get time. I resort to this approach when I'm on tight-deadline projects, by preparing my own HIIT workouts at home.
- While watching TV, you could use this time for cycling on a stationary bike, sitting on a Swiss ball and doing leg raises, lifting light dumbbells, doing squats and lunges, etc. Or even better, you could use each commercial break to put in a short HIIT workout.
- Walk, jog or ride your bike to go shopping in your neighbourhood.

Barrier 2: 'I'm too mentally exhausted to exercise.'

It is very normal to feel mentally, emotionally and physically scattered, especially when we are juggling multiple roles such as parenting, caretaking and being a full-time professional. While it is important to listen to our bodies and not push ourselves into any activity that causes more stress, exercise in fact, is a great energizer and stress buster.

The Solution

You need to know that exercise energizes us by releasing the feel-good hormone (endorphin) in our brain, which rejuvenates the body and mind. Try scheduling exercise at times of the day when you feel less mentally exhausted. Try to keep it short and simple during stressful days. Don't worry about metrics such as your timings during your run, etc. Also, listening to peppy music while exercising can alleviate stress. If you still don't feel like exercising, take a walk instead. And make sure that you don't forget to take at least a day's break every week to avoid feeling overwhelmed. There have been many occasions when I've felt mentally burnt out. But I have specially made time to exercise on such days knowing well that once I start the workout, my fatigue will start to dissipate, and completing the workout will leave me feeling refreshed and ready to deal with the challenges ahead. Exercise never fails to pep me up.

Barrier 3: 'I get no break from kids.'

For mothers, squeezing in exercise between taking care of kids, their homework, managing household, doctors' appointments and meeting workplace demands, among other things, can feel overpowering. And to be able to add exercise to this routine may feel nearly impossible. The good news is that there are ways to navigate this life-situation.

The Solution

Kids love it when their parents play with them. Not only will you get some exercise, but there'll also be some real-time parent–child bonding too. So, here are some fun workout ideas for you and your kids: jog; play juvenile games like hopscotch (I have enjoyed doing this when my son was growing up); put on some fun music and shake a leg with them; run with them while they're cycling; go for a nature walk; if you have a toddler, go for a walk with them in the stroller; attempt fun home workouts together, such as squats, planks, mountain climbers, leg raises, Spiderman planks, etc.

Barrier 4: 'I travel a lot for work.'

A lot of us miss out on exercise when we travel. If it's a one- or two-day trip with a jam-packed work schedule, missing exercise may not be a big deal, but if it's a longer travel, exercise can definitely become a happy part of it.

The Solution

It's actually easy to add exercise during travel, as most hotels have gyms and swimming pools. You also have roads to walk or run everywhere. So, here are some ideas to exercise while travelling:

- Work out in the hotel gym.
- Pack a resistance band, Theraband or jump rope, and design a short HIIT (explained later) workout using these props.
- Exercise to a YouTube workout video.
- Go for a run.
- Do two–three circuits of bodyweight exercises like squats, lunges, crunches and push-ups in the hotel room or in a nearby park.
- Do a few sets of Surya Namaskar (Sun Salutation).
- Perform a 15–20-minute full-body stretching routine.
- Put on your playlist and gyrate to the energy of music.
- Swim, splash and play in the hotel pool.

So, on your next outstation trip, don't forget to pack your sports equipment along.

Barrier 5: 'I am not motivated to work out', 'Exercise is boring', 'I have no willpower to exercise', 'I'll start next month'.

It is very easy to procrastinate exercising, especially if you're at the point of starting your fitness journey. Even the smallest of impediments may seem like boulders in the way of starting exercise. The key to beating procrastination and boredom is finding an exercise form that seems pleasant and undaunting, and that caters to your current fitness level too.

The Solution

It's only the start that is the toughest. If you can manage to get yourself past your front door for a week or two, exercise is very likely to become a habit.

Here are a few steps for you to motivate yourself to exercise:

- Think of a health or fitness goal you may have, such as to stay healthy, lose a few inches to fit into a favourite dress, become stronger, be able to run a marathon one day, etc. This goal could become your 'why' for exercising.
- Break your goal down to a few achievable goals, like losing two kilograms in a month, or being able to do a 5 kilometre run in a month.
- Experiment with different exercise classes by availing trial sessions.
- Engage in the exercise(s) that give you joy.
- Start small. Increase workouts gradually in volume or intensity so that you don't feel overwhelmed. This will help you to exercise by moving the needle bit by bit.
- Find an accountability partner to keep you motivated, such as a gym buddy, a running group member or your spouse.
- Remember, whenever you lose motivation, revisiting your personal goals is a great way to get reinspired to exercise. I like what someone once said, 'You will never have this day again, so make it count.'

Barrier 6: 'I have health issues.'

Health issues or debilitating injuries can often demotivate us from exercising for the fear of aggravating our issues. However, you should know that there are enough exercise options available to suit almost any type of illness.

The Solution

If you have ailments like asthma, osteoporosis, heart-related issues or a history of spine injury, take the opinion of your doctor to guide you to the type of exercise best suited to you. For instance, aqua aerobics or walking in water in a swimming pool may be recommended for people with arthritis and osteoporosis. Once you've consulted your doctor and established the type of exercise that is most suitable, start slow and easy. This will keep you motivated to exercise.

Barrier 7: 'I'm clueless about how to start.'

This feeling is completely natural, as starting anything new can be confounding in the beginning. Therefore, deliberating on things such as what your health presently looks like, what your wellness goals are, which are the exercises you think you might enjoy, are good starting points that can give you a clue as to how you can embark on your fitness journey.

The Solution

Here are a few cues to getting started:

- Talk to a fitness coach about different forms of exercise.
- Try out different exercise options available around you at the gyms, group fitness classes, swim sessions, etc.
- If it's the gym you choose, get a well-qualified personal trainer to help you exercise, or find a gym buddy who

is a fitness pro and can help you start out sensibly.
- If it's running that you're interested in, join a structured running group, as they have specific running plans as per the levels of the runners. Alternatively, if you know a runner friend who could help you start, use the opportunity to start running.
- If you're someone who prefers alone time during exercise, think about the activities that are individual in nature, such as walking, running, cycling, swimming, etc.

Barrier 8: 'Gym membership is too expensive.'

You don't really need a membership to a gym, a fitness class or a running group to exercise. There are numerous alternatives to working out anywhere on your own. All you will need is some comfortable sportswear, sports shoes and a strong will to start exercising.

The Solution

Some exercise ideas wherein you don't need to go to a gym are:

- Bodyweight strength training/conditioning circuits at home (given in detail later). Exercises such as squats, push-ups, burpees, lunges, mountain climbers and planks can be built into circuits. All these exercises work for multiple muscle groups, simultaneously.
- Strengthening circuits with basic fitness props, such as light dumbbells, resistance bands, ankle weights, Swiss balls, medicine balls, loop bands and jump ropes. You can make exercise circuits with any combination of this fitness gear. There are almost infinite workout videos on YouTube for every skill and fitness level as well as age and body type.

- Play a YouTube video and dance along or work out.
- If you prefer the outdoors, go for a brisk walk, jog, run, cycle or go on a day-long hike.
- Add movement throughout your day (discussed in detail later).

Barrier 9: 'I don't have family support to exercise.'

There can be situations where women face resistance from their family members to step out to exercise. This could be a result of the lack of knowledge about the importance of exercising, harbouring rigid cultural social beliefs against exercising, a joint family set-up, or in the worst case, chauvinistic outlook and insensitivity of male family members towards women. While these situations can be tricky to circumvent easily, there are ways to try and work around them.

The Solution

Some suggestions for breaking the 'no-exercise' impasse when you lack family support are:

- Sometimes, just a heart-to-heart talk with your close ones may open the doors for your fitness. Explain to them the numerous benefits of exercising, and how important it is for your mental, emotional and physical well-being. Make them exercise with you, if that strengthens your case in favour of exercising.
- Dance or play running games with your kids as often as you get the opportunity.
- Step out early in the morning for a walk if that is feasible, take the stairs or squeeze in a quick home workout when you're home alone.
- Volunteer to shop personally by walking to the grocery store rather than ordering through home delivery.

Don't feel guilty about giving enough priority to exercising, as it is a very critical self-care tool for your personal well-being.

Barrier 10: 'I'm already slim. I don't need to exercise.'

You may be thin without having much lean muscle mass that is crucial for being fit and healthy; or you may be thin while also carrying a relatively high fat percentage on your body; and in a worse scenario, you could be slim and yet suffer from health issues such as clogged arteries or type 2 diabetes. Even if you have none of the above issues at present and you're plain genetically thin, as it turns out, there are just too many health benefits of exercising that make it imperative for everyone (overweight and slim alike) to incorporate exercise or movement in their regular routine. Therefore, just being slim and trim doesn't define how healthy you may be. I've personally known some slim people who had no physical activity in their lives and suffered from many lifestyle illnesses like type 2 diabetes, asthma, joint issues and anxiety. When some of these people started an exercise regime, they were able to heal themselves to a great extent.

The Solution

Losing weight should not be the primary goal for exercising, it should be done for its countless benefits. If you're already slim, you could exercise to prevent illnesses and stay healthy, gain adequate muscle mass, look toned, have more energy through the day, and enjoy good mood, etc. Some of the exercise options to choose from if you're slim or skinny are strength training, yoga, Pilates, tai chi, brisk walks, short HIIT circuits or interval training, etc.

Barrier 11: 'I'm too old to start exercising.'

There are enough studies that confirm that it's never too late to start exercising. The US's Department of Health and Human Services confirms that 'even if you have had an inactive lifestyle, research suggests that you are never too old to benefit from exercise'.[55] Exercise is good at any age, and the more active you are (regardless of your age), the more health benefits you garner, such as decreased risk of type 2 diabetes, heart diseases, breast cancer, high blood pressure, metabolic syndrome, depression, etc.

The Solution

Even if you're starting to exercise for the first time in your 40s or thereafter, your body has the capability of getting stronger by building muscle mass.[56] You just need to be extra careful by starting slowly, at a low intensity, and with shorter durations. And if you do suffer from an illness, don't forget to consult your doctor before starting an exercise regime.

Starting slowly and gradually increasing the time and intensity of exercise will ensure that you are able to enjoy a painless exercise regime even during your veteran years. As aptly put by Dr Kenneth Cooper, the founder of Cooper Institute and also known as the father of aerobics, 'We do not stop exercising because we grow old, we grow old because we stop exercising.'

Benefits of Physical Activity

Many of us still consider exercise as mainly being a tool to lose weight. While exercise does help in losing weight by revving up the metabolism, this benefit is a very small part of a truckload of benefits that it bestows. If weight loss is the only goal for you to exercise, you need to know that what you eat has more impact on your weight than your exercise. All the exercise in the world won't help you lose weight if your nutrition is unwholesome and out of whack. If your nutrition is in check and you eat healthily, only then will exercise aid in healthy and sustainable weight loss. Losing inches is only one positive by-product of exercising. The whole truth about exercise is that it can enhance the quality of our lives in the form of many physical, cognitive and emotional benefits. Once you start working out (even at moderate intensity), you're bound to accrue the ripple effects on your overall well-being.

Here are some of the most amazing benefits of exercising:

- **Reduces stress and anxiety and lowers the risk of depression**: This by far, is one of the biggest benefits of working out. Exercise is a powerful therapy to uplift our mood in no time. There is enough scientific research confirming that regular physical exercise, even of moderate intensity, reduces symptoms of mild to moderate depression. Exercise has been my biggest go-to tool to fight stress and anxiety for many years now. Going for a run or hitting the gym for strength training has, without fail, restored my mental and emotional well-being.
- **Enhances cognitive functioning**: Exercise has the potential to prevent and delay cognitive decline and reduce the risk of dementia. Exercise also augments memory by enlarging the hippocampus in the brain.
- **Strengthens immunity and fights inflammation**: Even a 20-minute session of moderate exercise can stimulate the immune system to produce an anti-inflammatory cellular response that reduces inflammation, which is the precursor of most lifestyle

diseases. It, therefore, lowers the risk of cancer, viral infections, heart ailments, lowers bad cholesterol and high blood pressure.
- **Slows down our biological clock and the ageing process**: Exercise doesn't just make you *look* and *feel* younger, it actually *makes* you younger by changing the length of your telomeres, which are cap-like structures at the end of our chromosomes that protect them from fraying. Their length shortens as we get older. Progressive shortening of telomeres is associated with problems of ageing, degeneration of skin cells and other issues. However, a regular exercise regime lengthens telomeres and has an anti-aging effect at the cellular level that prevents age-related and degenerative physical as well as mental ailments.[57]
- **It benefits our bones**: It increases bone density and prevents age-related bone decline. Exercise (especially strength training) lowers the risk of osteoporosis and fractures by preventing bone loss.

Other health benefits of exercise include:

- It supports healthy weight and revs up metabolism by building muscle mass.
- It prevents muscle atrophy.
- It increases blood flow and oxygen circulation to keep the skin glowing.
- It improves the quality of sleep.
- It aids in digestion.
- It increases longevity.
- It increases stamina and endurance.
- It helps in raising self-esteem by enhancing body image.

- It increases balance and flexibility.
- It boosts confidence and self-esteem.

Last but not least, you end up inspiring others to take up exercising on a regular basis!

Movement Versus Structured Exercise

If you happen to be a fitness enthusiast who exercises for an hour each day, that's excellent! However, you may not be aware that exercising for an hour a day, *but* thereafter, remaining sedentary for the rest of the day is not really beneficial for your health. It's more important to put in a lot of movement *throughout* your day. It really does matter what you do during the rest of the day. If you're getting very little movement all day, and you land up sitting in an office chair or on a couch at home for most of the time, you're at a high risk of getting lifestyle diseases such as cardiovascular issues, high blood pressure, type 2 diabetes, etc.

Research shows that even for people who regularly perform high levels of activity, there is a threshold of 10 hours of prolonged sitting, beyond which our cardiovascular risk really goes up.[58]

Physical activity doesn't necessarily mean only 'structured exercise'. Exercise is a type of physical activity. Physical activity means movement, and movement is the key to fitness. Movement is a much wider term than structured exercise. Exercise is structured and repetitive, while movement is any physical activity that a person does which entails energy expenditure. For many people, it's actually easier to get movement into the day than to exercise due to various constraints mentioned in the 'Common Barriers to Exercising' section (p. 86). Movement is the key to our physical fitness and energy. It benefits our muscles, bones, joints, brain, heart, lungs and psychological health. Several movements (however leisurely) added up over a day can greatly impact our health in a very positive way.

If you're someone who's not particularly fond of a structured exercise regimen but are quite active throughout the day, this is a good situation to be in. It's all about regular movement, after all!

A great way to add more movement to our day is through non-exercise activity thermogenesis (NEAT). Once we understand the concept of NEAT, it can help us introduce a lot more movement to our day than we presently do. NEAT can especially motivate people who feel lazy or don't like the idea of exercising. That's because movement through easy ways is less overwhelming and intimidating than exercise.

So, what exactly is NEAT? As per the National Center for Biotechnology Information's definition, 'non-exercise activity thermogenesis (NEAT) is the energy expended for everything we do other than sleeping, eating or playing sports-like exercise.'[59]

Here is how you can add NEAT to your daily life whether at work or at home:

- Walk, walk and then walk some more. Squeeze in walk breaks through the day.
- Invest in a fitness tracker like pedometer or a smartphone that will prompt and motivate you to walk at least 10,000 steps a day as a standard norm.
- Try to move around every 25–30 minutes from your desk or couch.
- Park your car a little away from the destination and walk the rest of the distance.
- Ditch the elevator or escalator; take the stairs whenever you can.

- Use a cycle as your new mode of transportation to work or to the market, as far as possible.
- Stand up every now and then, and stretch your body for a minute or two.
- Run around with your kids and play with them.
- Walk your dog instead of assigning the duty to someone else.
- Indulge in gardening, if possible.
- Dance whenever you feel the urge to.
- Do a few exercises like leg and arm raises while watching TV.
- Have walking meetings and walking phone calls.

Every NEAT activity substantially increases the metabolic rate of the body as we need the energy to move even the smallest of muscles in the shortest range of motion. Research also confirms that people who move throughout the day are more likely to lose and keep off the unwanted calories as compared with those who are sedentary throughout the day.[60]

For people who have jobs where they need to sit most of the day, travel a lot or for those who are simply lazy, all is not lost. Hope appears in the form of NEAT. Structured exercise every day needn't be the only way to enhance your health and happiness quotient.

Here's my little rhyme to pep you up:

Exercise + micro-movements throughout the day
Keep lifestyle illnesses at bay
Just add more movement into your day,
And watch fitness and health walk your way!

So, the most ideal way to keep fit is to exercise regularly and move more often every day. Isn't that NEAT?

The Types of Exercise

While we are all well aware of the fact that running, cycling, swimming, weight lifting, yoga and Pilates are all forms of exercise, it helps to know which category of exercise each of these belongs to, and what are their individual benefits. This classification will give you a better idea of what is suitable to your health and personality. While there are many complex ways of classifying exercise, I shall keep them simple. There are five broad categories of exercises:

1. Aerobic training
2. Anaerobic training
3. Flexibility training
4. Balance training
5. Hybrid workouts

The most holistic approach would be to incorporate exercise at least from the first four categories into your weekly schedule by designing an ideal combination that works best for your body type and is aligned with your goal too. In fact, there is scientific research that confirms the importance of all these types of exercise to enhance your wellness.[61]

Therefore, I have explained each of these forms with examples so that you can pick the right exercises of your choice.

1. Aerobic training

It is also popularly called cardiovascular conditioning, cardiovascular endurance or just cardio exercise. As explained by Harvard Medical School, aerobic exercise is one that speeds up your heart rate and breathing for a sustained period of time.[62] Aerobic exercise involves large muscle groups in a rhythmic activity that you can sustain over a longer period of time as compared with anaerobic exercise. Your heart, lungs and muscles work in tandem, during this type of activity.

Your cardiovascular endurance is a big indicator of the state of your current physical health or fitness level. If a person can sustain a reasonably long cardio endurance session without feeling tired, this suggests that the person has a good fitness level. If you find yourself struggling with it, this means that you need to add at least two sessions of any type of aerobic exercise to your weekly exercise schedule. This will ensure that your heart, lungs and muscles work more efficiently to utilize oxygen intake, and this, in turn, will augment your health and fitness level.

Aerobic exercise is very effective in relaxing the mind, reducing the symptoms of depression,[63] building stamina, strengthening the heart and lungs, reducing the risk of strokes,[64] lowering blood pressure,[65] improving cognitive functions, helping you sleep better, reducing the risk of lifestyle illnesses like type 2 diabetes[66] and so on.

Some aerobic activities are weight-bearing, such as running, stair climbing and dancing, and can put a strain on your joints. Other aerobic activities are non-weight bearing, such as swimming, cycling, indoor rowing and elliptical trainers, which are more suited for people with joint problems.

Following are some types of aerobic exercises that one can do:

- **Endurance running**: All slow to medium effort runs, such as base runs, long steady-state runs and marathons. (I shall discuss this in detail later in the chapter.)
- **Endurance cycling**: When cycling is done at a slow to medium pace over a reasonably long time, it forms an aerobic exercise. The group cycling classes at the

fitness centres, known as spinning, usually employ a mix of low-, medium- and high-intensity cycling.
- **Lap swimming**: Lap swimming at a slow to medium pace for at least 30 minutes is an aerobic activity. It is one of the best aerobic exercises because it is very relaxing for the body due to the buoyancy of water that cushions the joints. The cooling effect of water is soothing to the body, despite the reasonable effort that this activity involves, and it counteracts the heat generated from the effort exerted during the activity.
- **Hiking**: If time is not a scarce resource for you, hiking is one of the most amazing endurance exercises not only for the body but for the mind as well. Unlike running, it is moderately paced, and yet you can get a great lower body workout due to the undulating and steep terrain that shows up off and on. Walking in the midst of nature, hearing the birds chirp, observing the flora and fauna, and breathing fresh air can be very therapeutic for the mind and body. It can boost your mood and reduce stress and anxiety considerably.
- **Power walking**: Power walking or brisk walking is an especially beneficial aerobic exercise for people with health or lifestyle issues, such as coronary heart disease, high blood pressure, obesity, metabolic syndrome, osteoporosis, etc. Its intensity is high enough to give you all the benefits of aerobic exercise, yet it is less intense than exercises such as running and dancing to keep you injury-free. Walking has more benefits than meets the eye. A good walk can do wonders for your physiological as well as psychological health. It can uplift your mood, alleviate stress and energize you. Walking reduces the risk of cognitive decline

and dementia. It heightens mental agility, enhances self-perception and helps you connect with yourself, leading to an engaged state of mind. Walking even improves our immunity. Paul D. White, the founder of preventive cardiology, had once said, 'A vigorous five-mile walk will do more good for an unhappy, but otherwise healthy, adult than all the medicine and psychology in the world.'

- **Dancing**: Dance is a great form of aerobic exercise if you're someone who doesn't enjoy going to a gym or some of the other aerobic activities. You're also spoilt for choice as there is never-ending innovation in movements and dance forms that keep the interest levels high. Some of the popular dance forms are Bharatanatyam, Kuchipudi, Kathakali, Odissi, Kathak, Zumba, Hip-Hop, Salsa, belly dance, ballet, etc. The list is endless.
- **Stair climbing**: You expend three times more energy while climbing stairs as compared with brisk walking. It's the most cost- and time-effective aerobic exercise to indulge in. What's more, if you're consistent, you're guaranteed a tighter and firmer butt and a pair of super-toned legs. Even gyms have this option nowadays in the form of machines that mimic the staircase-climbing experience.
- **Floor/step aerobics classes**: These group classes are high-tempo choreographed cardio workouts. Besides providing the usual aerobic exercise benefits, these classes are desirable for people who enjoy working out in groups and are looking for some motivation to exercise.

2. Anaerobic training

Anaerobic exercise is a high-intensity exercise involving quick bursts of activity that are performed at peak effort for a short period of time. During this type of exercise, a lot of energy is released in the body within a short period of time, and the oxygen demand of the exercise surpasses the oxygen supply. Basically, this process helps the body to build tolerance to the lactic acid that causes fatigue, and this in turn, improves muscle endurance.

Some of the benefits of anaerobic exercises are common with aerobics exercises, such as strengthening of the heart muscle, mood upliftment and relaxation, creating the ability to withstand fatigue, and reduced risk of lifestyle illnesses like type 2 diabetes. Other distinct benefits of anaerobic exercise are that it builds muscle strength and lean body mass, improves metabolism by building lean body mass, strengthens bones, and promotes healthy ageing by slowing the physical decline of bone density and muscular atrophy.

The following activities are examples of anaerobic exercise:

Strength training: Strength training is performing any exercise that drives our muscles outside of their comfort zone, compelling them to build back stronger, in readiness for the next challenge. The muscle that is being worked out contracts when resistance is applied to it. This builds muscular strength, muscular endurance and bone density. Strength training can be done either by using our own body weight or by using external weights such as dumbbells, barbells, weight machines in the gym, kettlebells and medicine balls, or using external resistance with resistance bands, TRX suspension, etc.

HIIT: High-intensity interval training, or HIIT as it is popularly called, involves repetitions or intervals of short yet high-intensity bursts of speed, with rest or slower recovery phases between each interval. Each burst is of a very high effort, getting the heart rate to 70-90 per cent of the maximum heart rate zone. These workouts are short and generally last for 20-40 minutes as they're really intense. HIIT workouts can be incorporated in running (tempo runs and shorter intervals), cycling and swimming. HIIT can even be a part of circuit training with body-weight exercises, such as burpees, jumpng jacks, mountain climbing, etc. Tabata is yet another type of HIIT training that is even shorter in duration. HIIT is an amazing way to improve cardiovascular conditioning, muscular strength, muscular endurance, stamina and agility and thereby accelerate weight loss.

Skipping or jump rope: Jump rope may appear like a kid's play prop, but it is a very potent exercise tool to boost quicker fat-burning, build muscle endurance, improve cardiovascular health, boost stamina, enhance physical as well as mental agility, and build all-around athleticism.

Plyometrics: Plyometrics is a type of exercise that trains muscles to produce power (strength + speed). Plyometrics primarily involves explosive moves and quick force production. It builds muscle strength, endurance, power, speed, agility and explosiveness, and is a great way to burn fat calories.

3. Flexibility training

Flexibility in simple words is the range of motion in our joint(s). It is the ability of our joints to move efficaciously through the complete range of motion. Being flexible means having supple muscles, tendons and connective tissues that can stretch and elongate easily through the body's available range of motion, allowing you to carry out movements like bending down to touch your toes, twisting your torso to glance behind or reaching your arm over your head.

Flexibility can be very specific to individual joints and muscle groups within your body. So, while some people have a remarkable level of flexibility overall, many people face tightness in some areas of their bodies. As we keep growing older, the natural range of motion of the body keeps reducing unless we follow a regular regime of flexibility training. When ignored, it can adversely affect a person's quality of life by causing injuries, and by impairing the body's balance, agility and coordination.

You can improve your flexibility by incorporating a stretching routine into your daily fitness regime. Some exercise types that increase our flexibility are:

Yoga: Yoga is one of the most popular exercises being practised around the globe, and virtually no exercise matches up to yoga as a mind-and-body practice. Through its postures and breathing techniques, yoga helps diffuse tension and restlessness and infuses a sense of calm and relaxation for the mind and body. Deepak Chopra, author and prominent advocate of alternative medicine, says: 'Through yoga, you can release the emotional toxicity stored in the body. Just as changing thought patterns can influence the body, changing the position of the body can influence the mind and facilitate emotional release. As you stretch your muscles and expand your range of motion, you shift the bodily patterns that trap emotional pain.[67]

Pilates: Pilates is another wonderful low-impact flexibility exercise type. Ruchi Kishore, a Mumbai-based celebrity Pilates instructor, explains that 'Pilates is a full-body workout that improves flexibility, focuses on core strength, eases back pain, improves posture, works on balance, coordination, pelvic alignment, joint control and stability, and is amazing for rehabilitation. Above all, Pilates is a blessing for people with neurological conditions.'

Tai Chi: Tai chi is a gentle, graceful and non-competitive exercise of Chinese origin. It comprises gentle, flowing and continuous movements.

Myofascial release: This is a very effective pain and soreness relieving technique that involves applying gentle yet consistent back-and-forth pressure onto the connective tissue. Myofascial release reduces muscle immobility and relaxes muscles, alleviates post-exercise soreness, relaxes contracted muscles, improves blood circulation, breaks lymph knots, increases joint range of motion, enhances overall flexibility and prevents the risk of injury. Myofascial release can be achieved by using tools such as foam rollers, trigger point balls, lacrosse balls and massage sticks.

Overall, compromised flexibility can adversely affect the quality of life by making day-to-day activities and movements very challenging. Picking your toddler up, reaching out on higher shelves to get something or simply scratching your back can be tedious and uncomfortable. Hence, I highly recommend stretching every day before and after exercise or attending at least two sessions of flexibility training per week.

4. Balance training

Balance training involves exercises that strengthen those muscles that help us maintain our balance, stability and coordination while staying upright. Balance exercises also prevent falls and injuries. They mainly involve the activation of core and leg muscles. Balance exercises can be reasonably challenging. Yoga, Pilates and tai chi include poses and exercises that require us to have proper balance. Balance exercises can also be performed with the help of a Bosu ball, kettlebell, stability ball, medicine ball and TRX.

5. Hybrid workouts

A hybrid exercise is any workout that combines two or more forms of exercise together to form a new type of exercise. These workouts are fusions of either two or more forms of the following exercises: aerobic, anaerobic, flexibility and balance.

Examples of hybrid workouts are as follows:

Circuit training: This hybrid workout includes circuits that alternate resistance exercises (bodyweight, dumbbells, kettlebells, resistance bands, etc.), with quick bursts of cardio exercises (jog on the spot, stationary bike, rowing machine, etc.). You can decide the number of circuits based on your fitness goals and stamina. If you're new to exercising, you need to learn individual exercises properly first before moving on to circuit training styles of workouts that are reasonably challenging.

CrossFit: This is an activity done in a group that incorporates elements from powerlifting, plyometrics, HIIT, calisthenics, bodyweight exercises, indoor rowing and other exercise forms. CrossFit is focused on high-intensity functional movements. It is a blend of cardiovascular endurance and resistance training. It involves the use of bodyweight exercises, such as burpees, air squats, box jumps and pull-ups. It also includes strength training moves, such as deadlift and thruster, that are done using equipment like barbell. CrossFit is a challenging workout regime, and therefore, not recommended for rank beginners.

Boot camps: Boot camps are military-style drills. A boot camp is basically an HIIT type of training with high-intensity circuits that blend elements of aerobic and anaerobic (calisthenics, sprints and resistance training) types of exercises. These sessions combine bursts of intense activity alternated with milder activity. Boot camps are demanding workouts, and thus, are not recommended for beginners.

How Much Is Enough?

It is recommended that you exercise at a moderate or greater intensity for 30 to 45 minutes on most days of the week.[68] While this may not seem much of an ask for some, it may feel like a formidable amount of time for others. The good news is that research has also shown that people who exercised for even as little as 15 minutes a day, were happier and more cheerful than those who didn't exercise at all. If you can't set aside a big block of time for a workout, breaking your exercise down into two or smaller sessions through the day is as therapeutic as a continuous hour of exercise. Even shorter bursts of vigorous 10-minute exercises can improve the quality of your life.

Do What You Enjoy

As is the case with diets, there's no such thing as 'one size fits all' even when it comes to exercise. From time to time, you'll have friends, acquaintances, social media influencers and others vehemently advocating their favourite workouts and fitness routines. If you happen to be new to exercising, you're very likely to heed and follow popular social advice on exercise. While it's super-awesome to get motivated to exercise, following someone else's exercise type and regime may not be the smartest thing to do.

Something that works for one person, may work for a few others, but will definitely *not* work for everyone. It's because all our bodies are unique, and react differently to different kinds of exercises. We all have different body types, metabolic rates and states of health. In fact, some exercises may do us more harm than good, especially if we suffer from certain health conditions.

You should definitely consult your doctor before embarking on any exercise regime. Thereafter, the best approach to start exercising is to try out different types of workouts, and observe how your body reacts to them. Note what's working for your body, and what's making you feel alive and energetic as well. Only then should you decide on an exercise or a combination of exercises to be blended into your daily routine.

Remember, it's a journey and should become a life-long pursuit to live a healthy life, not a short-term activity to lose weight or get in shape for an event. As you go through various fitness experiences, you will discover which exercises give joy to your mind, body and spirit. Such exercises will also be much easier for you to sustain. As explained earlier, many people stop exercising because what they were doing wasn't giving them joy.

Choosing Your Exercise

By now, you would have a fair idea about the major types of fitness activities available around you and what they're all about. However, if you're on the threshold of starting your fitness regime for the first time, you might still feel a bit overwhelmed by all the information above and need a bit of hand-holding. So, here are a few pointers that can guide you in choosing an activity that serves you best:

1. Select an activity suited to your health status. For e.g.: swimming may be best suited for people with joint issues, while weight-bearing exercises like running and stair climbing would not be suited for them.
2. Match your activity to your fitness goal. Answer the questions asked under the section 'Identifying Your Fitness Goal' below to help you match your fitness goals to your activity. For instance, if you're looking to become more flexible, yoga is what you need. If you love challenges, long-distance running and cycling, triathlons and calisthenics may be your cup of tea.
3. Choose the activity that fits your personality and that you're most likely to enjoy. If you prefer alone time, activities like solo running, cycling, swimming, walking, strength training or bodyweight workout at home or in a park could fit the bill. If you are leading a highly stressful life, activities like yoga, Pilates and swimming will help relax you. If you're looking to make friends, group fitness classes like Zumba or a running/cycling group may work well for you.
4. If you're on a budget, there are a whole lot of activities that are very affordable or may cost nothing at all, like running, power walking, stair climbing, outdoor boot camps, certain group classes, etc.

Identifying Your Fitness Goal

So, how do you ensure what exercises would you really stay committed to? It's easy. You just need to answer *one* question to yourself: what is my big 'why' to exercise?

To know your 'why' for exercising, answer the following:
Am I exercising to...

- lose weight and fit into my favourite dresses that I haven't been able to wear in a long while?
- stay generally fit and healthy all through my life?
- stay energetic throughout the day?
- become stronger, and eventually turn into a lean, mean machine?
- be able to run a marathon?
- bust stress and remain happy and positive the whole day?
- boost your self-esteem?
- for all of the above?

Long-Distance Running

Long-distance running has always been my most favourite fitness activity, and hence, I couldn't resist adding a section on running. I was bitten by the running bug at the young age of 40. I met an acquaintance in 2008 who is a marathon runner, and my first-ever conversation about running that day got me excited about running a marathon one day. Within three months, I ran my first-ever half marathon (21 kilometres). What followed was a spate of half marathons, marathons and an ultramarathon (50 kilometres). Running can be addictive and there's nothing wrong with such a positive addiction. However, if you're at the threshold of exploring running for the first time, it is advisable that you focus on the basics at this stage, and keep adding more running ammunition through various techniques and programmes as part of your running progression. Therefore, I'm going to lay down just the basics of endurance running to help you get started.

Important Guidelines for the Running Enthusiasts

Widely acclaimed Mumbai-based ultramarathoner and revered running coach Daniel Vaz ('Coach Dan' as he is lovingly called) shares important guidelines for those who are starting out on their running journey:

1. Make sure you have medical clearance before you start running.
2. Buy a good pair of running shoes that are comfortable. Make sure they're not tight, are roomy enough to wiggle your toes and have good arch support.
3. Wear comfy clothes with sweat-wicking fabrics that keep you cool in summer. Layer up adequately in winters, but remember, it gets hotter as you run. So, don't overdo the layering bit.
4. Start gradually and go up in distance incrementally. Do not increase weekly training mileage by more than 10 per cent per week. That's the 10 per cent rule.
5. Don't set your training schedule in stone. Allow yourself a rest day once every week. Take a day off when you don't feel too good. It's foolhardy to run through the pain that can lead to a full-fledged injury.
6. Use a training plan vetted by a coach or train with a coach for optimum benefit and proper progression.
7. Never skip a five–10-minute warm up routine that comprises dynamic stretching to avoid injury.
8. Always follow a cool-down routine with static stretching after the run.
9. Hydrate well before, during and after each run to prevent bonking and dehydration.
10. Make sure you are not sleep-deprived.
11. Consume a combination of adequate carbs (complex)

and protein within an hour of a race, long run or speed workout. It helps speed up recovery.
12. While you should train frequently, beware of overtraining. It can cause burnout and injury.
13. Be prudent with your running pace when the weather is too warm and/or humid. Hydrate more than you would during better weather conditions. Listen to your body for any unusual signs such as dizziness and cramps. In case you do experience such symptoms, don't hesitate to abandon your run midway to prevent serious health repercussions.
14. Always run with vehicular traffic coming towards you (and not from behind you) to ensure your safety.
15. Strength train and cross-train regularly to improve your running and to avoid overuse injury.
16. Don't let running be stressful. Don't compare yourself with other runners or their pace/race times. Every runner is unique.

Benefits of Running

While running has all the benefits of aerobic exercises that were discussed earlier in this chapter, some added benefits of running according to Coach Dan are:

1. **Running provides the 'runner's high'**: It's a feeling of fulfillment a runner has after finishing a good run. Running leads to an improved mood immediately afterward. You can experience this even after a short 20-minute run.
2. **It boosts confidence**: When we're able to achieve our running goals, it raises our self-esteem which leads to enhanced confidence in other areas of life.
3. **It's a platform to widen one's social circle**: Running

with a group of runners or joining a running club comes with the package deal of making loads of health-minded friends who add joy and laughter to our mornings. For me, running has always been about making friends and bonding over running. I'm in total consonance with Coach Dan when he calls running mental and emotional therapy.

Harmful Effects of Overtraining

While exercising is definitely good for health and longevity, over-exercising can have the reverse effect.

Overtraining is a condition in which you exercise excessively. In such a situation, your body is unable to recover in the time it generally takes to bounce back. When we exercise too intensely (much beyond the normal progression rate) or for too long at a stretch, it can lead to the process of breakdown of muscle tissues which is called catabolism. This may lead to excessive physical as well as psychological stress, and it could sometimes take two or more weeks for complete recovery.

However, since each of us is a bio-individual, overtraining will be different for different people depending upon their current fitness levels. So, while endurance athletes can sustain exercising for a few hours at a stretch on multiple days in a week, many others may reach their training threshold within an hour of exercising at a stretch.

Exercise is a long-term physical and mental health insurance that sets you up for a healthier and fitter you all through your life. Over-exercising isn't a smart remedy to achieve your fitness goal. We need to understand that more is not *always* better.

I learned this the hard way a few years ago. There was a

phase during my earlier running days when I participated in almost every local race to beat my best time. Wins and podiums came in easy as there were fewer women running back then. Running had become intoxicating and I was clearly overdoing it, as if on a drug. I was playing with fire and flirting with injury and learned my lessons the hard way. As they say, one should pause, reflect and realign every once in a while; I should have too. But I did not. I suffered an Iliotibial Band injury and I had to stop running for almost six months.

While I recovered and got to run again, my point of sharing this with you is to convey the crucial message that can help you exercise injury free and stress free. Exercise hard if you must, compete and sign up for events, but don't become complacent by throwing caution to the wind. Always be mindful of the importance of proper rest and recovery between events and workouts, as too much too soon is a recipe for disaster. Choose a workout plan tailored to your goals that has a defined progression scheme and allows for adequate recovery between sessions.

Take a look at the multiple downsides of overtraining:

- Muscle loss
- Joint pain
- Muscle soreness
- General body ache
- Fatigue and overexertion
- Difficulty in sleeping, or insomnia
- Weakened immune system leading to frequent illness
- Anxiety, irritability and mood swings
- Sudden decline in exercise performance
- Increased incidence of injuries
- Lack of motivation or enthusiasm to exercise

Crucial Fitness Guidelines

*'If you listen to your body when it whispers,
you won't have to hear it scream.'*

Before you embark on your fitness journey, remember these important pointers for a strong and injury-free workout:

Consult a doctor: If you're suffering from any form of serious injury or a chronic health illness like cardiovascular diseases, osteoporosis or asthma, ask a specialist/doctor to prescribe specific exercises or modifications of exercises for you.

Always begin small: Whether you're joining a gym, starting running or beginning any other form of exercise for the first time, always start slowly. You may be young or a fast learner, but you still need to start easy. If it's the gym, start with small dumbbells or a bare barbell. If it's running, start with a walk-jog routine for maybe a two-kilometre distance. This will help your body get used to the exercise form, and guard you from injury or burnout.

Avoid too-much-too-soon: Exercising too much from the start or adding intensity too fast can be a major cause of burnout or injury. If that happens, you may be discouraged to exercise at all. So, be smart. Start easy and gradually increase the intensity of your workouts. Remember, however fit or strong we may generally be, we become more susceptible to injuries as we get older. It is because we start losing bone and muscle mass regularly as we grow older, and it takes longer for us to recover as compared with when we were younger. It just means that we need to make our exercise progression wisely.

Never skip a warm up: We're often in a hurry to start and finish the workout for the day and get moving with other things in life. In this flurry, many of us disregard a good warm up routine and start our exercise session on 'cold' muscles to save time. Remember, a five–10-minute warm up routine can save you a muscle injury that can sabotage your exercise routine for many days or weeks, and even make your day-to-day functioning difficult. So, add dynamic stretching before starting your exercise session to increase your body's core temperature and send blood to all major muscle groups in the body. Warmed-up muscles are better prepared to face the workout challenge ahead.

Always cool down: Incorporate a gentle cooling-down session with static stretching after a workout. This will slow down your breathing and heart rate to prevent dizziness. A cool-down routine also lengthens contracted muscles to their original size, which can improve the range of motion, and prevent muscle cramps and other injuries.

Don't miss workouts after being sore: Don't skip the next workout if you get exercise-induced delayed onset of muscle soreness (DOMS) because the best way to relieve soreness is to continue exercising after the specified period of rest. A regular workout regime after soreness will help the muscles to heal due to increased blood flow to the sore muscles.

Cross-train on and off: To cross-train is to exercise through a different mode of fitness activity/activities than your regular one. This method of exercising not only adds freshness to your fitness routine but also prevents overuse or repetitive stress injuries by allowing your muscles to recover. Cross-training also helps you get past the plateau that sets in due to indulging in the same form of exercise over an extended period of time. Cross-training accelerates weight loss too. For instance: if you strength train or run, then you can cross-train with yoga or swimming once a week.

Go for comfortable sportswear: While exercise is a great mental stress buster, it requires you to challenge yourself physically and step out of your comfort zone. It only makes sense that you support your workout effort by wearing comfortable shoes and clothes so that exercising is as pleasant an experience as possible. The most important component of sportswear is comfortable shoes that fit you well. Women should not forget to invest in sports bras. These are absolute essentials for averting injury and preventing sagging.

Hydrate well: We sweat and lose fluids while exercising, without sometimes being aware of it. Along with the fluid loss, we also lose electrolytes that are essential for the normal functioning of our bodies. This can cause dehydration. Therefore, hydrate adequately before, during and after the workout.

I have a good feeling that I've motivated you enough to set your fitness goals the moment you complete reading this section on fitness, and start your fitness regime from tomorrow. Or maybe today itself?!

Never treat exercise as an unpleasant chore. You exercise because you care for your body, not because you want to beat it down. As someone has put it aptly: 'Exercise is a celebration of what your body can do, not a punishment for what you ate.'

Enjoy the freedom that comes with a fit and strong body. Go, exercise...one workout at a time...one day at a time...to infuse your body and mind with that quintessential feeling of well-being.

Are You Up for a Challenge?

This fitness challenge has been curated by Ishaan, the American College of Sports Medicine (ACSM) and National Academy of Sports Medicine (NASM)-certified, Mumbai-based fitness specialist.

Note: Check the internet and YouTube for posture correction and how exercises are done.

A Full Body Warm Up

20 reps each:

- Jog on the spot (2 minutes)
- Shoulder rotation
- Torso rotation
- Neck flexion and extension
- Leg swings
- Calf raises
- Chest flyes
- Alternate toe touches
- Side-to-side lateral bends pulling opposite arm to the side
- Cat-camel pose
- Forward lunge to reach

Workout 1 (beginners)

Equipment: A pair of 2 kg dumbbells, a pair of 1 kg ankle weights and an exercise mat

Three circuits and a break of two minutes between each circuit.

Exercises:

1. Jumping jacks (25 reps)
2. Wall push-ups (15 reps)
3. Dumbbell shoulder press (15 reps)
4. Sumo squats (15 reps)
5. Ankle-weighted lateral leg raises (15 reps each side)
6. Bicycle crunches (15 reps each side)
7. Superman (15 reps)

Workout 2 (intermediate)

Equipment: Jump rope, a pair of 3 kg dumbbells and an exercise mat.

Three circuits and a break of two minutes between each circuit.

Exercises:

1. Jump rope (30 counts)
2. Baby push-ups on the floor (15 reps)
3. Dumbbell shoulder press (15 reps)
4. Burpees (half or full) (10 reps)
5. Dumbbell double-arm triceps extension (15 reps)
6. Mountain climbers (15 reps on each leg)
7. Walking lunges (15 reps on each leg)
8. Plank hold (45 sec)

A Full Body Cool Down Routine

Hold each stretch for 20–30 seconds:

- Overhead reach
- Arm-cross shoulder stretch
- Chest stretch
- Overhead triceps stretch

- Standing side bend
- Standing quad stretch
- Standing cross leg touch down
- Standing hip flexor stretch
- Calf stretch against the wall
- Seated butterfly stretch
- Lying double knees stretch
- Lying lower back twist
- Cat-cow stretch
- Cobra stretch
- Child's pose
- Neck stretch

chapter 5

Sleep

Sleep is the single most effective thing we can do to reset our brain and body health each day—Mother Nature's best effort yet at contra-death.

—Matthew Walker, author of *Why We Sleep*[69]

Among the primary components that help sustain life, sleep is the most undermined. Despite being one of the cornerstones of overall health, sleep has somehow lost value in today's hectic world. A whole lot of us, in our crazily fast-paced environment, treat sleep as a luxury rather than a necessity of life, and millions of us (I'm not even exaggerating!) around the world are chronically sleep-deprived.

From a health-oriented perspective, the quality and quantity of sleep are as critical as a clean diet and regular exercise are for our mental, emotional and physical well-being. Suffice to say that you'll find it almost impossible to reach your true potential in any sphere of life without enjoying good-quality sleep on a regular basis. In fact, sleeping even an hour or two less each night can wreck your ability to function efficiently on a day-to-day basis, as sleep loss keeps adding to your 'sleep debt'.

Many of us push sleep to a much lower rung on the ladder to accommodate other, 'more important' things. Who would know this better than me! I've been through the dark abyss of sleep deprivation of a more perilous kind: insomnia. I've been guilty of abusing sleep and taking it completely for granted for many years. Having experienced sleep deprivation first-hand along with the outrages it had triggered in my body, I rate a good-night's sleep as one of the most fundamental pillars of our overall well-being and happiness. As a consequence of poor sleep hygiene, I suffered from psychosomatic issues, such as stress, joint pain, constant headaches and sluggishness through the waking hours that impacted my ability to think clearly. To add to my misery, my weight kept moving northwards and my athletic performance dropped. There was a time that I almost begged for sleep to return and make a truce with me. I tried every viable intervention suggested by doctors and well-wishers, but sleep just eluded me for what seemed like an eternity then.

If sleep deprivation leads to insomnia, it is also a warning sign of depression looming just over the horizon. According to Dr Rubin Naiman, the world-famous sleep and dream specialist, there exists a vicious cycle of sleep deprivation, stress and immunity. When our sleep is broken on a regular basis, it manifests through mental, emotional and physical stress in the body. This resultant stress then causes systemic inflammation affecting our immune system. Lowered immunity can then wreak havoc on other bodily systems, some of the most susceptible being the gut, the joints and cognitive health. And eventually, poor overall health can lead to unhappiness as a person perpetually fatigued due to sleep deprivation is more likely to feel cranky and edgy rather than happy. There indeed is a direct correlation between sleep quality and overall happiness.

How we feel when we're awake depends on what happens while we're sleeping. While sleeping, our body is working to support healthy brain function and maintain our physical health.[70] Deep sleep reboots our brain to function sharply by forming new neural pathways. Thomas Dekker, an English Elizabethan dramatist, had captured the importance of sleep precisely, 'Sleep is that golden chain that ties health and our bodies together.'

The bad news is that you can't make up for this sleep debt by sleeping extra over the weekend—like working overtime at the office to finish pending work. Shawn Stevenson, the author of the bestselling book *Sleep Smarter,* writes, 'Studies have shown that just one night of sleep deprivation can make you as insulin resistant as a type-2 diabetic. This translates directly to ageing faster, decreased libido and storing more body fat than you want (say it ain't so!).'[71]

As 'energy' bombards us through the day in its various forms, such as artificial light, sharp sound, movement and loads of information, our bodies' natural rhythms like the circadian rhythm (your natural internal process that regulates your 24-hour sleep–wake cycle) are disrupted, leading to broken sleep. We need to remind ourselves that we deserve rest to function optimally.

The good news is that you can certainly befriend sleep and woo it back into your life and nurture it. There are tools to repair sleep. I started incorporating big and small holistic sleep interventions incrementally to get me back on a path to recovery. With concerted efforts for more than a year to address my sleep wholeheartedly, my efforts finally started bearing fruit. I'm finally able to sleep most nights with the aid of certain daily tools. I can't explain the extent of joy and gratitude I feel in the mornings when I wake up feeling fresh after a good-night's sleep. I have a new-found respect for sleep today and plan to honour it ever after.

Another component of good sleep that affects our general well-being which not many people may be aware of is our rapid eye movement (REM) sleep. This is the second phase of our nightly sleep, non-REM sleep being the first stage. Dreams typically happen during the REM sleep stage. Dreaming, as per Dr Naiman, is as critical as sleeping. When we dream (during the REM stage), just like our gut digests and assimilates food, our brain processes memory and other information. Besides, dreams help in emotional healing, improve memory and reinforce learning. If we're consistently dream-deprived, memories are not consolidated, leading to memory deficit. We are also put at a higher risk of Alzheimer's and other forms of dementia. Needless to say that sleep deprivation adversely affects dreaming. Besides the usual suspects, certain medications like antidepressants and alcohol can also suppress dreaming.

Also, know that only sleep is true rest. Hiking, reading a book, playing golf, watching a movie or drinking alcohol are not forms of rest. They're stimulating recreation or a respite from something that we're trying to get away from temporarily, but *not* rest.

Benefits of Quality Sleep

Sleep is exceptionally therapeutic for our mental, emotional and physical well-being. Here's how:

1. Mental Well-Being (cognitive): Quality sleep helps us in:

- Enhancing learning ability for any new skill, such as a new language, a musical instrument, math equations, playing chess, etc.
- Staying alert through the day
- Sharpening attention, focus and concentration

- Making better decisions
- Increasing productivity and performance
- Improving problem-solving skills
- Enhancing creativity
- Sharpening the power of perception.

2. Emotional Well-Being: Restorative sleep has the power of healing us emotionally by processing and organizing our thoughts and feelings while we are in deep sleep. This helps us view things from a more positive perspective and react accordingly. Therefore, quality sleep helps in:

- Reducing emotional stress considerably
- Boosting mood by releasing feel-good hormones
- Creating a pause before reacting to a stimulus
- Resetting stressful experiences
- Improving our outlook towards life through increased optimism
- Providing an enhanced sense of well-being.

3. Physical Well-Being: There are innumerable benefits that accrue from a physical perspective when we sleep restfully on a regular basis. These include:

- Repair and recovery of heart by bringing down blood pressure to normal while we're fast asleep
- Regulation of the blood glucose spikes, thereby preventing type 2 diabetes
- Maintenance of a healthy balance of vital hormones—ghrelin (hunger hormone) that makes us feel hungry, and leptin (satiety hormone) that lowers food cravings when we are not hungry
- Increase in muscle mass that helps to keep our body weight under check

- Strengthening of our immune system by helping defend our body against harmful substances. Ongoing sleep deficiency can reduce the ability of our immune system to respond to threats
- Staying energetic and high on stamina through the day
- Restoring crucial functions in our body, such as muscle growth, tissue repair and release of growth hormones;
- Staying youthful and fighting ageing
- Keeping us alert and safe in life-threatening situations.

Both the quality and quantity of sleep affect every aspect of our daily life and overall health. So, while each person is unique, there are certain universally accepted guidelines about the number of hours of sound sleep required for our general well-being as laid down by the National Sleep Foundation.[72] Adults aged 18–64 need seven–nine hours of sleep, while adults aged 65 and above need seven–eight hours of sleep

The Consequence of Sleep Deprivation

In our fast-paced world, millions of people are suffering from chronic sleep deprivation and thus facing menacing consequences. What is unfortunate is that many don't even realize that sleep deprivation could be the prime source of various issues related to their health. What makes it even worse is the general sleep-management approach that we may be taking to address sleep issues: overusing sedatives and medications to help us wind down at night and overconsuming stimulants like coffee, tea and strongly caffeinated energy drinks during the day to keep us going. This creates a vicious cycle and an unhealthy dependence that could lead to another set of health problems, such as unwanted weight gain, lowered immunity, anxiety, loss of mental clarity, etc.

We can imagine the extent of the grave consequences of sleep deprivation through Walker's own words in his famous book *Why We Sleep*. He says, 'No facet of the human body is spared the crippling, noxious harm of sleep loss. We are socially, organizationally, economically, physically, behaviourally, nutritiously, cognitively and emotionally dependent on sleep.'[73]

If you're sleep-deprived, it affects the functioning of your circadian rhythm. Your circadian rhythm, in turn, drives your hormones and many other physiological and psychological functions. So, when your circadian rhythm is irregular or constantly disrupted, it wreaks havoc on your hormones and many other bodily functions.

The following are some of the health complications of sleep deprivation:

- **Lowered metabolism and increased weight gain**: It is a well-documented fact that sleep deficiency increases the risk of obesity. There are two hormones that regulate hunger in our body, **ghrelin** (hunger-stimulating hormone) and **leptin** (hunger-suppressing or satiety hormone). When we sleep less, ghrelin production is elevated while leptin production is suppressed. This gives rise to constant food cravings and activates the reward system, wherein you have strong food cravings. Over a period of many sleepless nights, you will start gaining weight as your appetite gets bigger and you indulge in untimely eating due to poor food choices and disrupted hormones.[74] This impairs insulin sensitivity leading to dramatic blood sugar spikes on the following day. And to top it all, when you're fatigued and groggy through the day, you're less likely to exercise regularly. This is a vicious cycle that feeds itself and disrupts all your attempts at weight management. As per a research on adult sleep habits, compared with women who slept seven hours per night, those who slept for five or fewer hours per night were 15 per cent more likely to become obese.[75]

- **Increased risk of lifestyle diseases**: Sleep deficiency adversely affects glucose metabolism, and the body is susceptible to stress by elevating stress hormone (cortisol) levels in the body. Raised blood pressure coupled with elevated stress can lead to lowered immunity and inflammation in various bodily systems. This increases the risk of illnesses like heart disease,[76] stroke, type 2 diabetes,[77] kidney disease, certain cancers, Alzheimer's disease, etc.

- **Decline in cognitive function**: As mentioned earlier, sleep deficiency is a recipe for slowing down mental performance in the form of impaired cognitive abilities to process new information, focus, memorize, recall details, make decisions, solve problems and think creatively. Resultantly, your productivity and overall performance will also decline.[78] A study published by National Centre for Biotechnology Information (NCBI) in April 2005 reported that a few physicians who were sleep-deprived took 14 per cent longer to complete a task, and made 20 per cent more errors as compared with those who had a full night's sleep.[79]

- **Increase in stress and mood swings**: Without sufficient nightly rest, you're likely to feel stressed, anxious, irritable and agitated. If left unaddressed for long, they can put you at risk of suffering from panic disorders and depression. In a study by University of Pennsylvania researchers, it was found that subjects who slept only for four and a half hours per night for a week reported feeling more stressed, angry, sad and mentally exhausted.[80]

- **Suppressed immune system**: Not sleeping enough can weaken our immune system. When it is impaired, we become more susceptible to catching colds and flu. Short sleepers are at a 50 per cent increased risk of viral infections. Without adequate sleep, our body produces fewer cytokines (a protein that targets infection), weakening the immune system.[81]
- **Increased inflammation**: There is enough scientific evidence that poor-quality sleep can result in chronic tissue-damaging inflammation in various bodily systems. This can cause our immune system to attack healthy tissues, causing cell damage, such as GERD in the digestive tract, rheumatoid arthritis in the joints and accelerated ageing.[82]
- **Increased fatigue**: Sleep deprivation can cause you to feel exhausted and sluggish the whole day. This happens because muscle repair only takes place during long and deep sleep.
- **Impedes athletic performance**: Because you feel fatigued before exercise, sleep deprivation can drain you of all motivation to exercise and knock down your performance.[83] This is noticeably true for endurance sports, such as running, swimming, biking, tennis and basketball, which rely on stamina, energy, speed and a quick reaction time.
- **Increased risk of accidents and injuries**: Lack of sleep can put lives at risk by an increased incidence of errors and induced micro-sleep (very brief and sudden bursts of uncontrollable sleep) at the wrong time. I've experienced bouts of exhaustion-driven micro-sleep

while driving in the past. I still shudder to recall the times when sheer luck saved me from serious accidents and ensuing injuries.

The adverse implications of regular sleep deficiency over an extended period of time may not be too obvious at first. But it may just be a matter of time before poor sleep hygiene starts taking a toll on various aspects of our well-being.

Factors Contributing to Sleep Deprivation

What and when we eat and drink (our nutrition), where we sleep and how we wind down (our environment), what routine we follow in the day (our circadian rhythm), and which energy inputs we consume (our energy exposure) determine the quality and quantity of our sleep.

Some of the prominent melatonin disrupting habits are:

- Eating closer to sleep time
- Consuming too much alcohol closer to bedtime
- Consuming too much caffeine during the day
- Regular use of antidepressants
- Nicotine consumption
- Exposure to blue light from gadgets
- Exercising close to bedtime
- High body core temperature
- Extreme room temperature
- High stress and anxiety levels

Steps towards Getting Better Sleep

Hopefully, I've succeeded in conveying a crucial message to you that a good-night's sleep should be non-negotiable for your overall well-being. And if you're someone who is like my past self, a sleep-deprived insomniac, then let tonight be the night to start implementing the first few steps towards better sleep hygiene.

It's pertinent to mention that sleep quality is mainly driven by melatonin levels (the hormone responsible for maintaining the sleep-wake cycle) and core body temperature. Therefore, it's critical for you to refrain from melatonin-disrupting habits.

Following systematic bedtime rituals will help you immensely in winding down and preparing your body and mind for sleep. Here are a few tips and bedtime rituals to slip into deep and blissful sleep at night effortlessly:

1. Optimize your sleep environment: Your bedroom should be a peaceful haven that makes you feel relaxed rather than stressed. Here are a few steps to make your bedroom sleep-friendly:

- Dim your home lights at least two hours before bedtime. If you wish to read before going to bed, use a 15-watt light. Install zero-watt red bulbs in your washroom and leave them on for night loo breaks.
- You could use blue blocker glasses to regulate light at night if you work a little late sometimes.
- Maintain a comfortable bedroom temperature. It should neither be hot nor too cold. The exact temperature is a completely individual preference as per your comfort.
- Bedroom walls should preferably be painted in soft and calming colours.
- Make sure your mattress and pillow are very comfortable, and your linen is breathable.
- Ensure that your bedroom is a quiet place at night, without distracting external noise. Use a fan for white

- noise or earplugs. You might even consider investing in noise-cancelling headphones.
- Keep your bedroom dark by obliterating artificial lights. Use heavy blackout curtains, blinds or an eye mask to block out all light.
- Remove all electronics from your bedroom as electromagnetic rays (white/blue lights) from the gadgets affect sleep. This includes all screens: TV, computer and e-readers.
- Keep your bedroom clean and organized. Remove mental stressors like files and papers from the office, bills and pamphlets, and piles of unfolded laundry. Keep your bed tidy.

2. Stick to a bedtime routine: Go to bed and wake up at the same time every day to help your body synchronize your internal clock with your healthy bedtime routine. This will help the body release melatonin at a fixed time every night, thereby signalling your brain and body that it is time to sleep. Irregular sleeping times can alter your circadian rhythm and mess up your sleep.[84]

3. Follow a caffeine curfew post 4.00 p.m.: If you consume caffeine in the evening, it can keep your nervous system stimulated long into your sleep time. Caffeine levels can remain raised in your blood for a minimum of six hours.[85] If your evening cup of coffee is non-negotiable, try decaffeinated (decaf) coffee.

4. Have a digital sunset two to three hours before bedtime: Artificial blue-and-white light from screens confuses our circadian rhythm and suppresses melatonin production.[86] So, put the TV, computers, iPads and other screens off at least two hours before bedtime; three hours is even better. Ditch even your smartphone at least 90 minutes before sleep time. If keeping a mobile phone near you is unavoidable, put it on Night-Shift mode, reduce the screen brightness and put it on airplane mode for the night. If working on the laptop is unavoidable sometimes during your wind-down time, install software like Flux and reduce the brightness of the screen manually.

5. Avoid eating heavy meals and drinking late in the evening: Eating a large and spicy meal closer to bedtime can disrupt restful sleep due to discomfort from indigestion. Eating too close to bedtime can increase core body temperature. It is best to have the last meal of the day about two hours before your bedtime. Drinking alcohol closer to sleep time is known to disrupt the body's circadian cycle, cause snoring, increase the risk of sleep apnoea and decrease the production of melatonin.[87]

6. Avoid liquids closer to sleep time: Although it's great to drink adequate water every day from a hydration perspective, drinking too much close to your bedtime can disrupt sleep by leading to the dreaded middle-of-the-night bathroom trips.

7. Exercise regularly, but not too late: While regular exercise helps in getting a good night's sleep, exercising closer to your sleep time can disrupt sleep. This occurs due to the stimulatory effect of exercise on the body and mind. The core temperature of the body is elevated, and the body starts feeling alert instead of feeling drowsy.

8. Increase natural daylight exposure in the day: Exposure to sunlight or natural bright daylight during daytime keeps the internal clock rhythm healthy, which finally helps in maintaining the sleep–wake cycle and the quality and duration of your nightly sleep. In fact, sunlight exposure is known to activate the parasympathetic nervous system and regulate the circadian rhythm.[88]

9. Limit erratic or long daytime naps: While up to 30 minutes of power naps can sharpen your cognitive ability, taking long untimely naps during the day can mess up with the quality of your nightly sleep.[89] Avoid naps especially if you already have trouble sleeping at night. If you must nap, take a shorter nap (for about 20 minutes) in the afternoon.[90]

10. Avoid stimulating talks and activities at bedtime: Exciting or stressful discussions are best left outside the bedroom as these can stimulate your brain and hinder your sleep. When you're emotionally charged or anxious, stress hormones (cortisol and adrenaline) are released that can cause you to become restless through the night. Being excessively energized at night is called a hyperarousal state. Ruminating at bedtime leads to this state.

11. Resort to restorative rituals before bed: If you feel generally stressed or restless around bedtime, follow a short ritual of mindful activities as these tools activate the parasympathetic nervous system that signals the brain to relax and rest. These are:

- Belly breathing, like 4-7-8 breathing
- Guided sleep imagery meditation
- Journaling to quieten 'monkey brain'
- Listening to calming instrumental music
- Reading a book
- Performing relaxing yoga-based stretches
- Taking a warm and long shower
- Getting a deep tissue massage from time to time

- Using aromatic candles or an aromatherapy diffuser
- Spending time with loved ones.

12. Track your sleep habits: What gets tracked, improves. You could self-audit the quality and quantity of your sleep and your sleep routine by maintaining a sleep journal, a sleep-tracking smartwatch or on a phone app (there are many sleep-tracking apps now). Look for patterns such as food triggers, excessive blue light exposure, stressful situations causing your mind to become hyperactive, late exercising, a big dinner close to bedtime, etc. Tracking can help you spruce up your sleep hygiene by being your accountability mechanism.

Dr James B. Maas, the author of *Power Sleep: The Revolutionary Program That Prepares Your Mind for Peak Performance,* says, 'The only way to repay your sleep debt is to get more sleep. You can't repay years of sleep debt by one night of good sleep, any more than you can compensate for years of overeating by a one-day diet.'[91] Research has shown that it can take up to four days to recover from one hour of lost sleep while it can take up to nine days to wipe out sleep debt.[92]

We shouldn't lose faith in our inherent ability to sleep and become overdependent on stimulants, antidepressants and artificial sleep aids. With good reason, Dr Naiman supplicates us with his words, 'We need to fall back in love with sleep.'

So, let's exploit this gift to its full potential starting tonight. Sweet dreams and sleep tight!

Are You Up for a Challenge?

Use a checklist

Pick out 10 big or small recommendations that you don't already follow from the toolkit under the title 'Steps Towards

Better Sleep' (p. 135) and follow them for a week. Notice the changes in the quality and quantity of your sleep. Tweak the list every week on the basis of what is working and what is not.

Carry out a digital sunset

If you're someone who is sleep-deprived because you're addicted to screens till late at night (whether to watch TV or check your social media updates), carry out a digital sunset stringently.

- Switch off the TV at least two hours before sleep time.
- Install the blue light-blocking app Flux (or a similar app) on your phone which you should activate two or three hours before bedtime.
- Set an alarm for about 90 minutes before sleep time. When the alarm goes off, put your smartphone away for the night.

Make a journal entry

In your sleep journal, note down the following details on waking up the next morning about the previous day. Track these for a week. Reviewing this information would reveal some sleep barriers and help you overcome them:

- The time you went to bed
- An approximation of the time you could actually fall asleep
- How many times you woke up during the night
- How long did it take you each time to fall back asleep?
- How many times did you wake up for the loo trip?
- What time did you wake up in the morning?

- How many naps you took in the day, and how long was each nap?
- What time did you eat your last meal?
- How many cups of tea or coffee did you drink?

chapter 6

Social Connections

Being deeply loved by someone gives you strength while loving someone deeply gives you courage.

—Lao Tzu, ancient Chinese writer and philosopher

Human beings are inherently social, and therefore, their social life is one of the most important influences on their mental and emotional health. From the moment we are born, we depend for our survival on the quality of our relationship with our primary caregivers—parents (where the first bond is usually with our mothers). As we grow older, our social circle increases to include friends, extended family, relatives, neighbours, teachers, classmates, roommates, colleagues, spouses, exercise groups, acquaintances, colleagues, faith-based groups and other communities.

While technology may have changed the way people interact with each other in their daily lives, it hasn't altered the basic human need to form supportive bonds with other people. Without positive, genial and enduring relationships, a person's overall well-being will be put in jeopardy.

Akin to the need for practising mindfulness, eating nutritious food, exercising and sleeping, human connection is also a very vital area of our lives. It embodies the experience of kinship and a sense of bonding with other people in various supportive relationships. Therefore, this area also needs to be thriving for a person to live a fulfilled life.

Connection is established in a relationship when two or more people interact with each other, and each person feels valued, seen and heard. They feel nourished after engaging with each other. We all know that life gets hard sometimes. During such tough phases, nothing feels more reassuring than having someone close to share our fears and insecurities with. These are the people who listen to us with patience and without judging, who give us their full attention and presence, and who uplift us when we need a little encouragement. After all, laughter and happiness are highly contagious.

I am, by nature, an outgoing person, thriving in the company of a large circle of friends. During my stay of over 10 years in Gurgaon (now Gurugram), I had established a huge social circle via the people in my neighbourhood, the mothers of my son's friends, members of the fitness classes that I used to conduct, my gym buddies and my running friends. I was enveloped in the warmth and joy of their friendships with regular opportunities to socialize with them. This was a huge factor in keeping me buoyant and joyous.

However, once I moved to Mumbai, I realized what an impact my social circle had on my psyche. The solitude I felt hit me hard. Not having any connections to count on while being in the grip of loneliness in the initial months of settling in, made the situation worse. I also had no family or relatives around besides my husband, since my son was in a residential university campus. I felt a pall of gloom settle over my being and life felt very dull for someone used to fun and laughter enveloping her perpetually. I soon realized that if I continued to wallow in self-pity, I could end up depressed. That's when I shook off my inertia, pulled myself together and proactively joined a running group, and joined a gym. This helped me meet new people with similar interests, and many of my exercise acquaintances ended up becoming my friends. Today, I am well-settled socially.

This experience of moving away from friends, feeling lonely and lost, and then making new friends, made me realize the important and critical role of such friendships on our emotional and mental well-being, which many of us may take for granted. We need to take cognisance of our social life or the lack of it, and ensure that it is in balance in order to keep us in good emotional health. Many people who feel stressed and unfulfilled in life may not even realize that lack of meaningful connections may be the cause of their unhappiness. They may continue to focus on the other crucial areas of life such as maintaining a good diet, getting sufficient sleep, exercising on a regular basis, etc. No doubt, all of these are great tools to manage stress and become healthier. However, they also need to realize that building and nurturing relationships is just as important, if not more. It is one of the foundational tools for enhancing our emotional well-being.

The next important insight that dawned on me in due time was that social happiness is not just about the number of connections that we build. It is more about the quality of these social bonds, and how we mutually contribute to each other's happiness and positivity in life. It helps to devote adequate effort and time to build relationships to a deeper level. I think it's better to have fewer yet more nurturing relationships rather than having a hundred friends, if none of them are really deep and dependable. While an outgoing person may be happy with numerous friends, some introverted people would feel fulfilled with a few but deep connections. I do know quite a few such people, and over the years, I too have personally moved from being a people's person to being a 'few people's person'. It's a happy place to be for me as now I feel that there's more balance in this crucial domain of my life.

Thinking about the human need to interact with others, I'm reminded of Tom Hanks's character in the Hollywood movie *Cast Away*, where he somehow manages to retain his sanity on a deserted island by befriending a volleyball, on which he draws a face and talks to it all the time. Even this mock companionship gave him sufficient courage and strength to endure extreme loneliness, which would have killed him otherwise. I'm sure there are living examples in the normal world where loneliness has adversely affected peoples' sanity.

The strongest relationships are those where there is mutual and genuine concern about each other's happiness and well-being. They are a source of strength and inspire hope. In today's modern-day and age, many of us are just focussed on online social interactions. While these are fine and maybe the only means of keeping in touch with those who are in distant locations, nothing compares to personal or face-to-face connections, which are much more meaningful and beneficial.

Another very important point we need to know, acknowledge and remember is that one person cannot satisfy all our relationship needs such as the need for love, affection, friendship, guidance, advice, companionship and intimacy. Therefore, it is not fair to have unreasonable expectations from our important connections to be everything to us, even if that someone is our significant half. Wanting everything from a single relationship can be disastrous for that relationship as too much would then be riding on it. This is the reason why we need to establish connections with a number of people. For instance, even if you have a very caring spouse, you need friends to rejuvenate you.

Benefits of Meaningful Relationships

Relationships that are meaningful provide us with a slew of benefits. Dr Emma Seppälä, author of *The Happiness Track: How to Apply the Science of Happiness to Accelerate Your Success* (HarperOne, 2017), says:

> People who feel more connected to others have lower levels of anxiety and depression. Moreover, studies show they also have higher self-esteem, greater empathy for others, are more trusting and cooperative and, as a consequence, others are more open to trusting and cooperating with them. In other words, social connectedness generates a positive feedback loop of social, emotional and physical well-being. Unfortunately, the opposite is also true for those who lack social connectedness. Low levels of social connection are associated with declines in physical and psychological health as well as a higher likelihood for antisocial behaviour that leads to further isolation.[93]

Thus, these are the benefits of relationships:

- **They are mood enhancers**: Meeting friends over coffee or accompanying them for a long walk, calling up a friend on the phone, joining a running or walking group, or having a chat with an acquaintance, are all ways of socializing. Connecting socially with people reduces our sense of loneliness. Loneliness is a big reason for anxiety and depression, especially in the case of women. Socializing has been one of the best stress busters and self-care tools for me whenever I've felt jaded and low. All the laughter and chatting (not necessarily serious and meaningful) helps in jacking up my dopamine levels in an instant. The cheerful company can envelop us with reassuring warmth, thus adding buoyancy to our mood.

- **They reduce mental stress**: By making us feel that we belong and are cared for, relationships bring down stress levels, boosting our emotional health. Chatting and laughing with others takes our minds away from our daily stressors by injecting an element of fun into our lives. It releases oxytocin and endorphins, which are all hormones associated with love, pleasure, happiness and relaxation. Socializing with close friends and having a good time with them is an instant energizer and an anxiety-slayer. Some of us may not be very outgoing and may end up internalizing stress. While it's therapeutic to take time off occasionally from others for self-reflection, it's definitely *not* a good idea to withdraw ourselves completely from our friends and loved ones when we're feeling down in the dumps. The role of friends is extremely important during these times, as they can help us vent and process our negative emotions without judging us. This can take the edge off the intensity of negative emotions. While friends may not always have answers to our problems, their mere presence may be calming and uplifting.
- **They bolster self-worth**: When others accept us as their friend and support us, it reinforces our belief that we are valuable. As humans, when we get the feeling that we belong, it reduces stress and insecurity and helps us thrive. Social support also provides individuals, especially those who are highly stressed, with a sense of confidence to cope well with stressors.
- **They have a positive impact on physical health**: Out of the numerous benefits of socializing on our overall

health, enhancing cognitive functions is one of its top perks. Social connections can definitely slow down mental illnesses, such as Alzheimer's, as people with dementia need to engage socially to combat loneliness. Having strong social connections also boosts our immune function, as immunity increases when stress levels drop. And stress levels drop dramatically when we are happily engaged with others.

- **They provide an outlet for angst**: American poet and civil rights activist Maya Angelou had once said, 'There is no greater agony than bearing an untold story inside of you.' Many of us may be harbouring anxiety from our past traumas. This can be very overwhelming and can adversely impact our emotional health. In such circumstances, it is best to open up to someone we trust with our gnawing secrets. This can help us unwind emotionally. Keeping things bottled up inside for long can manifest itself in the form of chronic anxiety, depression and loneliness. Besides, when we talk to someone about our stress, we get to hear our own words and thoughts from a fresh perspective, and that in itself may mitigate anxiety. This moment of epiphany may also help us diffuse negative emotions and move on. Talking to a couple of very close and trusted friends and family about my childhood trauma helped me vent my pent-up emotions and was cathartic for me. Your confidante could be a close friend, a family member or even a counsellor. A caveat: choose your confidante wisely, as confiding in someone you don't trust completely, in a moment of weakness, can make you feel insecure, awkward and vulnerable later on.

- **They render social support**: Relationships can provide social support in the form of a support group. A support group helps people suffering from similar stressors to come together, interact with each other by sharing their thoughts and feelings, and then to help each other acquire coping strategies. Having a strong network of support through strong community bonds enhances both emotional and physical well-being. It is, in fact, a vital component of adult life. You could either join a support group that is relevant to you or start your own.

Invest Time in Nurturing Deep Relationships

It is no secret that connecting with loved ones is a potent mood enhancer. It reduces loneliness, which is a big reason for anxiety and depression in today's world. All the chat, laughter and catching-up can help us recharge our energy levels, dissipate stress and uplift our mood almost instantly.

Here are a few fun ideas to keep fond connections alive and thriving:

- Reach out proactively and keep in regular contact with loved ones who are living far away.
- Meet local friends and relatives over coffee, or invite them over for a meal.
- Enjoy a leisurely walk-talk session.
- Exercise together.
- Enjoy a weekend getaway together.
- Go on an all-women vacation.
- Organize an e-union/virtual union with long-distance friends.
- Never be too busy to attend your loved ones' phone

- calls or invitations to meet.
- Listen more and talk less.
- Be mindful and listen with full attention.
- Be more 'present'. Keep your phone out of sight and maintain eye contact.

While it's great to have friends and indulge in regular socializing for the upkeep of our emotional health, don't forget that some connections can leave us drained of our positivity. Consciously surrounding ourselves with people who give out positive vibes and uplift us rather than pull us down is absolutely essential for our overall health.

There is wisdom in motivational speaker Jim Rohn's words when he says, 'You're the average of the five people you spend the most time with.' The people you spend time with can influence and forge your attitude, thoughts, actions and success more than you could imagine.

Emma Seppälä also quotes Brené Brown, professor at the University of Houston's Graduate College of Social Work, who says, 'A deep sense of love and belonging is an irresistible need of all people. We are biologically, cognitively, physically and spiritually wired to love, to be loved and to belong. When those needs are not met, we don't function as we were meant to. We break. We fall apart. We numb. We ache. We hurt others. We get sick.'[94]

So, it's time to put our phones down and start interacting personally with the people in our lives. Since relationships fulfil us and are nourishment for the soul, we need to put loving energy into every important connection and treat them just the way we wish to be treated.

Are You Up for a Challenge?

1. Is there a close friend you have not spoken to in a long time? Reach out proactively over a phone call or set up a face-to-face meeting.
2. When was the last time you went on a date night with your partner? Schedule one if you have been putting this off endlessly.
3. Is there a senior relative who lives alone in a distant location? Surprise him/her with a video call.
4. Plan an online get-together with your school or college mates.
5. Call and talk to your friends on their birthdays instead of just sending them wishes on social media.

INSPIRATIONAL STORIES OF REAL WOMEN

Seema Rao[*]

Tejaswee, my daughter, was an extroverted, vivacious and super-confident girl—always on stage to compere school programmes, the head girl of her school and a voracious reader. She aspired to be an editor.

Everything was going wonderfully well for our family, until suddenly on 11 August 2010, our lives changed forever. My 19-year-old daughter lost her battle to dengue within two weeks of her falling sick. It was all over so quickly.

When Tejaswee was diagnosed with dengue, the worst thing that we could imagine was that she might need a drip soon. But instead, she was moved to the ICU in no time, and a doctor told me that she was indeed very sick. I was terrified, but not even once did I imagine that she would be snatched away from us so soon. That was unimaginable! That was, in fact, the end of the world. I did not, and maybe, could not go in that direction. Not even after she died.

It was difficult to accept that she was not going to be walking back home with me. I went into a state of denial, refusing to believe that Tejaswee was gone. I didn't cry either. I thought of all the ways it could be proven wrong. I sincerely hoped for it to be a horrible nightmare... I was willing to live through a long and real nightmare. I felt extremely helpless, and there are just no words that can describe the pain of losing

---

[*]These are a few women I had interviewed, and whose personal accounts I deemed relevant to be included in the book for the purpose of inspiring you, the reader. The women are telling their stories in their own words.

one's child. Crying, at that point to me, meant accepting and acknowledging that she was gone forever, that she was never coming back. This thought was just unacceptable then. Not crying was a defence mechanism that told me that she was around, that there was a way to have her back.

Crying was a luxury—I had cried when I lost my dad at the age of 74. But his death didn't destroy me. I hadn't walked like a zombie wondering how to go on when my life was actually over. But when Tejaswee died, I thought I had died with her and it was just my body moving, breathing and barely existing. I wanted to die, so the pain would stop. It was unbearable! I was living any mother's worst nightmare.

It took me a few years to process Tejaswee's death. A parent's mind takes a long time to process and accept their child's death. In the initial days following her death, I couldn't eat any food for a while, and wondered if I could starve myself to death. I even considered other ways of ending the pain, and the thought of death was comforting—that it was possible to end this excruciating pain by simply dying. I couldn't sleep either, had a sluggish short-term memory and was averse to meeting people. In effect, it was very tough to function 'normally'.

In the months following her death, I wanted five minutes to say goodbye to her, to ask her how she felt and if she was okay. I prayed for just one interaction with her to have the assurance that she was fine. I prayed for her to appear in my dream and assure me she was fine. I visited every temple to seek answers, making wishes. I met a 'medium' to connect with my daughter's soul. I even resorted to past life regression therapy. I would have done anything for one word from her.

Soon the pain came in waves. Sometimes it was so deep that I felt like I was drowning in grief. This was followed by a stage of numbness. I found this stage to be a relief, and would often write down what kind of thoughts I would have to cope with during the next wave of dark, suffocating pain. At first, the drowning was longer than the numbness, over the years, the phases of relief grew longer.

It was annoying when I was repeatedly offered pills when I had found that I could sleep somehow if I read a book. I used to leave the lights on, read a little, doze off, get up, read some more and doze off again; the nights passed like this. I felt better on and off.

As time passed, certain small and big interventions started giving me moments of solace, helping me heal slowly. Reading certain genres of books was food for my soul.

Over a period of time, I also started taking interest in bird watching and bird photography. Being amidst nature felt therapeutic and distracted me from thinking about Tejaswee. I even started a blog to help me process my emotions related to my loss.

Other small things that helped me included avoiding 'trauma triggers' like certain sights, conversations and experiences; connecting with other bereaved mothers; stepping out to meet people; eating healthy; and exercising.

In fact, certain forms of exercise really helped me ease the pain. As years went by, I started adding fitness activities to heal and feel better. I came to love hiking, cycling, walking and running.

I participated in a 15-day cycling trip from Kullu to Leh immediately after the first death anniversary of Tejaswee. The idea of going to the Himalayas, known to be the abode of the gods and saints, was appealing. I felt as if I could find some answers there. This cycling trip motivated me to exercise regularly and eat healthy, wholesome meals regularly so that I could be physically fit and ready to embark on this strenuous trip. Every little attempt helped in some way. At the very least, it was a distraction.

I've been a part of of a Gurgaon-based hiking group called Let's Walk Gurgaon for a few years now. I go hiking with the group to the Aravalli Hills every Saturday. I also walk for an hour (six kilometres or more) on the other six days of the week. While earlier I felt exhausted walking even up to my society gate, these regular hikes helped me build my stamina immensely. Hikes inundated me with happiness producing hormones, such as dopamine, serotonin and oxytocin, and I felt lighter and happier. There was bonhomie, acceptance, focus (on the walk) and (good) exhaustion!

After being sick on and off for several years post the trauma (which I believe may be psychosomatic illnesses), I feel much healthier today and have not taken any antibiotics or medication for the last two years.

I am presently honing my passion for photography. Taking pictures of birds requires immense patience and focus. For that period, there is no space for anything else in the mind, not even pain. It is a practise in mindfulness that requires absolute silence in the lap of nature. It provides me the much-needed tranquillity and calms my mind. It works very well for me and my husband.

In 2014, I created a grief support group, which gives grieving mothers a platform to share their pain and their experiences, to provide emotional support to each other, to learn to smile again, and to help each other cope in the best possible way. It helps them all to deal effectively with post-traumatic stress disorder (PTSD). Now, we all meet regularly in Delhi/NCR (National Capital Region), Bengaluru, Kolkata, and even Singapore and the US. We even plan trips together within and outside India. And we are there for each other.

I have evolved over the past few years. I don't take anything for granted anymore. I choose my friends wisely. I believe that life is uncertain, and therefore, 'live in the present'. I try to fulfil my dreams and aspirations as if this could be the last day of my life.

We now have another daughter (through adoption)—our rainbow child—who we've named Kia Tejaswee.

Neha Koppikar

A chirpy, happy-go-lucky girl and an eternal optimist, I was the favourite child of my parents. I was so fond of dancing that I needed no excuse to hit the floor; I would just dance at the drop of a hat! Like any other teenager, I too had many dreams and aspirations, such as pursuing an MBA, wanting to train to be a professional dancer, learning swimming, trekking through the mountains, checking out career options, establishing a career, finding a life partner and so much more.

However, all my dreams changed when I was in the second year of my graduation. I had just celebrated my nineteenth birthday when my world came crashing down! In a freak accident, a train ran over my legs—crippling me for life, stunting my dreams and aspirations forever. I am an above-the-knee amputee now.

The moment is still fresh in my memory. I was lying on the railway track, conscious but in shock, wanting to move and shout but unable to. I felt something odd about my body, and then the realization hit me that I had lost my legs. I was in deep agony and I wished hard that the next train would run over me and end my agony forever because the thought of life ahead without legs was just too unbearable and unimaginable. But that didn't happen, and in those moments, my future flashed in front of my eyes: I was sitting in a wheelchair while my disconsolate parents were wheeling me around all my life.

I was confined to the bed for the next six months, forced to lie straight like a wooden log, doing everything on the bed. My family (parents and brother) used to clean me up, as the wounds did not allow me to sit upright or attempt anything on my own. The period of healing the external wounds was very painful. I survived with numerous surgeries, umpteen bottles of blood, and the care of doctors and nurses at the hospital. But the bigger challenge was the internal healing, as I was severely wounded mentally and emotionally. My spirit was completely broken, as I felt life had come to a standstill for me. From a buoyant and effervescent teenager, I had morphed into a desolate dependent who felt like a three-year-old needing to be looked after 24/7.

With such a bleak outlook, it was difficult to think straight or imagine a future for myself. I couldn't even describe the mental and emotional trauma that my family had to undergo, seeing their beloved child in such a grievous state! They were by my side, at every step of the way, even as I was totally helpless. If my parents needed to go somewhere, they had to arrange for a 'babysitter' for me. It was the most devastating time for me and my family.

When a person faces an unspeakable tragedy, their first instinct is to enter a state of complete denial. It happened to me too. At that point, I just couldn't reconcile with the fact that I had lost both my legs. I thought of it as a nightmare that would end soon. I vividly remember the moment when I saw myself, for the first time in the mirror, after a few months. I was horrified and heartbroken! The very first thought that entered my mind was, 'Is this the way I will look for the rest of my life?'

Once the state of denial passed, came the state of anger—towards life, towards those around me. For people closest to the victim, the phase of anger is the most difficult one. My family could feel my pain, but they didn't know how to handle it.

Then came the state of bargaining, during which I often found myself second-guessing the situation. Thoughts such as

'If only I had done this,' 'If only I hadn't done that,' 'I would've even been fine if I had lost only one leg,' or 'If only I were amputated below my knees, I could've at least walked with the help of prosthetic legs,' made me feel even more helpless and like a loser.

Then came the realization phase with dreadful thoughts, such as 'I have lost my legs forever,' 'I will be wheelchair-bound forever,' and 'This reality is never going to change.' And with this realization came the onset of depression.

There comes the stage of acceptance eventually, where you have to either make peace with your situation or go down a dangerously negative path that can affect your sanity.

What impeded my emotional recovery was people's perception of me after my accident. They would look down on me—some with pity, others with contempt—and a sense of worthlessness prevailed over me. Even my friends abandoned me, and their rejection took a severe toll on my self-esteem. I became very unkind to myself. Lying in bed, all day and night I would cry, cursing myself and my destiny, extremely unsure of what the future held for me.

At one point in time, not being able to bear my condition, even my family plunged into depression. This hit me really hard. I could not take the pain of my parents any longer, and that was the day that I decided to pull myself together!

That was a moment of epiphany for me. I started prepping myself through positive self-talk, telling myself that I cannot keep lying in bed and blame destiny for the rest of my life. I was alive, and I had to make the efforts to be in the best physical and mental state possible so that I could become as independent as was possible. I realized that since I was the one facing this trauma, it was me who had to fix it too, or else, I would keep feeling like a victim all my life. I knew it wouldn't be easy, but I was sure of one thing: I would try, no matter what. I had to pick up the broken pieces of my life, arrange them together in the best possible way and move on.

As I embarked on my path to emotional recovery and more self-reliance, my first thoughts were to learn to walk again, albeit with the help of external aid such as the Jaipur Foot. The Jaipur foot is a rubber-based prosthetic leg designed for people with below-the-knee amputations. However, this did not work out since I have a bilateral, above-the-knee amputation. Then, I attempted using prosthetic legs, but unfortunately, this too didn't work out as envisaged. The only option left for me was to try a manual wheelchair.

The next step was to complete my graduation since the accident had interrupted my studies. I enrolled in a B.Com. degree in the first year again to give my life a fresh start. Along with my studies, I started helping with household chores with the aid of my manual wheelchair. Once I completed my graduation, I started taking tuitions to feel a little more independent. I even picked up work with a few smaller organizations; however, things didn't work out due to various challenges. I also met with a few rejections, not because I was not capable, but because they didn't have the barrier-free environment conducive to my condition.

However, I did not let these rejections defeat me, and this positive shift in my thought process started making me feel much better. I started smiling again so that my family too could feel better. I also veered towards spirituality which gave me immense peace of mind.

I got married in 2006, nine years after my accident. In these nine years, a few broken relationships left me hopeless and vulnerable. I wasn't sure if I would ever find a caring life partner. But by God's grace, Kailash Koppikar found me through a matrimonial website where I put in all the details without any filters. The decision to marry him turned out to be the biggest blessing of my life. He is the most loving, caring and supportive husband I could have hoped for! In fact, he is my strength. He has nurtured me and given me immense courage to lead this life with utmost confidence.

Our daughter was born in 2007 and we were ecstatic looking at our little bundle of joy. But taking care of a newborn was a huge challenge for me; from feeding her, to giving her a bath, to rushing to her every time she cried, I had to learn to do all this in my own unique way. My daughter is 14 now and admires me as a very strong and gritty woman.

In 2011, I got an electric wheelchair. It turned out to be a huge blessing for me as it gave me the independence to bustle around the house doing chores, go to my office (situated at an elevation of about 90 metres) and commute within my locality on busy roads—all by myself.

Around the same time, I also started chanting the Buddhist mantra *'Nam-myoho-renge-kyo'* which emphasizes humanity, gratitude and treating each individual with respect and dignity. Daily chanting of this mantra gives me immense hope and fills me with positivity.

While my family and spirituality help my mind to stay positive and happy, I go to the gym and do yoga regularly for the health and well-being of my body. I feel super energetic after a workout. It releases all the negative energy there is.

I have transformed into a much stronger person today without any self-consciousness related to my physical state. The daily practice of gratitude has made me value what I have. I count my blessings rather than focus on what I don't have. I also have much more empathy towards everyone around me.

It's not that I never break down and never crave for my

previous self. There are times when I yearn to feel the wet grass under my soles, trek through the high mountains, ride a bicycle on a Sunday morning, drive a car... It's just that I've learned to bounce back quickly without wallowing in self-pity, thinking of all the things I can still do (despite having every excuse not to). I do it because I want to do it all—leading as fulfilling a life as I possibly can, constantly pushing myself out of my comfort zone.

I implore other women facing similar circumstances not to give up on life despite the challenges they face. They have a right to enjoy life as much as everyone else. Biases will always be there, but they should strengthen themselves mentally. They should engage in activities that fuel their heart and feed their soul by pushing the physical limits to the extent their bodies can allow. This will help them lead a more fulfilling life brimming with self-worth.

My Story

I did not have a rosy childhood filled with carefree laughter, dolls to play with and a family to spoil me silly. I have no recollection of my mother fussing over me or hugging me protectively when I'd run to her to feel safe. She suffered from schizophrenia when she lost her 16-month-old baby (my brother) to electrocution when I was in grade three. After almost a year, she was sent to a mental asylum to 'be taken care of'. Needless to mention that she never recovered!

My father, on the other hand, was a terror around the house. He was a firm proponent of corporal punishment at the first sign of insubordination by his three children, me being the eldest. We lived in a perpetual state of anxiety, fearing punishment for the most benign violations.

The memory of being thrashed by him with his leather belt till I screamed in pain and begged for mercy is etched forever in my psyche. My crime? A benign lie—a lie that fuelled an inferno inside him. I had gone to watch a Hollywood movie with my friends (all girls) in grade 12 and had lied to him that I was going to a friend's place. We were not permitted to go and watch movies with friends, and watching a Hollywood movie was somehow equated to watching a 'blue film', and viewed as highly immoral by my father.

Getting spanked by him while growing up was a regular affair for me and my siblings. The physical blows were aggravated with psychological blows when he often berated us by hurling the grossest of expletives, and whacked us in the presence of his friends, relatives and neighbours—it did not seem to matter to him who happened to be around when he felt enraged by our 'disobedience'. He often found innovative (read dire and dreadful) ways of threatening us if we dared not to comply. I still remember a spine-chilling incident that features in my top-10, stress-evoking memories. I have no recollection of what I did to offend him, but my father threatened to brand me with the iron kitchen tongs that he heated on the gas stove and advanced towards me, making me scream in panic and sheer horror, begging him for forgiveness.

Such incidents caused immense psychological angst and low self-esteem that stayed with me for years to come. But this was the least of the mental traumas that I experienced during my childhood. What damaged my spirit was the sexual abuse that I suffered at the hands of men while growing up. Some were my own relatives, and others, my father's friends.

With no mother figure in my life, I was easy prey for child-molesting perverts with human faces. There was just no escape for me. My house was like a free boarding and lodging place for my father's poet friends who would stay with us for days, even months. Sometimes, my father would even leave us in the 'safe custody' of these 'uncles' when he travelled for a day or two. And this was not all!

Almost every school vacation, we were packed off and 'offloaded' to some close or distant relative's house. Many of these holidays were spent in an utter state of anxiety and distress, trying to dodge the advances of a few lecherous uncles.

Each day was a struggle to 'stay safe'. Every morning, I would wake up with the terrifying thought of being violated yet again. What made it worse was that these experiences remained bottled up inside as I had no one to confide in. I was scared of informing my aunts about their husbands' conduct. And at home, I couldn't complain to my father either, for he was someone I couldn't trust, and feared a horrible thrashing for 'making stuff up'. I had nowhere to run from my perpetrators as I was almost certain that I would face a fate worse than I already had. In short, I trusted no one enough during my childhood and teen years to help me deal with this abuse.

One of the two things I'm grateful to my father for is that he sent us to a renowned residential school for five years. Apart from the vacations, those five years were the 'safest time' in my growing-up years.

Suffering a childhood chequered with persistent sexual abuse, being a recipient of fits of fierce rage replete with cringeworthy expletives, and experiencing brutal, sometimes nerve-wracking beatings, left me emotionally scarred. I was unable to process my negative emotions as I was just a child with a vulnerable mind, and as a consequence, I had a very low sense of self-worth and self-confidence. I grew up being very insecure, timid, gullible, withdrawn, and most of all, without a sense of individuality. I had no strong value base to fall back upon, and no role models whatsoever in my life.

The second thing that I'm even more grateful for to my father is his insistence that I send in my application for induction into the Indian Armed Forces. The Indian Navy was inducting women officers for the first time in the executive branch in 1992. Prior to 1992, women officers were inducted in the Navy only in the medical stream). I complied and unwittingly secured my one-way ticket to freedom and safety. I think the desire to run away from the agonizing life must've been so overpowering, that it impelled me to give my absolute best shot at the Service Selection Board of the Navy.

I was selected and commissioned as a Naval officer. This turned out to be my passport to liberation from misery—truly the biggest turning point in my life!

It was in the Navy that I learnt that not all men are sexual predators. Not only did I feel very safe, I also met a man who taught me that love is pure. Apart from loving me selflessly for who I was, he also taught me to respect myself. He noticed the good in me that I never knew existed; in short, he helped me grow my self-worth from zilch. He is now my husband of 27 years.

The period of my life in the Navy was initially very challenging, although I was more than willing to face this kind of hardship compared with the ordeals from my past. It was physically gruelling for me as I had never played a sport in my life till then, and didn't think of myself as capable of enduring any physical rigour.

Here I was, lifting a heavy rifle and marching in the parade ground for hours in the blistering afternoon heat; running cross-country races when I had hardly ever walked a few yards without huffing and puffing; taking part in boat-pulling sessions where each oar felt like an elephantine electricity pole; rolling/somersaulting on the road on a full stomach as part of punishment sessions (they were usually scheduled post dinner) and so much more.

The Navy sowed the seed of fitness in me. The lesson I learnt was that our bodies are capable of weathering a lot more than we can ever imagine; that there's a huge inner reserve inside each of us; and it's the mind that needs to be convinced to release these reserves in tough situations. I would initially sulk, whine, make excuses and report sick because of being physically and mentally unfit, but my body quickly adapted to the duress. I may not have been the fittest in my batch, but I had become physically tougher and emotionally more resilient than ever before.

It was the first stage of my transformation from a timid

and frail girl into a woman with a strong sense of purpose and individuality.

While I was changing for the better, I wasn't left alone by the demons of my past; they still lay dormant inside me. Whenever these demons reared their ugly heads to resurface, they hit really hard, evoking a cocktail of emotions, such as anxiety, self-hate, low self-worth and rage. I desperately wanted to purge myself of the 'filth' on my body and soul by scratching a layer off of me, or I would sometimes feel as though I might explode if I couldn't erase the repulsive and revolting memories.

This carried on for a couple of decades until a few years ago when I couldn't hold it all anymore. I suffered a few bouts of terrible emotional breakdowns in quick succession. Although I had a loving husband and a doting son, and all the material comforts, I was very unhappy inside. It still seems surreal and divine intervention to me that my son (then 19 but an old soul) gave me the space and comfort to try and understand where the angst came from, and how I could flush it out of my system forever. It was my moment of catharsis. He had been experimenting with different forms of spirituality at that point and had introduced me to several mindfulness-based interventions such as journaling, meditation and positive self-talk.

Journaling brought me instant stress relief in the form of brain dumps. It helped me put a finger on the trigger points of emotional pain and press them hard as if to release lymph nodes in the mind. It helped me face the demons lurking in the depths of my subconscious squarely by voluntarily allowing them to surface. This process also helped me rationalize that my past was not my fault. It made me aware of the choice I always had: to detach myself from my past and move on to enjoy my present.

Meditation too was akin to a deep tissue massage for my mind and soul. It soothed my frayed nerves, helped me reduce the incessant negative chatter in my brain, and led me inwards to a place of divine peace. Meditating showed me the way to process my strong negative emotions, such as anger, anxiety and self-hate. And this is when my self-healing started.

Daily affirmations and positive self-talk have helped me build my almost non-existent self-esteem. They have taught me to be compassionate with myself and to celebrate the good in me.

Certain books on spirituality and mysticism have been food for my soul. A daily reading habit has a soothing effect on my psyche and is now a part of my daily joy.

It is my daily ritual of meditation, gratitude journaling, visualization and deep-breathing exercises that has brought about immense healing and transformation at the soul level. All the above interventions have given me a new perspective to life where I no longer feel like a victimized damsel in distress. With the new-found resilience, I'm learning to push through the pain, and count the myriad blessings that each day holds for me.

While the above mindfulness-based interventions help heal my heart and mind, physical activities, such as endurance running, strength training and trekking to the mountains aid me in staying physically robust. As a result, I could run numerous marathons and even complete a couple of Ironman 70.3 distance triathlons.

Today, what feeds my soul, and which I know to be my life's purpose, is a deep desire to help other women discover sustainable tools to become healthier and happier, and to unfetter their spirit to become the best versions of themselves they possibly can be.

It's not that I've completely stopped feeling upset about my childhood memories, but my past doesn't gnaw at my spirit as intensely as it used to. I may experience fits of anger that overwhelm me but these bouts are few and far apart. I no longer wallow in self-pity and don't feel helpless anymore. I've realized that I'm not the only one who has suffered such a fate. There are many who go through a lot more trauma in life.

I've almost completely severed away that painful phase of life, which I feel was the only way of moving forward and leading a normal life. I realized that carrying childhood wounds into adulthood can affect relationships and happiness, and that it serves no good. I now know that while we may have been the products of our past, we don't have to become its prisoners by letting it dictate the way we navigate our lives.

Thus, I've come a long way, and it is a beautiful journey ahead!

SECTION II

chapter 7

Purpose of Life

The two most important days in your life are the day you are born and the day you find out why.

—Mark Twain, American author and publisher

'Purpose of life'—I had never really understood the true essence of this extensively used phrase until a few years ago. Even when I chanced upon it in a book or a newspaper article, I never gave it a second glance or read, until self-awareness dawned upon me. It was probably philosophical mumbo jumbo to me, and at best, signified what I was meant to do in my professional life. When I look back now, I know that I hadn't yet discovered *the* purpose, and this was one of the reasons why I felt so emotionally scattered and unfulfilled in life.

I didn't just stumble upon my purpose of life one morning over a cup of coffee. My purpose revealed itself gradually over a couple of years as I started to become restless, high-strung and perplexed, and I started feeling like a headless chicken in my day-to-day work. In hindsight, these basically were hints that what I was doing wasn't really gratifying to my spirit. I was being nudged to look deep inside and search my soul for answers to what pursuit would give me true happiness. As my daily rituals of meditation, gratitude, deep breathing and journaling started picking up pace and became ingrained into daily habits, my purpose of life too started taking firm shape in my mind's eye, until it became too strong for me to ignore.

Today, I truly know what it means to 'pursue your passion'. It has provided a new meaning to my life. I feel excited to wake up in the morning with a sense of purpose for my day. It keeps me charged like no stimulant in the world can. It doesn't bother me in the least what others think of what I'm doing or not doing. And best of all, now, I really know the meaning of being happy in the present moment. With a focus on my dream and a song in my heart, I move forward on my journey towards my soul goal, being more and more of who I'm authentically meant to be!

It is my belief that we are genuinely happy in life when we're living true to our purpose, and sharing the unique gifts that we possess with the world. Only then does life seem to flow effortlessly. As if through some synchronicity, things start falling into place, we start choosing the right careers, right relationships, right friends—who are in alignment with our true purpose of life. I wholeheartedly identify with the simple-sounding yet profound words of Abraham H. Maslow, the famous American psychologist, when he said, 'What one can be, one must be.'

I also know that when we purposely ignore our life's calling, life nudges us hard, and sometimes knocks us down in not-so-pleasant ways. This is to compel us to apply brakes, take a moment to pause, know that we are not yet living our life authentically and then look at life with a whole new perspective. It is only through the inexplicable breakdown of my health in the recent past that I was compelled to pause and review my life anew. When the discomfort in my body forced me to take a total break from any exercise for a while, it gave me time to introspect. There was more silence in my life than before which allowed me to go deep inside, to talk to what the 'real me' was trying to convey to me, to learn some crucial life lessons and to gain a whole new perspective on life.

Life gives all of us such chances from time to time to review our lives with a new lens, and then gives us the choice to seize the moment, learn and grow, or to keep living an unfulfilled life.

A life without dreams and passions is mere existence. It's like a garden without flowers or a bird with broken wings that cannot fly! Having a burning passion can give us the energy to live a joyous and fulfilling life. So, if we ever had a passion that we let grow cold, we need to reignite it by fanning its flames. Or discover it first-hand. By following our passion, we're honouring our true calling. Remember, every great achievement starts with a dream. And as Walt Disney says, 'All our dreams can come true; if we have the courage to pursue them.'

Hence, now that we know that pursuing our life's dream is crucial to our overall happiness, let us go ahead and discover our purpose of life—the true path to real happiness.

While 'follow your passion' may sound like a super-inspiring quote, it doesn't give clarity on where and how to begin. Therefore, I'm sharing a process with a set of steps that may help you identify your dream and then pursue it successfully.

Before starting, we need to know that achieving our life's most passionate goals needs real work to transform our dreams into a beautiful reality. We should be willing to welcome and embrace discomfort. Sometimes, it may just feel much easier to procrastinate on our dreams. To overpower procrastination and fuel our dreams, we need to step out of our comfort zone and be willing to face our fears.

The first step towards facing and overcoming our fears is to believe strongly in ourselves, even if it seems like a daunting task. Our negative thought process is likely to caution us against making progress, warning us that the task ahead is too arduous for us to succeed. But then, we need to remind ourselves often that life begins outside our comfort zones. We need to inculcate self-trust and tune into our internal compass, and ignore the insecure voice inside us that applies brakes every time we try to step out of our 'safe space'.

Here are 15 time-proven steps that you can take to pursue your life's passion, and make your blazing dream a beautiful reality.

Step 1: Be Sure of Your 'Why'

Your 'why' is your life's burning passion…your most precious dream…your soul goal…your soul's calling…your ikigai…your life's mission! Knowing our 'why' and pursuing our goals can give us a clear sense of direction in life. When we come face to face with our innermost passion, it embellishes life with a sense of purpose and makes it much more meaningful. A strong 'why' can also help us remain on track in the face of inevitable challenges. Knowing our 'why' is also extremely crucial for our overall well-being. One of life's greatest gifts is honouring our calling as it enhances the joy of everyday living. It even helps us declutter many areas of our lives, which, in turn, brings a sense of calm and reduces stress considerably.

A purpose-driven life can keep us very focussed and attentive on matters that are most vital, propelling us to push beyond our comfort zone, regardless of the obstacles. It can also save us from squandering precious energy on mundane pursuits and trivial distractions.

So *how* exactly do we discover our purpose of life?

The first step is to stop searching for it outside of us. Looking at our external world for cues will fill us up with negative energy of desperation and anxiety. Such negative emotions rob us of the mental silence that is critical to help us listen to what our intuition or inner voice is saying. Our intuition or our 'highest self' already knows all the answers and we need to start trusting it. Start paying attention to what this inner guide is saying to us. What are the ideas it keeps throwing at us from time to time as subtle hints? But, sometimes this inner pilot could be whispering something that we may think is far-fetched. Something we may think is not possible in our current reality, and so we start ignoring it.

If you haven't really had episodes of hearing your inner voice, even a frail distant whisper, you can start invoking and strengthening your inner voice through daily mindfulness tools, such as meditation or spending time alone amidst nature. Ask yourself every day during mindful moments, 'What is my life purpose?' Believe me, your intuition will become stronger over time, and it will speak to you in a more distinct tone that will be hard to miss.

For many years, I missed out on the joy I feel today because I hushed the whispers from my inner voice as being unrealistic at that time. But I am happy to have honoured it finally and now, things seem to move in a flow and life seems so beautiful.

We need to stop living a 'default' purpose that someone else may have planned for us, is an outcome of our circumstances or is aligned with the beliefs we may have been fed of what a good life means.

If trying to know your 'why' intuitively sounds a bit perplexing and uninspiring, try another method. Write down all the goals you have in the present moment as well as in all time frames. Then, identify two or three goals from this list that really fire you up. Now, close your eyes and repeat these in your mind several times and notice which one of these makes your heart flutter. The one that gives you the most joy while being repeated in your mind is your life goal in all probability.

Once you realize your 'why' and are very sure that *this is it*, commit yourself wholeheartedly to your life goal. The moment you commit to it, providence will move to help you make your dream a reality. Know that synchronicities will start happening once you've discovered your 'why' and have decided to pursue it earnestly. Synchronicity is a word coined by psychologist Carl Jung that he referred to deeply meaningful coincidences which mysteriously occur in our lives. When we experience synchronicity in our lives, we start having experiences that seem much too significant to be considered as mere day-to-day occurrences. These synchronicities may show up as some vital cues in the pursuit of our goal or in the form of opportunities that are aligned with our chosen path.

Don't wait for others or factors outside of you to 'decide' *your* life goal for you. This can be very disempowering. It is only when you honour your calling that you will experience:

- A more meaningful existence
- Greater self-awareness
- Heightened joy, peace and serenity
- The courage to step out of your comfort zone.
- Being true to your core values
- Increased integrity
- A sense of empowerment and liberation
- A lot of positivity
- A sustained flow

Step 2: Write Down Your Soul Goal on Paper

Once you know your 'why', the next-best thing is to put it down on paper. Until we record our precious dream in writing, it will remain just a dream. When we write down our big dream, we get more clarity on how to accomplish it. It makes our dream seem more palpable and attainable. It gets us significantly closer to making it a reality by manifesting it. From this point, we'll be able to start mapping out our journey towards our dream.

Step 3: Have a Strong Self-Belief

The difference between succeeding and failing at achieving our life's passion boils down to one simple thing: self-belief.

Only if we believe deep down in our hearts that we can achieve something, can we really put in full effort and make things work. Without self-belief, we would constantly downplay our abilities. And when things get tough (which they surely will at times!), we would be more likely to stay motivated and not give up. If we lack self-belief, we become more prone to procrastinating and telling ourselves that our dreams are beyond our reach.

Therefore, once we're certain about our burning desire, and have written it down in black and white, it's really crucial to have the self-belief that we *can* achieve it. This eventually will help us step out of our comfort zone by taking risks and navigating through a multitude of challenges. However, as easy as it may sound, for many of us (including my former self), our circumstances make it tough to have any self-belief. An unhappy childhood, traumatic experiences in the past, abusive relationships, etc., are some of the reasons why some people may have low self-worth and hence lack self-belief. Also, never let naysayers talk you out of your dreams. Remember, if *you* don't believe in yourself, no one else will.

The question that arises then is: how do we develop self-belief?

We need to indulge in positive self-talk to condition ourselves to shake off all self-doubt and fear. Fear is always a part of any attempt to change or transform. Every achiever encounters fear in the beginning, and yet, uses positive self-talk to surmount fear and strengthen self-belief. History is rife with numerous such examples. In fact, the stories of some real women in this book validate this. Our belief in ourselves will help us build our self-esteem and confidence, and these are critical in reaching our goals.

Self-belief gets strengthened through positive self-talk and positive self-affirmations. Self-affirmations are strong and effective statements spoken to ourselves that reinforce our belief in ourselves. One can start with these examples listed below:

'I am worthy of everything I dream of...'
'I am smart enough to accomplish my goals...'
'I have the power to change my life...'
'I learn and grow with my challenges...'

Such affirmations can prevent us from becoming our own critics and help us start believing in our abilities. Once we stop being self-critics, our self-confidence will emerge and self-worth and self-belief shall follow. What will also help us build self-belief is remembering our past accomplishments and recalling how we overcame obstacles on the way to these accomplishments. I always remind myself of my Ironman 70.3 triathlon journey of positive self-talk, visualization and self-belief that led to an almost unrealistic dream becoming a reality. This instantly bolsters my confidence in my abilities.

We could also use the 'Cookie Jar' method, which is a technique of using our past achievements to motivate ourselves when we're struggling. This was propagated by David Goggins in his book *Can't Hurt Me*.[95] As per this concept, we make a list of all our victories and triumphs along with the obstacles and challenges we have overcome. Each of these achievements is a 'cookie'. We put them in a mental jar and whenever we are feeling low, we pull out a cookie and munch on it mentally to remind and motivate ourselves of what we have already achieved in life. Our Cookie Jar can provide us the mental strength and energy to move forward. David transformed himself from an obese 297-pound young lad into a Navy SEAL who held a Guinness World Record for completing 4,030 pull-ups in 17 hours! As he puts it succinctly in his book:

> That's one reason I invented the Cookie Jar. We must create a system that constantly reminds us who we are when we are at our best, because life is not going to pick us up when we fall. There will be forks in the road, knives in your back, mountains to climb, and we are only capable of living up to the image we create for ourselves. Thus, whenever your self-worth takes a beating and your self-belief feels shaken up, just 'count your diamonds'.

Jack Canfield, American bestselling author and motivational speaker, puts it as follows: 'In order to believe in yourself, you first have to believe that what you want is possible.' He mentions four important steps to help us believe in ourselves:

- Believe it is possible:[96] Believe that you can do it regardless of what anyone says or where you are in life.
- Visualize it:[97] Think about exactly what your life would look like if you had already achieved your dream. (Explained in Step 6)
- Act as if:[98] Always act in a way that is consistent with where you want to go.
- Take action towards your goals:[99] Do not let fear stop

you, nothing happens in life until you take action. (Explained in Step 11)

He says, 'The mind is such a powerful instrument; it can deliver literally everything you want through the power of positive expectation.'

Step 4: Carry out a Self-Appraisal

Once we have bolstered our self-belief that it is within our power to achieve our life's purpose, it's time for a self-evaluation. This step is needed because positive thinking and self-belief alone can't help us attain our dreams. There is more effort needed. Self-evaluation can help us ascertain where we stand in the present moment in relation to our goal. It will also motivate us further, bestow the energy needed on the way and help us generate a plan to accomplish our goal.

At this step, we need to take stock of what our inherent strengths are and how these can be leveraged while pursuing our dreams. We are also required to think of what obstacles can come in the way of our efforts because there will be challenges. So, envisaging, and then preparing ourselves mentally and physically for these challenges will propel us forward. We will also need to keep a lookout for the opportunities that align with our goal. These opportunities may sometimes look like lemons (sour and unpleasant). It is up to us to ignore them or to make savoury lemonade out of them.

This is how self-evaluation can help us:

- Getting in touch with our present reality
- Analysing our inner and outer strengths
- Taking stock of potential mental and physical obstacles
- Identifying actions needed to overcome these challenges

- Exploring multiple pathways and opportunities to reach our goal
- Reducing stress by giving us a clear sense of direction
- Channelizing our time and energy in the right activities
- Instilling superior habits in alignment with our goal
- Keeping us motivated in pursuing our dream

Armed with the outcome of this self-evaluation exercise, we can now move into drawing a road map for our path ahead.

Step 5: Create a Road Map for Your Dream

After we have carried out a self-appraisal, we need to strategize and lay out a detailed plan for bringing our dreams to fruition.

A road map is a valuable guide to help manoeuvre the twists and turns on the path ahead. Knowing what our path looks like and how we intend to tread on it is critical in our journey of realization. This will also keep us inspired to make steady progress towards our dreams.

However, it's very important to remember that even while we equip ourselves with a road map for the journey ahead, our path may still digress from time to time. So, expecting deviations and preparing ourselves mentally for the occasional falls and stumbles on the way by building multiple pathways to reach our goals at the planning stage itself will save us a lot of anxiety and time.

Here are a few important components you could build into your road map to give it a solid foundation:

- Make a visual representation of your strategic plan.
- Break down your goals into sub-goals that are SMART [**S**pecific, **M**easurable, **A**chievable, **R**elevant and **T**ime-bound].
- Define milestones and set dates for each sub-goal.

- Brainstorm specific actions for each bite-sized goal. Explore tools like vision boards, mind maps, daily trackers, planners, calendars, reminders and checklists.
- Consider resources like mentors, coaches, books, blogs and courses.
- Mentally prepare for obstacles and build multiple pathways.
- Establish productive habits to make optimum use of your time. (refer to Chapter 8, titled 'Happiness Habits' for more details)
- Build a system to review progress daily, weekly, monthly and annually.

Step 6: Visualize Your Dream Vividly and Often

After building an unshakeable belief in your ability to achieve your dream, it's time to manifest it by visualizing it. Visualization is a mindfulness exercise where you imagine and create the outcome that you desire. It involves seeing the goal as already complete in your mind's eye. This step will help manifest intention into reality. Visualizing in vivid detail how your dream unfolds step by step unto fruition will shift your thought patterns and help your mind focus on searching for solutions to all the obstacles that may show up in your way.

I cannot emphasize enough the importance of visualization in my life. It has helped me achieve many milestones (big and small), and the most notable of them all is the visualization for my Ironman 70.3 event, which I have described in detail in Chapter 2 titled 'Mindfulness'.

The process of visualization is as follows: Find 10 minutes (or more) of undisturbed time, preferably on waking up. Sit in a comfortable position. Close your eyes. Imagine your life's dream as vividly as you can. The key to effective visualization is to create the most graphically detailed picture to focus on in your mind's eye. Visualization is most effective when practised regularly.

As Jack Canfield says, 'See what you want, get what you see.'

Step 7: Have an Accountability Partner

After you've garnered enough belief in yourself and have started visualizing your dream regularly, it's time to invest in one or more accountability partners. There will surely be times in your journey when you'll face daunting challenges, and feel thoroughly confused and unsure of the next step. You will be inundated with fears, insecurities, disappointments and self-doubt. It can be a daunting task to handle these situations all by yourself. These are times when having an accountability partner (one or more) can be invaluable. They're there to encourage you, keep you on track and not let you give up on your dream. They will be there to back you with their ardent support and give honest feedback. They're the people who believe in you wholeheartedly, support your dream fully, and have your best interest at heart.

Make sure you choose an accountability partner who:

- Is totally trustworthy
- Makes you feel comfortable when you share your deepest dreams
- Believes in you and your dream
- Gives you honest and critical/constructive feedback
- Helps you stay committed to your journey
- Holds you accountable and helps keep you on track
- Stands by you through your ups and downs
- Is non-judgmental and very supportive
- Challenges you to push yourself beyond your comfort zone

- Introduces you to a new perspective
- Helps you in any decision-making process
- Is your biggest cheerleader and keeps you motivated
- Lauds your efforts and celebrates your milestones

An accountability partner can be a spouse, partner, close friend, coach, mentor or even your child (as in my case). You may have one or several accountability partners.

Step 8: Break Your Big Goal into Smaller Goals

Many a time, it is easy to navigate well up to the point of visualization, and thereafter, get stuck for want of clarity on where to really start and what the first action step should be. Sometimes, it might all seem too overwhelming if the life goal is too big. At this point, the big goal needs to be broken down into multiple bite-sized goals to prevent a feeling of overwhelm and to attain clarity on what needs to be prioritized. Hence, we need to now break down our soul goal into small actionable steps to propel us forward and maintain momentum.

A great concept to help keep us on track is called 'Goal Setting to the Now'. This was introduced by Gary Keller and Jay Papasan in their highly acclaimed book *The ONE Thing*. It is a process of methodically breaking down the 'Big Goal' into smaller goals in a time sequence. Here's how they described it:

> By thinking through the filter of Goal Setting to the Now, you set a future goal and then methodically drill down to what you should be doing right now. It can be a little like a Russian matryoshka doll in that your ONE Thing 'right now' is nested inside your ONE Thing today, which is nested inside your ONE Thing this week, which is nested inside your ONE Thing this month. It's how a small thing

can actually build up to a big one. You're lining up your dominoes.[100]

This can help us determine what we need to start doing *now* in order to accomplish our long-term dream. It is a reverse engineering process of planning for the big goal by first working on the more immediate and smaller goals.

To understand our starting point, we must answer each of the questions below from the 'Goal Setting to the Now' process:

1. Identify our soul goal: Where do we want to be in five, 10 or 15 years?
2. Bring it closer to the present: Where do we need to be in three years to reach our soul goal?
3. Break it down to the annual goal: To get to where we should be in three years, what goals do we need to reach within a year?
4. Identify our monthly or weekly goals: What action steps do we need to take each month or week to help us achieve our annual goal?
5. Break it down to our daily goal: Based on our monthly or weekly goals, what's the one thing we can do today?
6. Based on our daily goal, what's the one step we can take *right now* to propel us closer to our goal?

We start taking small and precise actionable steps immediately based on our daily goal that is well-aligned with our ultimate goal!

Step 9: Set Timelines

Once you break down your soul goal into sub-goals and actionable steps for each day, it's time to set timelines for their execution. A timeline puts a timeframe on our dreams by giving us a sense of urgency. It makes us accountable for our dream and keeps us moving forward. A healthy way of using the timeline tool is to set a launch date (especially the month and year) for the realization of our big dream, and then, work backward from there. Thereafter, set deadlines for the sub-goals and milestones along the way.

Setting timelines for your dreams will help you:

- Get the momentum going and stay on track
- Put healthy pressure on you to complete each small milestone on time
- Overcome self-sabotaging habits like procrastination
- Prioritize your activities and make necessary trade-offs
- Channel your enthusiasm and energy in the right activities
- Shift your mindset from inertness to execution
- Bolster time efficiency by reducing time wastage
- Increase productivity by locking your attention on the goal
- Stay accountable to your dream
- Boost your sense of accomplishment

Timelines have always worked very well in my case. Whenever I've had too much free time to spare without strict deadlines for a project, I've always become a wee bit too carefree and indolent. At times, I've even procrastinated on that work, eventually working under pressure at the last moment for having neglected it earlier. Having learned from my tendency to become lackadaisical at times, I now always work under timelines whether they are set by someone else or are self-imposed. This practice has no doubt, made me much more efficient than I was a few years ago. I have also realized that time is a limited resource that we need to use most judiciously.

Step 10: Step Out of Your Comfort Zone

Our comfort zone is built out of all the things that provide us with a sense of safety, security and ease because they are familiar to us. And what is familiar is much less intimidating than the unknown. Being comfortable is our default mode as human beings. And while we dwell in the warmth of our comfort zone, our brain doesn't want anything to change.

We do need our comfort zone as our baseline or a reference point. However, just staying confined within the safety of our comfort zone is a death knell for our life's dreams. Staying cocooned in our safety bubble puts us at the risk of stagnation and decadence because discomfort equals growth.

Getting out of our comfort zone from time to time does create stress; however, it is the kind of stress that can help us be more creative and grow from there. It can even help us respond to life's myriad stressors when the going gets tough and unexpected things happen.

It's the fear of the unknown that keeps us from moving out of our comfort zone. Fear is real and it can cause anxiety and trepidation. But then, it's not until we face our fears squarely, and figure out how to conquer them, that we can really move in the direction of our dreams. Fear is a sign to move forward and grow, and not to step back and regress. Every time we step outside of our comfort zone, a bit of our fear shrinks and our self-confidence grows. By acknowledging fear and still choosing to move forward by doing what needs to be done, we're seizing the opportunity to fulfil our deepest aspirations.

As Phil Stutz and Barry Michels wrote in their great book *The Tools* that most people like to live within their comfort zones and that our *infinite* potential exists just on the other side of our comfort zone.[101] All the great things we're capable of achieving lie *outside* of our comfort zone. The barrier between our comfort zone and our infinite potential zone is a zone strewn with pain, fear, doubt, anxiety, etc. So, the tool that they suggest is known as Reversing Our Desire, which means that rather than trying to avoid the discomfort, we need to welcome it. So, instead of crouching in fear, we need to step forward and say 'Bring it on!'

So, when we are excited about our life's dream, yet feel apprehensive about taking the next step, we must remind ourselves that life is primarily about change and then put this tool to use. Moving out of our safe space from time to time is the only way, even if it is very uncomfortable sometimes.

I was a very timid person while growing up, suffering from a number of real as well as irrational fears, such as fear of the dark, fear of being alone in the house, fear of speaking in front of an audience, fear of disappointing someone by not living up to their expectations, etc. Resorting to certain mindfulness-based interventions, especially meditation, has dissolved a lot of my fears. I have definitely taken a few risks by stepping out of my comfort zone and these experiences have not only been extremely rewarding but have also bolstered my self-esteem and self-confidence.

As for stepping out of my comfort zone into an unknown space, I got to test my courage for the very first time when the opportunity for women to join the Indian Navy opened up in India for the first time. Hailing from the town of Agra, it was a major step for me to even contemplate joining the first batch of women officers in the highly coveted Indian Armed Forces. Stepping out and priming up for a very competitive selection process to be one among the 22 women officers to be selected from over 65,000 applicants from all over the country, was not just akin to stepping out of my comfort zone, but was more like jumping off a cliff without a parachute!

The feeling of elation I felt on being selected was surreal. Had I hesitated and not stepped past the intense mental discomfort due to lack of confidence and self-belief, I would've never known what my potential was.

You need to step out of your comfort zone because if you don't, you will:

- Never learn what you really are capable of
- Never face your fears squarely and transcend them
- Stagnate, and stop improving and growing
- Not take risks—'No risk, no reward'
- Not fail, and hence, won't learn valuable lessons
- Lose out on experiencing life to its fullest
- Never feel empowered and liberated
- Never strive to be the best you can be
- Let your dreams die...eventually!

Thus, the next time you have a calling to do something that will make you feel more alive, but fear is pulling you back, consider fear as the compass that is indicating to you where you need to go. At this point, be willing to move out of your own way as you may be the only one hindering your forward march towards your dream. Remember this: life begins at the end of our comfort zone.

Step 11: Take Action Steps Daily

Dreaming, visualizing and then coming up with a brilliant plan are important steps, but if you don't take consistent action towards your goal, it all comes to nothing. A dream without taking action is just that—a dream. To make our dream a reality, we need to actually live it through small daily action steps because inspiration and our creative energy respond to the action. If we wait too long between feeling inspired by our life goal and taking action to accomplish it, our self-confidence and momentum start eroding. Therefore, consistent action steps lay the foundation of our dreams.

Taking that first step may seem scary and daunting at first, but just dive in, and take the plunge! You'll start figuring out things on your way.

Follow these steps to build momentum and self-confidence to get moving:

- **Eliminate all excuses to not act**: They're just a part of our insecurities that are afraid of failure.
- **Set intention daily**: Intention setting at the start of the day can help you stay focused on your goals for that day.
- **Schedule time blocks**: Use a calendar or a planner to schedule big chunks of time for these tasks.
- **Prioritize tasks as ABCDE**: According to his book *Eat That Frog!*, Brian Tracy gives priority to all tasks as per A (must do), B (should do), C (nice to do), D (delegate) and E (eliminate).[102]
- **Take the first step**: Don't wait for the perfect moment. The first step is the most important action on your journey. From here, it'll become much easier to take the next step, and the next, and so on.
- **Remove all distractions**: Put off all notifications on your phone. You need undisturbed time to achieve significant output towards our goal.
- **Work during your most productive hours**: Working when you feel most alert and focused is a great way to get more work done in less time.
- **Review progress at the end of the day**: This will help you plan the next day's schedule in advance so that you get a head start.

Step 12: Be Ready to Fail! Focus on the Process, not on the Outcome

*If you are not willing to be a fool,
you can't become a master.*

—Jordan B. Peterson, Canadian clinical psychologist

It's sad to see that almost everybody celebrates success while overlooking the epic journey that led to that milestone. Every journey is embellished with a string of trials, tribulations, setbacks and failures. However, failure is generally looked down upon.

It is because of this universal outlook of frowning upon failure that we have come to dread failing. A lot of us are paranoid about taking risks and making mistakes. But we forget that without failure there is no progress. By sidestepping failure, we're not really living our lives to their fullest potential. Failure is a necessary ingredient that bestows us with life-altering lessons that ultimately transform our lives for the better.

If you want to accomplish your life goals, you need to realize that some amount of failure is inevitable. Yes, failing causes pain and agony, and yet, it is absolutely necessary and invaluable. It's a stepping stone to success and a critical prerequisite to growing as a person.

No one gets everything right the first time. Even the most successful people in life have failed multiple times before finally succeeding. Michael Jordan himself admitted:

'I've missed more than 9,000 shots in my career. I've lost almost 300 games. Twenty-six times, I've been trusted to take the game winning shot and missed. I've failed over and over and over again in my life. And that is why I succeed.'

Some of the famous achievers who failed a thousand times

before succeeding are Steven Spielberg, Steve Jobs, Sylvester Stallone, Bill Gates, Oprah Winfrey, J.K. Rowling, Henry Ford and Walt Disney.

The mindset of letting go of focussing on the result and enjoying the process is the only way to succeed in life. Failure is essential, transformational and inevitable! Failure is important because it:

- **Confers life-altering lessons**: Failure can guide us to identify and close the gap between where we are and where we want to be. It can help us revise our strategy creatively and find new pathways to achieve our goals.
- **Provides growth**: Failure helps us reflect, take things into perspective and grow by discovering the deeper meaning of why we do what we do. It can alter our frame of mind in a very transformative way.
- **Enhances resilience**: Failure gives us an opportunity to apply perseverance, tenacity and mental strength to overcome fear. Recovering from failure makes us more confident to face future hardships.
- **Builds strength of character**: It keeps us grounded, humble and compassionate. It makes us yearn to keep improving and focus on the process rather than the outcome.

J.K. Rowling, the critically acclaimed author of the highly popular *Harry Potter* franchise, once said: 'It is impossible to live without failing at something unless you live so cautiously that you might as well have not lived at all.' Certainly no one could have experienced and managed failure better than her, whose pitch for *Harry Potter* was rejected by 12 different publishing houses before it was finally accepted.

It is important to remember: only those who show up at the start line have a chance of winning. Don't let the fear of losing stop you from racing towards your goal. So, when you stumble or fall on your journey, get up, dust yourself...and begin again. Trust your journey!

Step 13: Review Your Progress Regularly

Once you start taking small but consistent action steps towards your ultimate dream, it's time to measure the progress you're making. It becomes absolutely essential to track your progress as it'll give you a clear sense of where you started and where you have reached so far.

It will then help you take corrective actions in case you find yourself veering off track. This course correction is necessary to narrow the gap between our dream and its realization.

Tracking progress regularly will help us acquire laser-sharp focus and ensure that our goals are translated into tangible action without losing that deep drive to hustle. This will eventually enable us to deliver what we promised to ourselves—the realization of our life's dream! The more frequent the tracking, the greater the chance of success. As Peter F. Drucker, legendary management guru, once said, 'What gets measured gets managed.'

Monitoring goal progress is a crucial process. It will help you:

- Get a clear sense of where you started and where you've reached so far
- Know where you currently stand in relation to your dream
- Close the gap between where you are and where you want to be

- Catch yourself veering off and course correct when you're slacking
- Identify areas for improvement
- Constantly refresh your strategy and action plan
- Get clarity on the next step you need to take
- Maintain a laser focus on activities that lead you to your dream
- Expand your chances of success

We could review our progress by taking cues from some time-tested methods such as:

- Employing a tracking tool like a calendar, planner, scorecard, checklist, etc.
- Carrying out a debrief consistently, ideally, at the end of each day, week, month and year.
- Reviewing what went well today, last week, last month, last year?
- Analysing what didn't go so well today, last week, last month, last year
- Deciding what we're going to do next.

There is no right or wrong way to review your progress—pick what suits you.

Step 14: Leverage the Power of Consistency

Consistency is simply showing up every day and putting in constant efforts with discipline and single-minded focus towards our big goals. It's not the things that we do on and off that lead us to success. Relentless pursuit through systematic incremental steps is what will eventually lead us to our dreams.

Having said this, the road to being consistent is definitely not easy. It is paved with slippery distractions and potholes of low motivation. Resistance will come from inside sometimes, and fear will surface from time to time. Don't let these barriers talk you out of your goal. Resistance is natural whenever there is a big change expected, and when you're trying to create something new.

However, this shouldn't dissuade you from your journey. It is only through unwavering focus and consistency, especially through the rough patches, that you will finally start moving at a fast pace on the road to success.

But, what does it mean to be consistent? How do we stay consistent and true to our goals? It means:

- Showing up day after day after day with absolute discipline
- Staying committed to our goal even if we don't feel inspired sometimes
- Repeatedly taking actions that lead us to our goals
- Establishing consistent work habits
- Focusing on the task at hand in the present moment
- Not getting distracted, not multitasking (it leads to attention deficit) or procrastinating
- Relentlessly pursuing our dreams

Step 15: Celebrate Your Wins (Big and Small)

We generally tend to celebrate 'big' accomplishments, but rarely take time to savour the numerous tiny wins that eventually help us reach our big goals. Of course, it is great to accomplish big goals, but they may take a long time to be achieved. By remaining centred only on our larger goals at the expense of the smaller wins, may demotivate us and make us fall off the wagon.

For instance, we may wish to publish a book one day. However, writing a few lines a day may seem humdrum and uninspiring. But that's how we build a practice of writing daily.

We must never forget to celebrate the few lines every day, a page tomorrow, a chapter thereafter and so on. This is because it's a series of these few lines and pages day after day that will eventually make the book a reality.

Any measurable progress (however small) towards our big goal is a 'win'. Acknowledging and taking time to savour and marking off every milestone on the way to our big goal can prevent us from burning out.

Celebrating our wins while on our way to achieving our big goals will:

- Boost our sense of emotional well-being by reducing stress
- Help us stay motivated by giving us a dopamine spike
- Provide us the much-needed hope and optimism
- Evoke positive feelings and shape our perspective favourably
- Help remind us of the progress we are making
- Bolster our confidence
- Keep us aligned with our big goal

The celebration doesn't have to be something super-elaborate, but significant enough for us to look forward to. Oprah Winfrey, the famous American talk-show host and philanthropist, once said, 'The more you praise and celebrate your life, the more there is in life to celebrate.' We could always celebrate our wins by:

- Rewarding ourselves with a massage, pedicure, etc.
- Journaling about our feelings
- Surprising ourselves with a gift (a coffee mug or a book)
- Taking time to express gratitude in our own, unique way

- Scheduling a fun night out
- Indulging in our favourite meal
- Going out for coffee with a friend
- Sharing our progress with people we love
- Taking some time off to rest, recover and recuperate

Before I end this chapter, I want to share with you that goals and life purpose are not set in stone. They are likely to evolve over time as you age, build on your repertoire of skills and knowledge, undergo varied life experiences, and face new circumstances and challenges. Remember, roadblocks are fuel for growth if we're willing to have a beginner's mind to learn from them. So, don't get disheartened...

... just take a pause
... honour how far you have come
... recalibrate your life
... re-evaluate your goals
... realign with your core values,
... and move ahead!

Are You Up for a Challenge?

Challenge 1

Below are a few questions that you can ask yourself to help you identify your purpose in life. Some are straightforward while others may be tough. But no one ever said that identifying one's life purpose is going to be easy.

- If you already had all the time and money in the world, what would you like to do in life?
- If you were guaranteed to succeed, what is the one thing you would do?

- What would you dare to do, even if you might fail?
- What is it that you love doing so much, that you would do it for free or even pay to do it?

Challenge 2

Ask yourself the following three questions:

- What are you deeply passionate about?
- What are you really good at and love doing?
- How can you serve others and get paid for it?

The intersection of these three answers will give you a clear indication of the potential purpose of your life. This exercise could require multiple iterations over a period of time. This is derived from the Hedgehog Concept that was introduced by Jim Collins in his book *Good to Great*.[103] While he mentioned it in the context of businesses, we can apply it in our personal lives as well.

chapter 8

Happiness Habits

Motivation is what gets you started.
Habit is what keeps you going.

—Jim Ryun, American Olympic athlete

All the tools in this book will be of no use if they lie rusting in your toolbox—your brain! They need to be integrated into your daily routine for them to have the desired impact on your life. The best way to deploy these tools is by building certain habits—I choose to call these the 'happiness habits', as choosing these will infuse your life with happiness.

We often hear and read about infinite tools and interventions to make life healthier and happier in books, media, blogs and motivational talks. We feel super-inspired to change—as if we could use them that very moment! However, when the next day arrives, and we get on with our daily grind, we seldom revisit these tools that start rusting in our memory bank. In no time, we are back to being what we were...*until* we start making habits out of these tools before they're lost forever in some deep, dark recesses of our memory.

Habits are extremely critical in helping us install impactful rituals and routines into our lives that enhance the quality of our overall well-being. Once they're installed, they can run on autopilot without us having to summon our willpower every now and then to do things that we need to. The thing with willpower is that it is a limited resource, and thus, can deplete over time if we constantly need to use it on a day-to-day basis. This is where habits come to our rescue.

There are some time-tested systems to instill habits that will operate on their own on a daily basis, without taxing us mentally. If installed wisely, they can bring immense peace to our lives and save us a lot of time as well.

James Clear, the American bestselling author, explains in his book *Atomic Habits* that:

> Building better habits isn't about littering your day with life hacks. It's not about flossing one tooth each night or taking a cold shower each morning or wearing the same outfit each day. It's not about achieving external measures of success like earning more money, losing weight, or reducing stress. Habits can help you achieve all of these things, but fundamentally they are not about *having* something. They are about *becoming* someone.[104]

Thus, it becomes imperative for us to start with the pertinent question: 'Who do I want to become?' This question is the ultimate driver for our habits. So, pause now, put the book down and calmly reflect on this question right away. Who do you want to become? A strong athlete or an accomplished writer? A great spouse or a parent or a colleague? A fine homemaker? An effective executive or an entrepreneur? A healthy and happy person?

While contemplating this pivotal question, you must also keep the following declaration made by Clear in *Atomic Habits* in mind: 'The more you repeat a behaviour, the more you reinforce the identity associated with that behaviour. In fact, the word identity was originally derived from the Latin word *essentitas*, which means being, and *identidem*, which means repeatedly. Our identity is literally our "repeated beingness".

'Your identity is literally your *"repeated beingness".* It is indeed a powerful phrase, one that can change your life for the better. Your *identity*, as Clear explains, emanates from your *habits*. Therefore, if you want a new identity, repeat the desired behaviour as often as possible. If you want to repeat the desired behaviour as frequently as possible, you need to live with your new identity. This is how identity and habits are intimately interconnected.

However, the question that now arises is: how do we install new habits? Changing habits is generally not a cakewalk. But the problem isn't you. The problem is with the way your brain works with regard to this. Researchers at the Massachusetts Institute of Technology (MIT) concluded that: 'Neurons that are located in the habit formation region of the brain fire at the beginning of new behaviour, recede while the behaviour occurs, and then fire again once the behaviour is finished. Over time, patterns form, both in behaviour and in the brain. This can make it extremely difficult to break a habit.'[105]

The good news is that you can form new habits with the help of certain well-tried suggestions which are laid out in this chapter.

In my own case, I've had many subpar habits in my life that have come in the way of my health and happiness. Over time, I've been able to change a lot of these habits, especially those related to my nutrition, sleep and spending time on social media. Although I'm still a work-in-progress, I have learned a few very effective ways that have helped me replace these inferior habits with valuable ones.

So, before examining the habits that we need to change

to become happier, let us first look at the tools that we can employ to make habit-changing an easier process:

1. **The ABC of Habit Formation**: In his book *Tiny Habits*, Dr B.J. Fogg, an American bestselling author, talks about the remarkably powerful concept of 'tiny'.[106] He explains that tiny can be mighty. We need to first identify the behaviour we want to make a habit of. We need to make it extremely easy so that it's impossible to fail. Then, we need to find the space where it fits naturally into our routine. Thereafter, we need to nurture its growth. For example, if you want to start meditating on a daily basis, start with one or two minutes of meditation every day. Or, if you want to run a marathon, start by running and walking a kilometre every day. Tiny, incremental actions will make you feel motivated to do the activity more regularly as it doesn't require employing your willpower. And then, you can slowly build and increase the duration and intensity of your new habit. Dr Fogg recommends the ABC system of installing habits:
    - **A—Anchor** Moment: It is an existing routine, like brushing your teeth. If you attach the new behaviour that you aspire for, to this Anchor Moment, it shall always remind you to execute this tiny behaviour.
    - **B**—New tiny **Behaviour**: A behaviour you desire in your life. Carry out this 'tiny' behaviour (e.g. two minutes of meditation) immediately after the Anchor Moment (e.g., brushing your teeth). This is too tiny to fail. So, the moment you brush your teeth in the morning, you meditate for two minutes. As you repeat this process day after day, you will be able to increase the duration and make it into a daily habit.
    - **C**—Instant **Celebration**: Once you accomplish that tiny behaviour, you should celebrate instantly in your

own way, such as pumping your fist and saying, 'Yes! I did it!' Celebrating such small wins creates positive emotions and takes us closer to our ultimate goal (In this case, making meditation a daily habit).

So, remember the ABC of Tiny habits—**A**nchor, **B**ehaviour and **C**elebration.

2. **The Four Laws of Behaviour Change**: Another system that you can consider for installing habits is the 'Four Laws of Behaviour Change' introduced by Clear in his book *Atomic Habits*. According to Clear, 'The Four Laws of Behavior Change are a simple set of rules we can use to build better habits. They are (1) make it obvious, (2) make it attractive, (3) make it easy, and (4) make it satisfying.'[107]

Let us see how we can use these four laws in an activity (let's say, running) that we intend to do:

- **Law #1—Make it obvious**: Use intentions such as, 'I will go for a run in the *neighbourhood park* when I get up *in the morning*.' Note that the 'when' and 'where' are very vital. If you are precise, you increase the odds of implementing your intention of going for a run. You can also make the cue obvious by 'designing your environment'. Perhaps, you could arrange the running clothes and shoes the night before, and keep them in plain sight so that you see them as soon as you get up in the morning.

- **Law #2—Make it attractive**: Think about all the research demonstrating the benefits you want: a rush of energy, an alert mind or a good mood throughout the day. A good way to bolster any habit is by joining a group of people where your desired behaviour is seen as normal behaviour, which in this instance, would be a running group.

- **Law #3—Make it easy**: Do you want to know the easiest way to make it easy? You can start very small—like running and walking just one kilometre to start with. On days when you're not too motivated to run (and there will surely be a few), tell yourself that you're going for a short walk instead. Once you step out and begin, you are bound to build momentum and have a decent run.
- **Law #4—Make it satisfying**: Give yourself an immediate reward after performing your new habit. It could be as gratifying as enjoying fresh coconut water with your running buddies after you finish your run.

It is worth noticing that both the bestselling authors—James Clear and Dr Fogg—talk about two common means for establishing a new habit—starting tiny or small, *and* celebrating it or making it satisfying.

Let us now have a look at some potent and effective constructs that can empower us to integrate first-class habits into our lives.

1. If-Then Algorithms

A powerful tool to instill habits is to implement 'if-then' algorithms by anchoring a desirable habit to an existing habit. It is along the line of the concept of having an anchor moment in Dr Fogg's book *Tiny Habits*. For example, if you want to start meditating in the morning, you can anchor it to your habit of getting up in the morning when the alarm goes off.

So, the algorithm will be: *If* I get up in the morning on hearing the alarm, *then* I will meditate right away. In the other example of running, if laziness is keeping you from stepping out regularly for a run, the algorithm could be: *If* I brush my teeth in the morning, *then* I will put on my running gear and step out of the house for a short run.

2. Focus on the process: Habits can take time to get embedded into your routine. Establishing a habit could take anywhere between two weeks to even a month—it varies from person to person and on the type of habit—easy to complex. As Hal Elrod, an American author, keynote speaker and success coach, wrote in his book *The Miracle Morning*, when you first set out to establish any new habit, it will go through three phases.[108]

(a) **Phase 1 (Days 1-10)—Unbearable**: If you decide to meditate first thing in the morning, even if it is for just one minute, at first it will appear almost painful. It will suddenly disorient your normal routine.

(b) **Phase 2 (Days 11-20)—Uncomfortable**: After a few days of 'enduring' this activity, you will enter a phase where you won't find it unbearable, but are likely to still feel uncomfortable.

(c) **Phase 3 (Days 21-30)—Unstoppable**: A few more days of persistence and persevering through discomfort, you will reach a phase where you'll become unstoppable with regard to your mediation habit. At this stage, you would've started experiencing the incredible benefits of the habit and would be fully motivated and charged to continue doing it on autopilot.

So, focus on the 'process' of habit building and you can keep adding to your repertoire of habits and spiral your way up in all aspects of your life. You will not need to use your willpower for these habits thereafter.

3. Do it daily: When you start a new habit, the initial days will prove to be a huge challenge, as you're likely to feel quite unsettled with your daily routine being disturbed. It's because we all are resistant to change as humans and love to stay in our comfort zones. Introducing something new can initially appear a bit stressful. So, the thumb rule for establishing a habit is to be consistent and *do it daily*. If you do happen to miss a day for any reason, definitely don't miss another one in a row.

4. Plan your day the night before: Planning your day the night before can take a whole lot of guesswork out of the day, and that, in turn, will curb the stress around establishing a new habit. It will enable you to proactively schedule not only work-related stuff but also your important daily habits. You can prepare a list of your important tasks and self-care habits, and schedule them in a calendar. The calendar could be a physical planner or a digital one, as per your preference. I love to write things down on paper, so a physical planner is my preferred tool for planning for the next day.

Also, you will generally have more control over your early-morning and late-evening time slots rather than the middle of the day, when there are more activities planned already, and hence, more distractions. So, it is helpful to schedule self-care habits for early morning and late evenings. Also, schedule your deepest work in the first half of the day, when your mind is most fresh and energy levels are at their peak.

5. Create time blocks: Time blocks are large chunks of continuous time that you spend on specific tasks and responsibilities. Time blocking is a very efficient method of time management. For work that requires deep thinking and reflection, you need lengthy slots of undistracted time. For this, you could schedule time blocks of 60–90 minutes where you could remove all distractions, such as your phone and online distractions and put in deep work. This should be followed by a break for a few minutes, where you recover by indulging in calming activities, such as taking a power nap or going for a short walk, but not going online to jack up your brain, as surfing the net or checking your notifications are not calming activities.

Most of us are familiar with and would've faced exhausting consequences of 'too much work and too little time'. Time is one of the most valuable assets we have in life. So, poor time management can potentially cause stress, anxiety, irritability, mood swings, fatigue, reduced focus, lack of sleep, and at worst, depression. This is where time blocking can step in to assuage our stress. Time blocks can help us get the most out of our day by helping us plan our hours systematically when we're inundated with a heavy workload each day. It can also help us track how we are spending all our time in a day.

This kind of task scheduling can put us in control of our day by helping us plan and prioritize work in a more systematic manner. It increases focus, efficiency and productivity. Not only will it help us enjoy our current work more, but it will also free up more time for us to focus on our relationships and self-care activities, such as exercising, reading, etc. Being able to make time to indulge in activities that give us joy will inevitably reduce stress and anxiety.

Here's a step-by-step time blocking guide for your reference:

- Invest in a planner/diary/app that has hour-to-hour slots.
- Make a complete list of your jobs related to work, home, family, social and self-care commitments.
- Categorize them into high, medium and low, and then, prioritize the top 10 tasks.
- Enter the time needed to complete each task.
- Transpose these jobs into specific time slots in your daily planner on the previous evening itself.

- Schedule two-three deep time blocks of about 60-90 minutes each. Use the morning deep work time slot for the most important work.
- Schedule short breaks every 30 minutes for a quick stretch or walk to give your brain and eyes a breather.
- Set up separate smaller time slots for 'reactive' tasks only after at least one deep work slot.
- Use a preferred time-management strategy such as the Pomodoro technique. The Pomodoro technique is a time management system that can motivate people to work within the time they have at their disposal. It uses a timer to split work into blocks of typically 25 minutes in length, separated by short breaks.
- Keep an 'overflow day' aside in a week to prevent you from feeling overwhelmed if and when you fall behind on tasks.
- Review and amend your time blocks as needed. No one can be perfect all day, every day, so move things around on the planner, if needed.

Note: While the above system works well for me, feel free to devise your own unique time blocking method.

6. Carry out a digital detox: Owing to the fact that many of us are into professions that require extended online presence every day, a complete withdrawal from the use of technology is absolutely unrealistic.

However, there are a staggering number of us whose faces are constantly glued to our screens. This is not just related to work commitments alone but is also a result of being habituated to mindless scrolling through our social media notifications, watching video forwards and news on loop, and so on. There is a perpetual dopamine rush in our brains from these activities, and we become restless from the 'Fear of Missing Out' (FOMO).

Digital obsession is associated with a number of psychological problems, such as anxiety, depression and loneliness. This constant fixation with screens may even be a sign of a serious disorder called social media anxiety disorder. As a result, we're missing out big time on cultivating deep relationships, as there is minimal human interaction. It can even adversely affect our physical health, as too much screen time causes eye strain, muscular discomfort and joint pain.

Taking frequent and mindful digital breaks can work wonders for our mental and emotional well-being by filtering out a lot of noise from the mind. This is now known as the 'Joy of Missing Out' (JOMO).

Some of the Joys of Missing Out are:

- Enhanced self-awareness
- Increased focus and productivity
- Reduced anxiety
- Lowered risk of depression
- Improved relationships
- Enhanced sleep
- Better prioritization of tasks

Here are a few ways to take digital breaks

- Do not start your day by opening emails or social media first thing on waking up.
- Set digital boundaries by giving yourself a separate daily screen-time allowance.
- Turn off notifications or alerts while doing important work.
- Declutter regularly by closing tabs that you don't need

immediately, and deleting social media apps that hinder your productivity.
- Take regular screen-less breaks by indulging in self-care activities, such as developing 'offline' hobbies, stretching, practising deep breathing, reading and meditating.
- Monitor your daily screen time and internet usage by using relevant apps on your devices.
- Follow a 'digital sunset' by shutting all screens at least an hour before bedtime
- Put your phone away and be completely 'present' while doing deep work, eating, spending face-to-face time with family and friends, exercising, etc.

For many of us in the present scenario, constant and incessant social media consumption is as addictive to our minds as sugar is to our palate. Till not so long ago, I wouldn't sleep without checking my WhatsApp notifications expecting new messages and checking whether the messages I sent had the eagerly awaited 'blue ticks', and had been responded to. And then, I would invariably be lured by the incessant stream of forwards...*just* for a bit...but then the 'bit' somehow always expanded into an hour or more.

Mornings were no different. Even before I could focus my eyes, my hand would reach out for my phone as if on autopilot and it would be a rerun of the night before. Besides disrupting my calm mind during the day and my sleep at night, I realized that it was eating into mammoth chunks of my time that could've been used more productively. It really felt like a sugar craving—the more I ate, the more I wanted!

Now, it's been a couple of years since I've got a handle on my digital fixation. I generally don't use my phone for any purpose other than for calling and receiving calls until noon, and until I've put in a few hours of deep work. I have worked on my 'digital sunset' too, even though I flounder sometimes. The outcome? Increased output, minimal irritability, plenty of mental peace, more time to pursue things that give me joy, much better sleep, and so much more!

If the story of your life also runs similar to mine before my digital-detox phase, try keeping your hands off your phone (at least off social media) for a couple of hours after you wake up and a couple of hours before your bedtime. It's bliss!

7. Declutter your home...and your mind!

Surprising as it may sound, less mess equals less stress. Getting rid of excess clutter around our daily existence not only helps us organize our homes, but also mollifies our high-strung nerves. As it turns out, amassing a lot of 'stuff' doesn't provide lasting happiness. On the contrary, it can make us feel stressed and weary! Cluttered surroundings with incessantly added layers of 'stuff' adversely impact our energy levels. They can weigh us down and make us feel stagnant and stuck.

When we let go of the things that no longer serve us or bring us joy, all the energy that has been trapped in them for so long, is set free. The spaciousness created around us can provide a great sense of relief and elation, and most importantly, clarity. So, go ahead—clean up your closets, your drawers, your kitchen cabinets and whatever else, and get that extra load off your home and your mind.

Finally, I would say that you need to adopt a learner's mindset when it comes to changing a habit. When you're trying to establish habits and things are not going as expected, just analyse what happened when you were not able to do what you said you would do. Don't beat yourself up when you slip up. For instance, if you haven't been able to sit to meditate for a few days despite wanting it so hard, don't be harsh on yourself. It can demotivate you further. You need to have plenty of self-compassion to help yourself during such a personal transformation. We either win or we learn—this is a mental process followed by some of the best athletes and sportspersons in the world. Just analyse what you could do to improve and start again. And then, just start again! Every day is a good day to start again!

So, start building habits, and get into the habit of building such habits. I love what Warren Buffett, renowned American business magnate, investor and philanthropist, had said, 'Chains of habit are too light to be felt until they are too heavy to be broken.'

Are You Up for a Challenge?

1. Identify a **keystone habit**—that singular habit which provides the most solid foundation to your entire day and life. Then start taking steps as described in this chapter to install this habit into your daily routine. For example, waking up early or starting exercise.
2. Identify the one **damaging habit**—that habit which throws you off balance. Then start taking steps to uninstall it from your life. For me, it was checking social media as soon as I got up in the morning. Now, I make it a point to be *creative* before I am *reactive* and do not access social media before 11.00 a.m., by which time I have put in at least two hours of creative time. What is it for you?
3. Install at least three **'if–then' algorithms** to ensure that some of the important self-care habits that you identify start running on autopilot without consuming too much of your willpower.
   - if I get up in the morning, then I will...

- if it is nearing my bedtime, then I will...
- if I have important work to complete but am feeling tempted to go online just for a few minutes, then I will...

4. If and when you stumble in the process of installing habits, which you definitely will, repeatedly whisper **'let me start again'** to yourself, get back on track and restart the habit. It will surely take a few iterations before you can install the 'master habit'—that of installing new habits!

chapter 9

Self-Care

If your compassion does not include yourself, it is incomplete.

—Jack Kornfield, author and Buddhist practitioner

In today's scenario women juggle several responsibilities at home and in office—childcare, senior care, domestic chores, deadlines at work, children's studies and extracurricular activities, scheduling doctor visits and the list goes on. As a result, they often end up deprioritizing their own needs. Before they realize that their plate may be on the brink of overflowing, odds are that they will eventually become frustrated and resentful. This bitterness will likely show up in the form of tension, irritability, poor health and a general sense of unhappiness. When we don't prioritize self-care, we're very likely to feel like a victim of our circumstances, thus hampering the quality of life and making us feel unfulfilled.

I have met numerous women over the past years who feel sheepish at the mere suggestion of self-care activities. Take the example of a relative of mine (a teacher by profession). She is someone who runs on the incessant treadmill of getting breakfast ready for the family before leaving for work, returning from school to resume her domestic duties of tending to her terminally ill mother-in-law, doing laundry, cooking dinner, and if time permits, running a few errands outside. A big chunk of her weekends is generally spent on planning, coordinating and organizing the upcoming cultural events and functions at school. Gauging her high physical and emotional stress levels, I suggested she avail deep tissue massages on a weekly basis, for it works wonders on a tired body and mind. She almost felt scandalized, responding that she couldn't even imagine wasting precious time indulging in 'such' activities.

Get Past 'The Guilt'

My relative is not alone in feeling guilty at the thought of taking care of herself. Many women feel that self-care is nothing but an act of selfishness. They feel awkward to shift the balance suddenly from caring for everyone else to caring for themselves, often finding it a frivolous waste of time.

We have to understand that nurturing ourselves is *not* akin to being self-centred or selfish unless we are vehemently ignoring other critical areas of our lives. Self-care is very essential for our survival and well-being. Only when we regularly take care of ourselves can we be in a good mental frame and physical state to show up powerfully for others day after day.

The next time you experience guilt pangs at 'self-indulging' thoughts, such as needing a massage or spending a bit more time in a warm shower, think about how these activities can benefit all the 'stakeholders' of your life including yourself. Think of how such tools can dissipate stress and leave you feeling rejuvenated. For instance, imagine yourself returning from a deep tissue massage, feeling completely relaxed, cheerful and more 'present'. Then imagine how very relaxed you would feel taking care of your family or others thereafter. Wouldn't it ease your daily grind significantly?

By taking good care of ourselves we are also serving as role models for our children, so that they too can understand the importance of self-care and thus, practise it to enrich their own lives.

Self-care is also a critical way of empowering ourselves in a culture where women are disenfranchised as a norm. Although things are changing, it is still at a slow pace.

Anureet Sethi said to me, 'As psychotherapists, we strongly propagate self-care. Self-care is actually prioritizing yourself and taking time out to nurture your passions and interests. Somewhere down the rat race, we have forgotten to indulge regularly in self-care as a means of mental wellness.'

Be Your Own Best Friend

Do you think you could be genuinely compassionate to others without being compassionate to yourself? If you don't treat yourself with love and respect, how can you love and respect others from an authentic place within you? Loving starts with ourselves. Isn't that 'self' someone who you would be spending your whole life with? Self-care activities are essential to start the process of finding and tuning into our authentic selves.

Also, understand that if you're someone who needs a lot of regular self-care (more than some others you may know) to nourish your overall well-being, it's perfectly fine and you're not alone. Don't view yourself as someone fragile, and as if something is wrong with you. It's counterproductive to compare yourself with women who seem stronger than you and don't use much self-care. A big reason why many women appear not to need so much self-care is that as women, we can push through a lot of discomforts and ignore the red flags our body and mind may be giving to us. Remember, willpower and energy are limited resources, and the body or the mind may break down some day as a consequence of weakening resolve and mental strength. Every one of us has a different threshold for enduring mental, emotional and physical wear and tear.

Types of Self-Care

Personally, I need a lot of self-care on a regular basis. I need to indulge in activities that soothe my frayed nerves and nourish my mind, body and spirit. In fact, the tools and techniques that I am going to talk about here help me re-energize myself so wonderfully that I show up the next day with renewed verve and vitality, ready to take on the world!

Before we delve into a plethora of self-care habits, we need to acknowledge that due to our bio-individuality (uniqueness as individuals), self-care can mean different things to different people. Also, due to our unique personal circumstances, some tools may work for us better than the others.

We need different types of self-care tools to satisfy diverse types of self-care needs. These would be in the form of psychological, physical, spiritual and mental self-care needs. Remember that many self-care activities mentioned below may overlap under different types of self-care needs because of their myriad benefits.

1. **Psychological self-care**: These types of activities cater to our need to feel emotionally refreshed. They revive us emotionally by helping us feel, accept, connect and process the full range of our emotions without the need to judge them. Some examples of these self-care activities are:

    - Writing in a journal
    - Blogging

- Socializing with friends
- Reading an engaging book
- Creating art such as painting, dancing, sketching, knitting, etc.
- Watching a movie with our family
- Listening to uplifting and soothing music
- Saying 'no' when we feel like saying so
- Owning and caring for a pet
- Going on a weekend getaway with family or/and friends
- Dressing up for an occasion
- Decluttering your daily schedule by delegating less-important jobs
- Seeing a therapist

2. **Physical self-care**: Physical self-care is a very broad spectrum of activities that enhance our physical well-being. Remember, these self-care activities will not only benefit our physical health but will have a ripple effect on our mental and emotional health as well. Some ideas are:

   - Spending some time in the sunlight
   - Eating a nutritious and wholesome meal
   - Indulging in regular exercise
   - Playing a sport that we like
   - Getting a deep tissue massage
   - Sleeping seven–eight hours every night
   - Pampering ourselves with a new haircut or a pedicure/manicure
   - Taking a long and indulgent shower
   - Window shopping
   - Taking a walk during lunch breaks
   - Going for a day-long hike

- Relaxing through aromatherapy
- Hydrating well through the day
- Walking barefoot on grass
- Drinking calming teas or infusions
- Getting a health check-up done

3. **Spiritual self-care**: Indulging in spiritual self-care activities is the surest road to sustained happiness. Spiritual self-care includes activities that help us get in touch with and nourish our spirit. Spiritual self-care doesn't require us to be religious. We could believe in God or a spiritual being, or could be an atheist; either way, we can reap tangible benefits from engaging in spiritual self-care practices. These could include:

   - Meditating
   - Contributing to causes we care about (giving or volunteering)
   - Gratitude journaling or praying
   - Spending time in nature
   - Practising positive self-talk and self-compassion
   - Doing deep-breathing exercises
   - Practising yoga
   - Walking barefoot on grass
   - Going for high-altitude treks
   - Spending time in silence, self-reflecting, Just 'being'!

4. **Mental self-care**: Self-care activities that can positively stimulate the mind and the intellect, and augment the cognitive power of the brain, qualify as mental self-care exercises. Some of the examples include:

   - Reading a book
   - Solving a puzzle like crossword or Sudoku

- Playing chess
- Visiting a museum
- Learning a new language
- Learning to play a musical instrument.

My personal favourites are meditation, gratitude journaling, deep breathing, indulging in regular exercise, walking at least 10,000 steps every day, reading a book and getting a deep tissue massage.

A caveat: to experience maximum benefit, you need to be fully present and mindfully engaged during the self-care activity that you're indulging in.

Spending Time on Screen Is not Self-Care

It's a delusion that screen breaks can relax our minds. In fact, screen time is a very big stressor. Looking at other people's lives that they project on social media has been known to cause anxiety, insecurity and low self-esteem, and among other things, it can desensitize us to our immediate environment. Spending too much time checking notifications and other people's statuses can lead to immediate attention deficit, procrastination, missing deadlines and social disconnect—all of which are recipes for an unhappy life.

Exclusive 'Me Time'

Spending quality time alone is not a lonely pursuit. Spending time with ourselves while the whole world continues to hum with activity helps us rest, replenish and refresh ourselves. This can be achieved simply through activities such as walking barefoot in the grass, taking a silent yet mindful trail walk, reading a book while sitting on a park bench or sipping coffee while sitting on our favourite couch at home. As the English author Steven Aitchison puts it, 'A caterpillar must endure a season of isolation before it turns into a butterfly. Embrace the time you have alone, it will only make you stronger.'

You Are Enough Just the Way You Are

While you embark on your self-care journey, don't ever forget that you are enough just the way you are. Remember not to pay attention to any mental gremlins that make you feel inadequate in any way. Self-care is required not because you are incomplete in any way, but as an approach in life to recover your balance and equanimity in today's super-engaged and high-paced life. This pace of life can put an inordinate amount of emotional, mental and physical strain on you and throw you off-balance at times.

Therefore, step off from time to time from the incessant treadmill of daily grind to smell the roses. Incorporate self-care as a 'way of life' and give yourself a chance to thrive. Delve frequently in the activities that help you assuage stress, make you come alive with joy and help you operate from a place of calm amidst life's myriad challenges. Treat yourself with love, respect and compassion, and truly enjoy being a woman. This is a wonderful investment in yourself, your family and others whom you care for.

Are You Up for a Challenge?

- My top three self-care tools are exercise, meditation and journaling. Which are yours?
- Which are the eight self-care habits (two from each category) that you love and would like to incorporate

in your life? Take small steps to incorporate these into your life (as explained in Chapter 8 ['Happiness Habits']).
- What one thing can you start doing from today that can reduce your stress?
- What one thing can you stop doing immediately that aggravates stress in your life?

chapter 10

Female Hormones

*I'm not afraid of storms,
for I'm learning how to sail my ship.*

—Louisa May Alcott, American author and poet

I love the imagery that I had once read about female hormones. It compared female hormones to a beautifully synchronized ballroom dance that flows smoothly, wherein both partners support each other step to step; until one partner goes out of step and ends up stamping on the other's foot, breaking the harmony and causing pain.

Female sex hormones (oestrogen and progesterone) work together in an incredibly complex system. If one gets 'out of step', it displaces the other hormone as well as many other bodily systems, like a bull in a china shop! Imbalanced hormones have the power to upset the great harmony that our bodily systems enjoy when they are working in tandem.

Despite the fact that hormones are responsible for regulating many crucial bodily processes including our mental and emotional well-being, sadly, most of us are unaware of the pivotal role they play in our bodies. I am no exception to this, and remained clueless until about a decade ago. It was my curiosity about the overall well-being of my body that led me to research about them.

Understanding our hormones and then nurturing them can save us a lot of emotional and physical stress. It can help us stave off many health conditions, such as chronic stress, anxiety, depression, irritability, a feeling of overwhelm, weight gain, insomnia and lower metabolic rate. And in extreme cases, certain hormonal conditions, like menopause, can make some women feel suicidal.[109]

However, unlike general belief, hormonal imbalances don't just occur as a result of obvious causes such as certain foods in our diet and environmental toxins. Hormonal disruption can also happen as a result of imbalances in one or various critical areas of our lives such as home environment, career, relationships, poor sleep, nutrient deficiencies, lack of or too much physical activity, etc.

So, before we learn a few smart tricks on how to balance and nurture our hormones, we need to first recognize the two hormones that are unique to women.

Oestrogen and Progesterone

Oestrogen and progesterone are the two main female sex hormones that are secreted by the ovaries. When imbalanced, they can create discomfort and health issues either by being too high (oestrogen or progesterone dominance) or too low (oestrogen and progesterone deficiency). Imbalance in one or both can create discomfort and distress during various stages of a woman's life, such as premenstrual syndrome (PMS), pregnancy, perimenopause (before menopause stage) and menopause.

Common Life Phases with Hormonal Imbalance

Many of my female clients have felt anxious, depressed, angry and agitated for 'no apparent reason', as they would share with me. After having a heart-to-heart talk, I would realize that they had no serious malady, just a flurry of hormones vexing them for attention. Most of these women were going through one of the following life-phases that are nesting grounds for hormonal imbalance:

- Premenstrual Syndrome (PMS)
- Perimenopause and menopause
- Pregnancy

Since pregnancy is an entire subject in itself and needs professional medical intervention, I shall keep it out of the discussion here. Let us learn the basics about the other two phases.

Premenstrual Syndrome (PMS)

PMS is a condition that almost all women who menstruate go through. It affects more than 90 per cent of women across the globe. The exact cause of PMS is not known; however, hormonal imbalance is believed to trigger PMS symptoms. It is thought to be a result of oestrogen dominance and a decline in progesterone levels that adversely affect the levels of serotonin (the 'feel-good' hormone) in the brain. Because each one of us is unique, the intensity of PMS symptoms varies from person to person.

While some women have it easy and can just breeze through their periods, for others it could feel as intense as labour pain. Those who suffer from the dreaded period blues (and that's quite a staggering number), may endure a combination of symptoms, such as cramps, bloating, nausea, constipation, fatigue, breast tenderness, food cravings, moodiness and irritability.

I have personally experienced an extremely painful PMS from the time I started menstruating until the time I joined the Indian Navy in 1992. My period always brought extreme misery with sharp abdominal and lower-back pain and cramps. It used to be so bad that I would stay in bed crying, with legs raised on the wall and a hot water bottle against my lower back for heat fomentation.

However, just as I started my rigorous training in the Navy in 1992, all the discomfort just disappeared. My period would come and go quietly without creating any turbulence in my life. It was a breeze. The point of mentioning this is that while there was absolutely no physical activity in my life before my Naval stint, I had a lot of PMS discomfort. But once there was regular physical activity since 1992, the discomfort receded and ceased for good. I also attribute my difficult PMS episodes to my heightened stress and anxiety emanating from traumatic situations and fears during my growing-up years. This too disappeared when my life felt safer and more meaningful after joining the Navy.

Primary Symptoms of PMS

Some of the typical symptoms of PMS are:

- Abdominal bloating and weight gain
- Abdominal and lower-back pain and cramps
- Tenderness of breasts
- Anxiety and/or depression
- Mood swings, irritability and emotional outbursts
- Food cravings
- Fatigue
- Trouble falling asleep or sleeping too much

- Headaches
- Constipation or diarrhoea
- Acne
- Sensitivity to light or noise
- Trouble with concentration
- Change in libido
- Social withdrawal

During a painful PMS, many women loathe even the mention of the word 'exercise', especially if lethargy and fatigue are the uninvited guests lodging inside the body. However, research reveals that exercise can be great therapy for symptoms of PMS.[110]

Even if you don't feel up to exercising as per your usual workout routine, too much bed rest may not be a good idea. Adding some gentle movement can distract you from the discomfort, and some easy stretches can invigorate you by alleviating your pain and discomfort. Certain yoga stretches are particularly effective in easing period pain and cramps. These are:

- Balasana (Child's Pose)
- Marjariasana (Cat Pose)
- Supta Matsyendrasana (Supine Spinal Twist)
- Ustrasana (Camel Pose)
- Supta Baddha Konasana (Reclined Bound Angle Pose)
- Apanasana (Knees-to-Chest Pose)
- Viparita Karani (Legs-up-the-Wall Pose)
- Savasana (Corpse Pose)

Natural Ways of Handling PMS Discomfort

While most dietary guidelines to balance hormones are common to PMS and menopause, there are some dietary interventions that can specifically alleviate PMS stress. These are:

- Adding foods rich in nutrients such as calcium, magnesium, vitamin B6 and omega-3 fatty acids.
- Eating foods like eggs, tofu, dried beans, legumes, lentils, whole grains (oats, finger millet, barley, brown rice, quinoa and buckwheat), fatty fish, seeds, dried fruits, nuts, banana and dark chocolate.
- Eating more fibrous foods, especially vegetables like broccoli, leafy greens, beans, sweet potato and carrot.
- Reducing salt, dairy, caffeine, saturated fats and spicy foods like pickles.
- Eliminating sugar, refined flour, fried foods and packaged foods with preservatives, trans fats and alcohol.
- Managing stress through self-care tools (More details in Chapter 9 titled 'Self-Care.')

Perimenopause and Menopause

Perimenopause is a three–five-year transition period just before a woman reaches menopause. During this stage, the production of female hormone, oestrogen drops dramatically. The menstrual cycle becomes highly irregular and unpredictable. This lowers a woman's chances of becoming pregnant. Perimenopause can start at any time after mid-30s in its natural course, and is marked initially by a drop in the progesterone levels and oestrogen dominance. It is during this phase that women start experiencing a difficult PMS if they haven't been already, and experience typical menopausal symptoms that send the female hormones in a tizzy. It's a phase that marks the gradual move towards menopause.

Menopause or 'the change' is the time in a woman's life

when her menstrual cycle ceases completely and ovulation stops, marking the end of her reproductive years. This usually happens between the ages of 45 and 55.

While many consider menopause to be an illness because of its distressing symptoms, it is just an inevitable phase in every woman's life. However, since the oestrogen levels decline further during menopause, it increases the risk of certain diseases, such as heart disease, blood pressure, diabetes and osteoporosis.

Since hormones ebb and flow drastically during menopause, it can be a very distressing period for some women, although symptoms vary from person to person. Most women at this time in their lives are managing multiple roles such as helping their children settle down in life, taking care of old and ailing parents, handling the pressures of home, marriage and professional life (for many), and of course, their own health. While they're in the midst of dabbling in all these roles, when menopause arrives, it can take a huge toll on them in the form of physical, emotional and mental stress. Sometimes, the symptoms can be so intense that medical interventions may be needed.

Common Menopause Symptoms

As mentioned earlier, each woman is unique, and therefore symptoms would vary in intensity, duration and effect on each woman based on individual health and fitness levels, and discomfort thresholds. The most common symptoms of menopause are:

- Hot flashes, night sweats and chills
- Stress, anxiety and depression
- Severe mood swings with bouts of anger, aggression, irritability or crying

- Weight gain and water retention due to lower metabolic rate
- Feelings of overwhelm, hopelessness and gloom
- Sleep deprivation or insomnia
- Migraine headaches
- Memory lapses, brain fog and reduced ability to concentrate
- Loss of libido
- Soreness of breasts
- Vaginal dryness
- Urinary incontinence or frequent or sudden urge to urinate
- Decreased muscle mass and bone mass
- Dryness of skin
- Hair thinning or hair loss
- Changes in body shape, such as loss of fullness of breast and butt, and shifting of weight from butt and thighs to the tummy
- Increased hair growth on the face, neck and chest
- Heart palpitations
- Pain and stiffness in joints
- Lowered self-esteem and self-worth due to poor body image
- Increased incidence of urinary tract infections
- Heightened risk of some diseases such as osteoporosis, breast cancer, hypertension and stroke

Natural Ways of Easing Menopause Discomfort

While the symptoms of menopause can be severe for many women, it is absolutely possible to mitigate them with the help of certain lifestyle changes, such as:

- **Reducing caloric intake:** Eating slightly fewer calories

per day can help control weight gain triggered by hormonal imbalance, as caloric requirements reduce during and after menopause.
- **Reducing the intake of certain foods**: (list given under the 'Common Hormone Disruptors' section below).
- **Including critical nutrients**: Adding certain foods rich in hormone-friendly nutrients can reduce menopausal discomfort. These are omega-3 fatty acids, lean protein, fibre (fruits and vegetables), calcium, magnesium, B vitamins (especially vitamins B2, B6, B12 and B9-folic) and vitamin D (unfortunately, there are very few food sources of vitamin D. Sunlight is its strongest source). These can help in boosting energy and managing mental health along with many other benefits.
- **Taking essential supplements**: If your diet is deficient in essential nutrients, consider taking supplements *but* only after consulting your physician.
- **Staying hydrated**: Drinking enough water (at least eight glasses) throughout the day, especially to deal with hot flashes.
- **Exercising regularly**: Just like dietary changes, exercise is one of the most effective means of reducing menopausal stress, creating positive energy and keeping excess weight off. It also helps in preventing osteoporosis, staying fit, balancing hormones and preventing many other lifestyle diseases. Yoga is especially known to be therapeutic during menopause.
- **Practising mindfulness**: Mindfulness activities like meditation, focussed breathing, practising gratitude and journaling can be very helpful techniques in alleviating mental symptoms such as stress, anxiety, depression, mood swings, anger bouts, irritability, etc.

These interventions help to take the focus off negative emotions and physical symptoms of menopause, and help to appreciate the positive things in one's life. (More details in Chapter 2 titled 'Mindfulness'.)

- **Getting seven–eight hours of sleep each night**: Sleep is very therapeutic in balancing hormones. If you don't sleep adequately each night, your body will produce the stress hormone cortisol that can aggravate menopause symptoms further. For more details on how to sleep better, refer to Chapter 5 titled 'Sleep'.)
- **Investing in other means of self-care**: Our bodies deserve some pampering and tender care at this time and stage. Self-care can mean different things to different women as self-care too is bio-individual. Therefore, regular self-care during menopause through what you like doing can help ease psychological stress to a great extent. (More details in Chapter 9 titled 'Self-Care'.)

While menopause is an absolute reality in each woman's life, it doesn't need to be feared or loathed. Our attitude towards it can make a lot of difference in our ability to handle it. If we view it with anger and irritation, the symptoms will feel stronger and more exaggerated. If we view menopause from a place of self-acceptance and calmness, and as being a part of our complete selves, an intrinsic part of our lives, we're sure to feel much more in control of our situation.

Interventions to Keep Hormones in Harmony

While both PMS and menopause may have slightly different balancing protocols, and there is 'no one size fits all' for every woman, there are some recommendations that could work universally. These are:

- Eating top hormone-balancing foods like turmeric, leafy green vegetables, cruciferous vegetables (cabbage, broccoli, cauliflower, bok choy, etc.), pomegranate, walnuts, seeds (flaxseeds, chia, sesame and pumpkin), wild-caught salmon, coconut oil, ghee, avocado, fresh berries, garlic and olive oil.
- Consuming only organic and local foods without hormones, toxins and GMOs, especially if consuming meats, dairy and seafood.
- Avoiding certain foods (comprehensive list in the section 'Common Hormone Disruptors' below)
- Eating healthy omega-3 fats. Fats are the building blocks of hormones. A low-fat diet can actually make it harder for the body to produce the hormones it needs.
- Taking essential supplements. If your diet is deficient in recommended quantities of essential nutrients, like magnesium, calcium, omega-3s and vitamin D, consider taking supplements of these nutrients after consulting your physician.
- Sleeping well by listening to the body when it is tired and wants to rest.
- Managing stress through all the tools laid down in the different sections of this book. (Also check more options in Chapter 9 titled 'Self-Care'.)
- Avoiding environmental toxins (listed in the comprehensive list in the section 'Common Hormone Disruptors' below).
- Replacing plastic and inferior metal containers with steel, glass containers or ceramic containers for cooking and eating.
- Empower yourself with positive self-talk. This is an amazing way of easing menopause-related stress. Tell

yourself often that you're healthy, you can be healthier, and that there is nothing 'inherently' wrong with you. This will take a huge weight off your shoulders and allow your body to heal naturally.

Common Hormone Disruptors

By now we know that our sex hormones need to be synchronized so that we stay emotionally and physically healthy especially during stages such as PMS, reproduction and menopause. This is possible if we first understand who the culprits are that upset the apple cart of our hormones.

Hormonal 'troublemakers' could show up in the shape of some foods, environmental toxins, certain medications, drinking water, stress emanating from multiple areas of our lives, excessive usage of plastic products that release toxins, poor sleep and certain nutrient deficiencies, among other things. I have tried to categorize them in a manner that is easy for you to understand:

1. **Foods that topple hormonal balance**: We need to beware of certain foods that aren't in complete agreement with our hormones. When consumed during PMS and menopause, they can aggravate symptoms such as stress, anxiety, irritability, inflammation, water retention and insomnia. These foods include:
    - **Refined sugar and refined flour products**: Too much sugar and simple carbs in the diet can throw off oestrogen balance in a woman's body.
    - **Caffeine**: Too much caffeine can irritate and aggravate hormones. Caffeine stimulates the adrenal glands to secrete cortisol—the stress hormone. And stress is not good for hormonal health. Too much stress along

with caffeine can cause inflammation and glucose intolerance.
- **Alcohol**: Frequent consumption of alcohol is associated with blood sugar deregulation.
- **Other foods**: Foods like white salt, fried foods, too many saturated fats, and hot and spicy foods.

2. **Non-organic produce**: These include foods with synthetic hormones, pesticides, hormones, herbicides, phytoestrogens, DDT (dichloro-diphenyl-trichloroethane), dioxins, etc. These toxins can be found in foods like meat, fish, dairy, eggs, soy, fruits and vegetables. They are all endocrine hormone disruptors.
3. **Plastics**: All plastic especially food storage containers, packaging material and toys, can be toxic due to their bisphenol A (BPA), brominated flame retardants (BFR), oxybenzone and phthalates content.
4. **Processed and packaged foods**: Refer to the section in Chapter 9 titled 'Self-Care' for the complete list.
5. **Mineral and vitamin deficiencies**: Certain micronutrient deficiencies like those of vitamin D, omega-3s, calcium and magnesium can disrupt hormonal balance.
6. **Non-organic personal care products**: Certain brands of soaps, toothpaste, face wash, sunscreens, hand wash, etc., contain contaminants like phthalates and triclosan.
7. **Non-organic cosmetics**: Certain brands of cosmetics like mascara, eye pencil, hair dye, lipstick, deodorant, etc. contain contaminants like phthalates and triclosan that are detrimental to hormonal health.
8. **Non-organic baby care products**: Certain brands of baby care products contain contaminants like phthalates and triclosan.
9. **Non-organic household cleaning products**: The presence

of industrial chemicals like per- and polyfluoroalkyl substances (PFASs) and phthalates makes them harmful for our hormonal health.

10. **Non-stick and metal coating**: Coating of cookware, and inner metal coating of food cans containing polytetrafluoroethylene or Teflon are harmful for our hormonal health when they break down on being heated.
11. **Pharmaceutical compounds**: Some of the medicines contain compounds like atenolol, diazepam and meprobamate that are harmful for hormonal, renal and heart health.
12. **Drinking water**: Drinking water that has been 'purified' with disinfection by-products like disinfection by-products (DBPs) is harmful for hormonal health.
13. **Household goods**: Many household goods like furniture, textiles and carpets have fire retardants, phthalates, polybrominated diphenyl ethers (PBDEs) and BFRs in them that can disrupt hormonal health.
14. **Firecrackers**: These have industrial chemicals like perchlorate that are harmful for the thyroid hormone.
15. **Electronics**: Electronics generally contain flame retardants, PCBs and BFRs that can cause imbalance in the hormones.
16. **Microwave and air fryers**: These are not hormone friendly. They can cause toxins to be released from plastics and metals. When plastic is exposed to heat, it can potentially cause 52 types of cancers. Radio waves from microwave ovens cause a lot of harm. It has unhealthy vibrations and radiation.
17. **Stress**: We spend a lot of time in our 'fight or flight mode' where the body gets the signal that we are in a perpetual danger zone like we're being chased by a bear. These

glands respond by pumping the hormone epinephrine (also known as adrenaline) into the bloodstream. Too much epinephrine affects physiological health.
18. **Overtraining**: Surprisingly, overtraining can bring a lot of stress to the body. Some people thrive by training hard, while for others, their bodies may respond to gentle exercise like yoga. A by-product of overtraining is the overproduction of adrenaline which suppresses the production of hormones and chemicals such as serotonin and dopamine.

While it is impossible to purge ourselves of all hormone disruptors in our homes as well as the environment, being aware of their presence in our lives is the first step in the direction of eliminating them. Thereafter, we can start by removing the ones we have more control over, such as the contaminated food sources. We can also take small steps towards cleaning up our homes of environmental toxins by keeping indoor air-purifying plants that remove toxins from the air we breathe.

Our hormones control many critical bodily processes and are pivotal for our mental and emotional well-being. If we don't make an effort to keep them in balance, they can become a trigger for many health issues, such as chronic stress, anxiety, depression, irritability, weight gain, insomnia and sluggish metabolic rate.

Suzanne Somers, an American actress and author, says, 'Our bodies are finely tuned machines, and if our hormone mixtures aren't "just right", everything goes into disrepair.'

So, take care of your hormones and help them dance synchronically together again!

'Are You Up for a Challenge?

Go through the list of various hormone disruptors in the 'Common Hormone Disruptors' section (p. 238) in the chapter. Try to clear your house of as many of them as you can to make your hormones happy for ever after!

INSPIRATIONAL STORIES OF REAL WOMEN

Nandita Chakraborty

It was 1996 and I was a regular college student doing my junior residency after completing my MBBS (Bachelor of Medicine, Bachelor of Surgery) degree.

Life as a junior resident involves long hours of work, and is busy and tough. Therefore, a minor symptom like cough didn't bother me much, even though it refused to respond to any medication. However, when it started interfering with my breathing, I could feel that something was wrong. Regular tests were done, and it was diagnosed as tuberculosis.

Treatment started, but my condition kept getting worse. Within five-six weeks, I became too weak to walk and eat, while my cough continued to get worse. I instinctively knew something was out of place.

The next few weeks entailed more and more tests as the diagnosis wasn't clear. Bronchoscopy and multiple biopsies later, the doctors reached a diagnosis. I was suffering from an autoimmune condition called Sarcoidosis (Besnier-Boeck-Schaumann disease). Back then, most doctors hadn't witnessed cases of Sarcoidosis. In fact, we had just read about it as a short passage in our medicine textbooks. Sarcoidosis leads to the growth of granulomas (inflammatory non-cancerous benign growth) in different parts of the body. I had this growth in my joints, and one was pressing against my windpipe. My treatment for tuberculosis was stopped and I was put on high doses of steroids. My cough reduced, and other debilitating symptoms also showed improvement. I started feeling better.

After a year of this treatment, although my autoimmune

condition got better, I started struggling with the massive side effects of the treatment itself. My hair greyed quickly, and my bones creaked (due to steroid-induced osteoporosis). My mouth and gut were lined with ulcers, and my blood pressure and blood sugar levels shot up. I couldn't bear the sunlight (due to photosensitivity). I developed severe depression (steroid-induced again), and although my physical symptoms were getting better, I wasn't feeling good mentally and emotionally.

In about 18 months, my treatment was gradually stopped because my autoimmune disease symptoms had improved. But all the past years of medical interventions left me with a weak musculoskeletal system, severe digestive tract issues, and obesity.

Soon, I got married to my childhood sweetheart and a few months later, I found out that I was pregnant. My pregnancy was closely monitored and by God's grace, all went well, and I was blessed with a healthy baby girl.

After about seven years, the granulomas returned with a vengeance. This time, I developed this growth on my neck. It grew to a size where it kept pressing on my recurrent laryngeal nerve, which eventually paralysed my right vocal cord.

I was just 38 then, and my world became silent inside me. I was very passionate about singing. Owing to my latest condition, I couldn't even speak audibly, let alone sing (which was a big blow to me). It required a humongous effort to speak, and my voice was very hoarse. The irony of this situation was that if I couldn't speak, people around me would also not speak to me. This can cause immense loneliness. I had to keep reminding people around me that I had lost my voice but not my ability to hear.

The steroidal treatment started once again. This time, the

side effects were far worse than before. Due to excessive use of steroids, I suffered from Addison's disease, more commonly known as adrenal insufficiency. It was tough to continue my medical practice as even my day-to-day chores became a challenge to accomplish at this point.

By the time I turned 40, in 2010, I felt dejected and hopeless about my life. It all seemed harsh and very unfair.

One fine day, I went to the nearby park and sat there for a very long time. I began ruminating about life, and the path that lay ahead of me. Somehow, it dawned upon me that I was unnecessarily worried about the future, whereas all we have is 'this moment'. I wondered why I was losing my peace in the 'now' by worrying about my future, which was unknown. This shift in my thought process opened doors of joy and happiness into my life.

As I reflected on my situation, I could see that there were five significant ways in which the universe helped me.

First and foremost, books walked into my life as my guru. To this day, whenever I am ready to learn a new lesson about life, an appropriate book appears in my life, as if by serendipity. I had once read a line and loved it: 'Pain is inevitable, suffering is optional'. It was by Haruki Murakami in his book *What I Talk about When I Talk about Running* (Vintage, 2009). These lines stayed with me. The words haunted me day and night. I truly understood that whatever was happening to my body was inevitable, but what story I made of it, and told myself and everyone else in my world, is optional. So, I had a choice to change my story.

Second, I met my yoga teacher, Dia Pinto. She explained to me the healing power of breathing. I joined her classes and that was truly a life-changing experience for me. My perspective towards many things in life changed for the better.

I even learnt voice modulation and started to speak without too much effort.

Third and very important was running. Once yoga became an intrinsic part of my routine, I was ready for the next jump. I wanted to explore running as a fitness activity. And as luck would have it, I chanced upon an article written by Rahul Verghese in *Sunday Brunch* titled 'Anybody Can Run'. Around the same time, I discovered a small group of runners in my neighbourhood, and started running with them. Running helped me immensely to calm my mind and develop a positive outlook towards life.

I ran my first 21-kilometre race at Airtel Delhi Half Marathon in 2011. I ran my next one at Standard Chartered Mumbai Marathon, December 2012. Soon, I ran my first full marathon (42 kilometres) in Gurgaon. I was truly happy. For the first time after a long while, I felt that my physical illness was just a small part of me, that I was much more than my illness. I was not only my body, but also my breath, thoughts and feelings. I felt as if I had acquired extraordinary courage to attempt anything I fancied. What was most significant was that I wasn't feeling like a victim anymore. I felt like a warrior. I knew I have my limitations, but they couldn't make me sad or unhappy anymore. Yoga and running nullified all negativity.

Fourth, I made vast lifestyle changes that were conducive to my physical and mental health. I changed the way I ate based on my own research on diet, slept before 10 p.m. and woke up at 4:15 a.m. six days a week. I incorporated strength training and CrossFit to my weekly-fitness routine. People in my life changed, and I started attracting people who were more aligned with my present ideology and lifestyle. My body changed and so did my thought process and words.

The fifth and the most gratifying chapter of my life opened up with charity and fundraising. Kushal Raj Chakravorty founded the Lotus Petal Foundation (LPF) in 2011. He rented a small place in a shopping arcade and started giving free education to six underprivileged children from the neighbourhood urban slums of Gurgaon. In 2013, I became a volunteer at LPF. Gradually, as the organization grew, I became more involved and started to take care of their Arogya programme, where I conducted weekly outpatient department (OPD) in school and took care of the health and nutrition of the students.

Today, LPF provides quality education, food and healthcare to more than 500 students, free of cost.

I became a fundraiser for LPF in 2014, and since then, I've been raising funds at the Airtel Delhi Half Marathon every year. The whole process of raising funds changes you as a person, and I have experienced it first-hand.

Meghana

I can never forget the summer of 2015, a period that changed my whole perspective towards life! I was 13 years old then and had been suffering from what seemed to be an ordinary viral fever. The first round of medical tests came out clean. The fever didn't subside even after 10 days. Besides, I started feeling a growing stiffness in my neck, followed by general confusion. Additional tests were done, and this time, I was diagnosed with meningitis—an infection of the covering membranes that surround the brain.

Being medical professionals themselves, my parents were aware that if they did not act quickly, they could end up fighting a losing war with a disease that could spell death to their daughter within no time. They did everything known within the medical fraternity to contain the disease and prevent it from accelerating.

With the help of innumerable health professionals and by the grace of the Almighty, I did survive. However, shortly after, I suffered a stroke and near quadriplegia, a condition that leads to the loss of movements and sensation of both upper and lower limbs. I couldn't move my body as I was paralysed, I couldn't open my eyes, I couldn't speak and couldn't eat normally. I was in a state of coma. In short, my world became completely dark and silent!

My parents consulted countless neurologists and neurosurgeons throughout the country and abroad to understand the extent of the damage and my chances of recovery. In fact, my mom tried everything under the sun to stimulate my brain through each of the five primary senses. While medical interventions were going on, she even explored alternative therapies and spiritual tools—whatever could give a ray of hope related to my progress.

To stimulate my brain through my sense of smell, she started giving me massages with aromatic oils with strong smells and strong fragrances. She started playing audios of Sanskrit mantras, binaural beats (illusions created by our brain when we listen to two different tones at different frequencies) and tanpura close to my ears. In her desperation to revive me, she started singing my favourite bedtime songs; within an hour of singing, she saw me breathing heavily, and there was an intense contortion in my face. My mother became ecstatic and hopeful of my chances at recovery, as she knew that having an emotional connection is probably one of the highest and most primitive orders of survival among living beings.

Then, she asked my brother and cousins to speak to me, even if I did not respond. Hearing the familiar voices of people I had grown up with, I finally started responding by wiggling my body. The emotional stimulation had started working, and I slowly started 'waking up' to these stimuli.

In an attempt to make me speak, my mother would make exaggerated phonetic sounds. I started responding by staring at her, and after a week of hearing it every day, I started making small sounds like 'mmm ma ma ma.'

She even experimented with Tibetan bowl-and-bell therapy because she had heard of its healing effects through the vibrations it created. It helped me improve my attention span a little, as I was able to open my eyes and stare at her for a while without blinking. Slowly, I learnt to talk again.

I soon started intense conventional physiotherapy, occupational therapy and robotic physiotherapy. I was now undergoing six physiotherapy sessions (two physiotherapies, two occupational therapies and two robotic therapies) each day. With the help of robotics, I started standing and then walking on a treadmill.

There's no denying that the sessions were excruciating. I had no balance, my back was too weak to hold me upright and I could hardly move my limbs because of severely impaired fine motor skills. The utter fear of falling while attempting to walk without having balancing skills yet, used to make me scream.

After almost a year, I could walk with the support of a walker and later with an orthosis. At one point, when I got tired and bored of physiotherapy, my mother decided to put me completely on holistic healing interventions. I soon learnt that recovery could even occur beyond the confines of a room.

I started attending Iyengar Yoga sessions to enhance my flexibility; easy horse riding to strengthen my back and improve my posture; kick-boxing sessions to strengthen my muscles and increase stability; drumming to enhance my hand–leg coordination; and craft classes to improve my fine motor skills.

While my physical pain was receding, my emotional state was anything but fine. I had lost an entire academic year due to my illness. Because of the stroke, my mental age decreased, and I lost friends. It is because I couldn't understand the social context of the language and mannerisms of my teenage classmates. I was more comfortable with children two years younger than me. It didn't make life any easier for me to walk around with orthotic shoes and a walker as a teenager. Owing to my inability to process the emotional upheaval my mind was going through, I suffered from anxiety, mood swings and crying spells.

At school, I had problems following the pace of instructions, as my retention ability was poor. There were other issues too—like not having fine motor skills for writing, as my right hand was more affected than the left.

What helped me get over my anxiety and fears was Vipassana. I was introduced to a teacher who had been practising Vipassana for more than a decade. It was unbelievable how that transformed me. It started to calm me down, my concentration in studies improved and I started feeling much better. I started eating healthy and avoiding junk food. It's truly amazing how beautifully I kept healing in mind and body with the help of holistic tools such as yoga, meditation and Ayurveda.

It has been five years ever since, and I no longer consider my illness as a dark phase in my life. Yes, it was tough while it lasted, but now it has become a milestone in my life. I've become more compassionate. I still remember all the elderly stroke patients at the hospital who would smile when I would give them a high-five with my more functional hand.

I look forward to going to school now, have made a wonderful bunch of friends, I go to the gym regularly and I've even completed a 10 kilometre walkathon recently.

All the above interventions—medical, holistic and spiritual, the emotional support of my family and our well-wishers, along with my 'never-say-die' attitude, showed me that there's light at the end of the tunnel. And today, that light shines ever brighter in my life!

Roshni Sharma

My story isn't about a larger-than-life transformation but about very 'everyday', 'low-key' issues that rarely ever raise an alarm. Nonetheless, they're as potent as a slow killing poison. They cripple your wings, destroy your ambitions and reduce your outlook towards life to an insignificant 'nothing'.

I have always been a homemaker in a typical Haryanvi family in Delhi, dedicated to housework and obsessed with cleaning, keeping busy from dawn to late night. Even if by some miracle, I ever got some free time, I would 'find' work for myself—washing, cleaning or cooking something 'extra'. I would sleep late, very exhausted from work, and rise very early with the stress of the new day's work. I hardly got any sleep and any peace of mind—this was my humdrum life—day in, day out.

I was perpetually on medication as I would fall sick at the drop of a hat. Over the years, I also piled up weight with this routine, but I was always casual about it. My attempts to lose weight were always half-hearted and erratic. I would try eating less for a few days but then give in to temptations again. I would try again some days later and then fail again. Whenever I felt frustrated, bored, overwhelmed or hopeless, I would try to overcome this emotional stress by turning to food. Although it was comforting, it added to the agony and guilt later. I felt I was falling deeper and deeper into this negative spiral, as I had no willpower and no self-worth to stop myself.

This cycle of erratic eating with attempts to eat less and then fail again went on for a few years. Whenever I failed, my self-worth went down a few notches. It gave rise to self-contempt, and I came down very hard on myself. There was a gnawing feeling at the back of my mind that 'I do not deserve a 'healthy life'. Over time, it turned into 'I don't deserve a good life', as my dissatisfaction with myself rubbed off on every sphere of my life.

Then came 2017— the worst period of my life. Even though everything around me seemed just fine—I had a loving family, we had a roof over our head and food on our table—I was breaking down from inside. As if that wasn't enough, I was now diagnosed with hyperthyroidism, high blood pressure, borderline diabetes, osteoarthritis and had a slipped disc.

My already unhealthy and unhappy life was now burdened with chronic conditions threatening my day-to-day mobility. As if that wasn't enough, I was also going through menopause which added a whole new dimension of physical and emotional trauma, with anxiety and mood swings added in good measure. Besides, I wasn't even motivated to exercise, as in my mind, I just felt that exercise was painful and not worth attempting in my present state of health.

It wasn't until the day when my son noticed the 86 kilograms of weight I had piled on that he felt something needed to be done soon about it. He was convinced that I needed to see a nutrition coach who could help me lose weight and improve things a wee bit. He introduced me to Tanuja Sodhi, a health coach, and that proved to be a turning point of sorts in my life.

Her approach wasn't of a doctor trying to diagnose but of a friend trying to understand. She asked me questions about my daily routine, my relationship with people around me, my relationship with food, my regular thought process and about my self-talk—aspects I had never given a thought to. For the very first time, I found myself articulating how I felt. It felt cathartic being heard.

She started by helping me realize the importance and value of holistic wellness. She emphasized that while eating healthy is the key to a healthy life, a healthy change doesn't come about until the negative mindset is turned around. She advised me to slow down, notice things, understand why I feel the way I do and practise mindfulness in everything. She advised me to begin the day with gratitude and positive affirmations—which in the beginning felt fake and pointless, but through constant interaction, she made me believe in it, and I persisted.

Soon enough, the affirmations began to become my reality. I felt a greater sense of self-worth, and I started looking forward to things. She urged me to go for walks, spend time amidst nature and spend positive, quality time with myself. As inconsequential as it may sound, it has had a significant impact on my life.

Today, I'm about 7 kilograms lighter, and I'm a regular morning walker. My cardiovascular health is way better. I'm able to walk much longer distances without running out of breath. I have participated in many running events including 5 kilometre and 10 kilometre distances. Biggest of all, I could gather the courage to sign up for a mighty challenge of running or walking 2 kilometres *every day* for 100 days, without missing a single day. I not only finished this challenge but finished first in my age category in the Delhi-NCR region by walking 250 kilometres in 100 days!

During this 100-day challenge, on one of the days, I had severe pain in my left knee, and walking even a single step was painful. The pain instigated me to play a little smart. I gave my phone to my husband and asked him to finish the walk for me, which he did. My 2 kilometres for the day was recorded. I had gotten away clean, and no one would have come to know. At least that was my assumption. However, something inside me just didn't feel right. The very same day, we were at a family function and I was a little lost because I felt guilty for having cheated. We returned home around 11.30 p.m., and as soon as I entered home, I asked my son and daughter-in-law to accompany me for a 2 kilometre walk. I started at 11.35 p.m. in the pitch dark, wearing a saree. But I finished my quota for the day. This incident has instilled so much confidence in me that I now walk around tall.

Completing this challenge has given me immense confidence. However, what got me through it, I believe, was the work done before the challenge. From total negativity and helplessness to supreme positivity and self-confidence, I feel like it's a new life for me. Of course, it isn't perfect, and more needs to be done, but this life has so much more 'life' in it—all achieved by altering thinking patterns ever so slightly, through small changes every day.

Small and consistent is sustainable and powerful!

Conclusion

Step out of the history that is holding you back.
Step into the new story you are willing to create.

—Oprah Winfrey, American talk-show host

The all-pervasive theme of this book is to create a balance in all the primary areas of our life, such as health, connection, social life, food, movement, spirituality, sleep, primary work, need for creativity, home environment, learning and personal growth, with the help of the tools laid out meticulously all through the book.

These interventions cover the whole spectrum—from being mindful, eating a clean and nutritious diet, putting in more movement each day, sleeping enough and restfully, nurturing close relationships, discovering our purpose of life, forming keystone habits and indulging in regular self-care, to looking after our hormonal health.

By now, we've also figured out that each one of us deserves a life of flourishing and happiness, and that this state of being is waiting to be embraced right outside our comfort zones. All we need to do now is to match our needs and inadequacies with the right tools and then consciously make a plan to incorporate these foundational tools into our daily lives.

I would also urge you to go inward and communicate with your soul to know what it yearns for. It will breathe purpose and direction into your life. Pursuing your life's dream will energize your actions and give meaning to your existence.

Giving ourselves something to strive for moves us from the passenger seat and puts us behind the wheel. It is so much more rewarding to be creatively engaged with the process of life instead of passively allowing our immediate external influences to dictate our place in the world. Having clear goals can also give us the much-needed clarity on what we should be doing earnestly and what we should be giving up as it no longer serves us.

Working towards dreams brings us face to face with challenges, and the process of overcoming these challenges compels us to unearth our inner strength and put it to use. Repeating this process over and over again builds self-esteem, and gives greater confidence to vanquish roadblocks that we will inevitably face along our journey. Life, from my perspective, is suboptimal if it is bereft of dreams and goals. They are drivers of my personal growth and pursuing them makes my soul dance with joy.

Equipped with so much information and myriad tools in your toolkit, you must wonder where to begin? I would recommend picking a couple of tools from each of the categories like mindfulness, nutrition and physical activity as a good place to start.

Mindfulness is a cornerstone habit that brings about a positive shift in our psyche, which in turn, preps us up for the forthcoming change. Tools such as meditation and journaling also bestow us with the inner strength to establish equilibrium in all the vital areas of our lives, setting in motion our metamorphosis into a healthier and happier being.

Take small yet consistent steps to form cornerstone habits that will make your transformation much smoother. Plan your day in advance to remove the guesswork. Schedule all that you have set out to do, and take daily actions towards your goals resolutely. Don't forget to review your progress regularly. And did I forget to remind you that digital detox is a great way to annihilate procrastination and deeply focus on what is important for you?

Above all, enjoy the journey of your transformation without stressing over the outcome of this journey. As Nelson Mandela, the South African anti-apartheid revolutionary, political leader and philanthropist, once said, 'I never lose. I either win or learn.'

Every day is yet another chance for us to readjust the sails of the journey called life. Therefore, I implore you to hold the reins of your life firmly in your hands, believe in yourself and the powers above, unfetter your spirit, spread your wings, take a leap of faith and soar high, to the life of your dreams!

You can!

Acknowledgements

First and foremost, thank you dear God. This book wouldn't have been possible without your constant divine guidance. You fueled my confidence every moment through my faith in you. You literally created this book through me. I owe you everything, and my heart throbs with love for you.

To my husband, Charanjit: I can't thank you enough for being there wholeheartedly for me throughout the process. The fact that I could finish this book within a tight deadline is a testimony of your incessant support. From reading all my drafts, to offering constructive suggestions, to making sure I ate and hydrated well, to never saying no to any of my unreasonable demands, you were right there for me. Love you, my sunshine!

To my son, Angad: my heart aches with love and gratitude for you. For the constant pep-talks to keep my confidence soaring, for the esoteric, other-worldly conversations that always leave me refreshed, for the incredible shoulder massages to melt away stress, for everything... literally! You're the best thing that ever happened to me. Thank you for choosing me as your mother.

To Joshua Rosenthal: my deepest gratitude to you and the Institute for Integrative Nutrition for the profound insights I gained through your course. I can't even begin to talk about the inner growth I've experienced. You're a part of the wonderful *synchronicities in my life.*

To Brian Johnson: I'm immensely grateful to you and Optimize for aligning me with my higher self and helping me to start living my life more authentically. Whenever I reminisce about the transformation I've experienced, I feel overwhelmed with *tears in my eyes*.

To Rupa Publications: thank you for believing in me yet again and offering me this fabulous chance to share my insights with the world.

Endnotes

1. Michael Camilleri, 'Serotonin in the Gastrointestinal Tract', *Current Opinion in Endocrinology, Diabetes and Obesity*, Vol. 16, No. 1 (February 2009): 53–59, https://bit.ly/3JC3kMV, accessed on 4 January 2022.
2. Tal Ben-Shahar, *Happier: Learn the Secrets to Daily Joy and Lasting Fulfillment*, McGraw-Hill Education; 1st edition (2007).
3. Cited in Savita Malhotra and Ruchita Shah, 'Women and Mental Health in India: An Overview', *Indian Journal of Psychiatry*, 2015, 57 (Suppl 2): S205–S211.
4. Herbert Benson, *The Relaxation Response*, Avon; Reissue edition (1976).
5. Sue McGreevey, 'Eight weeks to a better brain', *The Harvard Gazette*, 21 January 2011, https://bit.ly/3rY3Uxs, accessed on 18 February 2022.
6. Michael Speca et al., 'A Randomized, Wait-List Controlled Clinical Trial: The Effect of a Mindfulness Meditation-Based Stress Reduction Program on Mood and Symptoms of Stress in Cancer Outpatients', *Psychosomatic Medicine*, Vol. 62, No. 5 (September 2000): 613–22, https://bit.ly/3eL9hsy, accessed on 4 January 2022; Melissa A. Rosenkraz et al., 'A Comparison of Mindfulness-Based Stress Reduction and an Active Control in Modulation of Neurogenic Inflammation', *Brain, Behaviour and Immunity*, Vol. 27 (January 2013): 174–84, https://bit.ly/3FUNHh4, accessed on 4 January 2022.
7. Amishi P. Jha, Jason Krompinger and Michael J. Baime, 'Mindfulness Training Modifies Subsystems of Attention', *Cognitive, Affective, & Behavioral Neuroscience*, Vol. 7 (June 2007): 109–19, https://bit.ly/3FSDKkx, accessed on 4 January 2022.
8. Stefan G. Hofmann, Paul Grossman and Devon E. Hinton, 'Loving-Kindness and Compassion Meditation: Potential for Psychological Interventions', *Clinical Psychology Review*, Vol. 31, No. 7 (November 2011): 1126–36, https://bit.ly/3FVUp6w, accessed on 4 January 2022.

9. Fabrice B.R. Parmentier, 'Mindfulness and Symptoms of Depression and Anxiety in the General Population: The Mediating Roles of Worry, Rumination, Reappraisal and Suppression', *Frontier Psychology*, Vol. 10, No. 506 (8 March 2019), https://bit.ly/34og0a9, accessed on 4 January 2022.

10. Robert A. Emmons and Michael E. McCullough, 'Counting Blessings Versus Burdens: An Experimental Investigation of Gratitude and Subjective Well-Being in Daily Life', *Journal of Personality and Social Psychology*, Vol. 84, No. 2 (2003), https://bit.ly/3sWDhdk, accessed on 4 January 2022.

11. Lisa A. Williams and Monica Y. Bartlett, 'Warm thanks: Gratitude expression facilitates social affiliation in new relationships via perceived warmth', *Emotion*, Vol. 15, No. 1 (February 2015): 1–5, https://bit.ly/3JGBjne, accessed on 4 January 2022.

12. C. Nathan DeWall et al., 'A Grateful Heart Is a Nonviolent Heart: Cross-Sectional, Experience Sampling, Longitudinal, and Experimental Evidence', *Social Psychological and Personality Science*, Vol. 3, No. 2 (6 September 2011), https://bit.ly/3qOQF0k, accessed on 4 January 2022.

13. Patrick L. Hill, Mathias Alleman and Brent W. Roberts, 'Examining the Pathways between Gratitude and Self-Rated Physical Health across Adulthood', *Personality and Individual Differences*, Vol. 54, No. 1 (January 2013): 92–96, https://bit.ly/32PAyHT, accessed on 4 January 2022.

14. C. Nathan DeWall et al., 'A Grateful Heart is a Nonviolent Heart: Cross-Sectional, Experience Sampling, Longitudinal, and Experimental Evidence', *Social Psychological and Personality Science*, Vol. 3, No. 2 (6 September 2011), https://bit.ly/3qOQF0k, accessed on 4 January 2022.

15. Alex M. Wood et al., 'Gratitude influences sleep through the mechanism of pre-sleep cognitions', *Journal of Psychosomatic Research*, Vol. 66, No. 1 (January 2009): 43–48, https://bit.ly/3ET2hof, accessed on 4 January 2022.

16. Lung Hung Chen and Chia-Huei Wu, 'Gratitude Enhances Change in Athletes' Self-Esteem: The Moderating Role of Trust in Coach', *Journal of Applied Sport Psychology*, Vol. 26, No. 3 (2014): 349–62, https://bit.ly/3JBY0sJ, accessed on 4 January 2022.

17. David S. Black and George M. Slavich, 'Mindfulness meditation and the immune system: a systematic review of randomized controlled trials', *Annals of the New York Academy of Sciences,* Vol. 1373, No. 1 (June 2016): 13-24, https://bit.ly/3JEjyFf, accessed on 4 January 2022.
18. Trinity College Dublin, 'The Yogi masters were right: meditation and breathing exercises can sharpen your mind', *Science Daily,* 10 May 2018, https://bit.ly/3sVmO9p, accessed on 4 January 2022.
19. Valentina Perciavalle et al., 'The role of deep breathing on stress', *Neurological Sciences,* Vol. 38, No. 3 (March 2017): 451-58, https://bit.ly/3FXQuWX, accessed on 4 January 2022.
20. Southern Methodist University, 'New breathing therapy reduces panic and anxiety by reversing hyperventilation', *Science Daily,* 22 December 2010, https://bit.ly/3oZEjCB, accessed on 4 January 2022.
21. Hui-Ching Chien et al., 'Breathing exercise combined with cognitive behavioural intervention improves sleep quality and heart rate variability in major depression', *Journal of Clinical Nursing,* Vol. 24, No. 21-22 (November 2015): 3206-14, https://bit.ly/3FSvi4x, accessed on 4 January 2022.
22. Ibid.
23. Sang Hwan Kim et al., 'Mind-Body Practices for Posttraumatic Stress Disorder', *Journal of Investigative Medicine,* Vol. 61, No. 5 (28 February 2013), https://bit.ly/3FUMPZU, accessed on 4 January 2022.
24. Volker Busch et al., 'The effect of deep and slow breathing on pain perception, autonomic activity, and mood processing—an experimental study', *Pain Medicine,* Vol. 13, No. 2 (February 2012): 215-28, https://bit.ly/3zoTdGp, accessed on 4 January 2022.
25. Ibid.
26. Christophe André, 'Stress reduction, insomnia prevention, emotion control, improved attention—certain breathing techniques can make life better. But where do you start?' *Scientific American,* 15 January 2019, https://bit.ly/3FOnoJw, accessed on 4 January 2022.
27. Joshua M. Smith et al., 'Online Positive Affect Journaling in the Improvement of Mental Distress and Well-Being in General Medical Patients with Elevated Anxiety Symptoms: A Preliminary Randomized Controlled Trial', *JMIR Mental Health,* Vol. 5, No. 4

(October–December 2018), https://bit.ly/3zuG0fh, accessed on 4 January 2022.

28. Joshua M. Smith et al., 'Effects of Writing about Stressful Experiences on Symptom Reduction in Patients with Asthma or Rheumatoid Arthritis', *JAMA*, Vol. 281, No. 14 (April 1999): 1304–09, https://bit.ly/3eN0iqL, accessed on 4 January 2022.

29. Courtney E. Ackerman, '83 Benefits of Journaling for Depression, Anxiety, and Stress', *Positive Psychology*, 5 May 2022, https://bit.ly/3qKVQi3, accessed on 4 January 2022.

30. A.J. Adams, 'Seeing Is Believing: The Power of Visualization', *Psychology Today*, 3 December 2009, https://bit.ly/3eNPb0R, accessed on 4 January 2022.

31. Christopher N. Cascio et al., 'Self-Affirmation Activates Brain Systems Associated with Self-Related processing and Reward and Is Reinforced by Future Orientation', *Scholarly Commons*, Vol. 11, No. 4 (April 2016): 621–29, https://bit.ly/3zprA07, accessed on 4 January 2022.

32. Ibid; David K. Sherman and Geoffrey L. Cohen, 'The Psychology of Self-Defense: Self-Affirmation Theory', *Advances in Experimental Social Psychology*, Vol. 38, https://stanford.io/3zzMbPm, accessed on 4 January 2022.

33. Richard Cooke et al., 'Self-Affirmation Promotes Physical Activity', *Journal of Sport and Exercise Psychology*, Vol. 36, No. 2 (September 2013): 217–23, https://bit.ly/3sSYgOf, accessed on 4 January 2022.

34. Jennifer M. Taber et al., 'Optimism and Spontaneous Self-affirmation Are Associated with Lower Likelihood of Cognitive Impairment and Greater Positive Affect among Cancer Survivors', *Annals of Behavioral Medicine*, Vol. 50, No. 2 (April 2016): 198–209, https://bit.ly/3EQpUOg, accessed on 4 January 2022.

35. Belinda Wilson, 'Bio-individuality: The new and simpler health philosophy', *news.com.au*, 26 September 2014, https://bit.ly/3eK7Bzv, accessed on 3 January 2022; 'The Secret to IIN's Health Coach Program Is Now Scientifically Proven', Institute for Integrative Nutrition (IIN), 4 March 2021, https://bit.ly/3mPKnN1, accessed on 3 January 2022.

36. Marnie Soman Schwartz, 'Why Treating Yourself Is the #1 Secret to a Healthy Diet', *Shape*, 24 June 2016, https://bit.ly/3zhI2PX, accessed on 3 January 2022.

37. Jorge Alejandro Alegría-Torres et al., 'Epigenetics and Lifestyle', *Future Medicine*, 30 June 2011, https://bit.ly/3HlPTPc, accessed on 3 January 2022.
38. 'Genetics loads the gun, lifestyle pulls the trigger', *MedCrave*, 19 December 2015, https://bit.ly/3IageRb, accessed on 22 February 2022.
39. Mark Hyman, 'Why Calories Don't Matter', *Dr. Hyman*, https://bit.ly/3EP25WM, accessed on 3 January 2022.
40. Mark Hyman, 'The Most Damaging Food Lie We Have Ever Been Told', *Dr. Hyman*, https://bit.ly/3Hwls8S, accessed on 3 January 2022.
41. Dr Mark Hyman, '5 Clues You Are Addicted to Sugar', *Dr. Hyman*, https://bit.ly/3mSmQej, accessed on 3 January 2022.
42. Vasanti Malik et al., 'Long-Term Consumption of Sugar-Sweetened and Artificially Sweetened Beverages and Risk of Mortality in US Adults', AHA Journals, 18 March 2019, https://bit.ly/36oqBml, accessed on 3 January 2022.
43. Allison Aubrey, 'Reality Check: To Burn off a Soda, You'll Have to Run 50 Minutes', *The Salt*, 16 October 2014, https://n.pr/3ncjyTt, accessed on 3 January 2022.
44. Artemis P. Simopoulos, 'An Increase in the Omega-6/Omega-3 Fatty Acid Ratio Increases the Risk for Obesity', *MDPI*, 2 March 2016, https://bit.ly/3v6pbHn, accessed on 3 January 2022.
45. Vandana Dhaka et al., 'Trans fats—sources, health risks and alternative approach—A review', *Journal of Food and Science Technology*, 28 January 2011, https://bit.ly/3oUUe5e, accessed on 3 January 2022.
46. Megha Rajeev, 'The Best Kept Secrets in Marketing: Retail', *The Push Crew Journal*, 24 February 2017, https://bit.ly/3zk4GXQ, accessed on 3 January 2022.
47. 'Time to try intermittent fasting?' *Harvard Health Publishing*, Harvard Medical School, 1 July 2020, https://bit.ly/3JEzOpB, accessed on 3 January 2022.
48. 'The gut–brain connection', *Harvard Health Publishing*, Harvard Medical School, 19 April 2021, https://bit.ly/3HrWkQM, accessed on 3 January 2022.
49. S. Salminen et al., 'Influence of mode of delivery on gut microbiota composition in seven-year-old children', *BMJ Journals*, https://bit.

ly/3BDAzMe, accessed on 3 January 2022.
50. Kris Carr, 'How to Improve Your Gut Health', *Kris Carr*, https://bit.ly/3sXhC4V, accessed on 3 January 2022.
51. WHO, 'Physical inactivity a leading cause of disease and disability, warns WHO', World Health Organization, 4 April 2002, https://bit.ly/3sURJCt, accessed on 4 January 2022.
52. Long Zhai, Yi Zhang and Dongfeng Zhang, 'Sedentary behaviour and the risk of depression: a meta-analysis', *British Journal of Sports Medicine*, Vol. 49, No. 11 (15 May 2015): 701, https://bit.ly/3pNoz6p, accessed on 4 January 2022; 3.Lynette L. Craft et al., 'Intervention study of exercise for depressive symptoms in women', *Journal of Women's Health*, Vol. 16, No. 10 (7 December 2007), https://bit.ly/3ESW4bC, accessed on 4 January 2022.
53. Anne McTiernan et al., 'Recreational physical activity and the risk of breast cancer in postmenopausal women: the Women's Health Initiative Cohort Study', *JAMA*, Vol. 290, No. 10 (2003): 1331–36, https://bit.ly/3eQbHq2, accessed on 4 January 2022.
54. 'Exercise for Your Bone Health', National Institute of Health (NIH), https://bit.ly/3sUTbop, accessed on 4 January 2022.
55. Richard Weil, 'Senior Exercise: It's Never Too Late to Start Exercising', *MedicineNet*, 1 September 2020, https://bit.ly/3qI2Vji, accessed on 4 January 2022.
56. Sid Kirchheimer, 'It's Never Too Late to Start Exercise', *WebMD*, 13 May 2003, https://wb.md/3mWfxSW, accessed on 4 January 2022; 'It's never too late to start exercising', *Harvard Health Publishing*, Harvard Medical School, 1 June 2019, https://bit.ly/3sUUdAN, accessed on 4 January 2022.
57. Christian M. Werner et al., 'Differential effects of endurance, interval, and resistance training on telomerase activity and telomere length in a randomized, controlled study', *European Heart Journal*, Vol. 40, No. 1 (November 2018): 34–46, https://bit.ly/3zlOvcC, accessed on 4 January 2022.
58. Ambarish Pandey et al., 'Continuous Dose-Response Association between Sedentary Time and Risk for Cardiovascular Disease: A Meta-analysis', *JAMA Cardiology*, Vol. 1, No. 5 (August 2016), https://bit.ly/3sW7nOc, accessed on 4 January 2022.
59. James A. Levine, 'Non-exercise activity thermogenesis (NEAT)', *Best*

Practice & Research Clinical Endocrinology & Metabolism, Vol. 16, No. 4 (December 2002): 679–702, https://bit.ly/3F4TTSN, accessed on 4 January 2022.
60. Christian von Loeffelholz and Andreas Birkenfeld, 'The Role of Non-Exercise Activity Thermogenesis in Human Obesity', *Endotext*, 8 April 2018, https://bit.ly/3ET3Nq8, accessed on 4 January 2022.
61. 'The 4 most important types of exercise', *Harvard Health Publishing*, Harvard Medical School, 2 February 2022, https://bit.ly/32NNPkn, accessed on 4 January 2022.
62. Harsh Patel et al., 'Aerobic vs anaerobic exercise training effects on the cardiovascular system', *World Journal of Publishing*, Vol. 9, No. 2 (February 2017): 134–38, https://bit.ly/3sVAdxW, accessed on 4 January 2022.
63. James A. Blumenthal, Patrick J. Smith and Benson M. Hoffman, 'Is Exercise a Viable Treatment for Depression?' *Health and Fitness Journal*, Vol. 16, No. 4 (July/August 2012): 14–21, https://bit.ly/3zlaTmp, accessed on 4 January 2022.
64. Xuemei Sui et al., 'Longitudinal Patterns of Cardiorespiratory Fitness Predict the Development of Hypertension among Men and Women', *The American Journal of Medicine*, Vol.130, No. 4 (April 2017): 469–76, https://bit.ly/3mT2rFQ, accessed on 4 January 2022; Siobhan Gallanagh et al., 'Physical Activity in the Prevention and Treatment of Stroke', *International Scholarly Research Notices*, 2011, https://bit.ly/32Yjxey, accessed on 4 January 2022.
65. Ibid.; Xuemei Sui et al., 'Longitudinal Patterns of Cardiorespiratory Fitness Predict the Development of Hypertension Among Men and Women', *The American Journal of Medicine*, Vol.130, No. 4 (April 2017): 469–76, https://bit.ly/3mT2rFQ, accessed on 4 January 2022.
66. Sheri R. Colberg et al., 'Exercise and Type 2 Diabetes: The American College of Sports Medicine and the American Diabetes Association: joint position statement', *Diabetes Care*, Vol. 33, No. 12 (December 2010): e147–e167, https://bit.ly/334TZwo, accessed on 4 January 2022.
67. Deepak Chopra, 'Healing Emotional Pain with Yoga', 20 February 2014, *Chopra*, https://bit.ly/3mW9QEp, accessed on 4 January 2022.
68. Edward R. Laskowski, 'Answer to "How much should the average adult exercise every day?"' Mayo Clinic, 22 September 2021, https://mayocl.in/3uYDy0l, accessed on 4 January 2022.

69. Matthew Walker, *Why We Sleep: Unlocking the Power of Sleep and Dreams*, London: Simon & Schuster, 2017, p. 8.
70. 'Sleep Deprivation and Deficiency—Why Is Sleep Important?' National Institute of Health (NIH), https://bit.ly/3JHmmS7, accessed on 4 January 2022.
71. Shawn Stevenson, *Sleep Smarter: 21 Proven Tips to Sleep Your Way To a Better Body, Better Health and Bigger Success*, Model House Publishing, 2014.
72. Eric Suni and Abhinav Singh, 'How Much Sleep Do We Really Need?' *Sleep Foundation*, 10 March 2021, https://bit.ly/3LMC679, accessed on 4 January 2022.
73. Matthew Walker, *Why We Sleep: Unlocking the Power of Sleep and Dreams*, London: Simon & Schuster, 2017, p. 133.
74. Shahrad Taheri, 'Short sleep duration is associated with reduced leptin, elevated ghrelin, and increased body mass index', *PLOS Medicine,* Vol. 1, No. 3 (December 2004), https://bit.ly/3znSQfb, accessed on 4 January 2022; Rachel Leproult and Eve Van Cauter, 'Role of sleep and sleep loss in hormonal release and metabolism', *Pediatric Neuroendocrinology,* Vol. 17 (2010): 11-21, https://bit.ly/3Gc8CwB, accessed on 4 January 2022.
75. Harvard TH Chan, 'Sleep', https://bit.ly/3tihY4z, accessed on 28 February 2022.
76. Naima Covassin and Prachi Singh, 'Sleep Duration and Cardiovascular Disease Risk: Epidemiologic and Experimental Evidence', *Sleep Medicine Clinics,* Vol. 11, No. 1 (March 2016): 81-89, https://bit.ly/3mUdChG, accessed on 4 January 2022.
77. Daniel J. Gottlieb et al., 'Association of sleep time with diabetes mellitus and impaired glucose tolerance', *JAMA Internal Medicine*, Vol. 165, No. 8 (2005): 863-67, https://bit.ly/3eQOh3y, accessed on 4 January 2022.
78. Y. Harrison and J.A. Horne, 'One night of sleep loss impairs innovative thinking and flexible decision making', *Organizational Behavior and Human Decision Processes,* Vol. 78, No. 2 (May 1999): 128-45, https://bit.ly/32I6vlE, accessed on 4 January 2022.
79. Steven K. Howard, 'Sleep deprivation and physician performance: Why should I care?' 2005 April; 18(2): 108-12, https://bit.ly/3srkfLt, accessed on 28 February 2022.

80. A resource from the Division of Sleep Medicine, 'Sleep and Mood', Harvard Medical School, https://bit.ly/3qK0zQZ, accessed on 4 January 2022.
81. Nayyab Asif, Razia Iqbal and Chaudhry Fahad Nazir, 'Human immune system during sleep', *American Journal of Clinical and Experimental Immunology*, Vol. 6, No. 6 (December 2017): 92-96 https://bit.ly/3pSErVm, accessed on 4 January 2022; Eric Suni, 'How Sleep Affects Immunity', *Sleep Foundation*, 19 November 2020, https://bit.ly/3HPpDx1, accessed on 4 January 2022.
82. Tauseef Ali et al., 'Sleep, immunity and inflammation in gastrointestinal disorders', *World Journal of Gastroenterology*, Vol. 19, No. 48 (December 2013): 9231-39, https://bit.ly/3FXTcfa, accessed on 4 January 2022; Elsevier, 'Loss of Sleep, Even for a Single Night, Increases Inflammation in the Body', *Science Daily*, 4 September 2008, https://bit.ly/3mV5M7p, accessed on 4 January 2022.
83. Cheri D. Mah, 'The effects of sleep extension on the athletic performance of collegiate basketball players', *Sleep*, Vol. 34, No. 7 (July 2011): 943-50, https://bit.ly/3JFQTzp, accessed on 4 January 2022.
84. Hans P.A. Van Dongen and David F. Hinges, 'Investigating the interaction between the homeostatic and circadian processes of sleep-wake regulation for the prediction of waking neurobehavioural performance', *Journal of Sleep Research*, Vol. 12, No. 3 (September 2003): 181-87, https://bit.ly/3sXfNF6, accessed on 4 January 2022; Jonathan S. Emens et al., 'Phase Angle of Entrainment in Morning- and Evening-Types Under Naturalistic Conditions', *Chronobiology International*, Vol. 26, No. 3 (July 2009): 472-93, https://bit.ly/3HCUSv2, accessed on 4 January 2022.
85. Christopher Drake et al., 'Caffeine effects on sleep taken 0, 3, or 6 hours before going to bed', *Journal of Clinical Sleep Medicine*, Vol. 9, No. 11 (November 2013): 1195-200, https://bit.ly/3qQWZol, accessed on 4 January 2022.
86. Joshua J. Gooley et al., 'Exposure to Room Light before Bedtime Suppresses Melatonin Onset and Shortens Melatonin Duration in Humans', *The Journal of Clinical Endocrinology & Metabolism*, Vol. 96, No. 3 (March 2011): E463-E472, https://bit.ly/3sZHkWs, accessed on 4 January 2022.

87. F.G. Issa and C.E. Sullivan, 'Alcohol, snoring and sleep apnea', *Journal of Neurology, Neurosurgery and Psychiatry*, Vol. 45, No. 4 (April 1982): 353–59, https://bit.ly/3JIKIdW, accessed on 4 January 2022; R.G. Stevens et al., 'Alcohol consumption and urinary concentration of 6-sulfatoxymelatonin in healthy women', *Epidemiology*, Vol. 11, No. 6 (November 2000), https://bit.ly/3HALp7g, accessed on 4 January 2022.
88. 'Seasonal affective disorder (SAD)', *Mayo Clinic*, 14 December 2021, https://mayocl.in/3pON03s, accessed on 4 January 2022; Eric Suni, 'Light and Sleep', *Sleep Foundation*, 3 November 2020, https://bit.ly/3HCL4AW, accessed on 4 January 2022.
89. J.R. Depaulo Jr et al., 'Bipolar II disorder in six sisters', *Journal of Affective Disorders*, Vol. 19, No. 4 (August 1990): 259–64, https://bit.ly/31s14qi, accessed on 4 January 2022.
90. Rajiv Dhand and Harjyot Sohal, 'Good sleep, bad sleep! The role of daytime naps in healthy adults', *Pulmonary Medicine*, Vol. 12, No. 6 (November 2006), https://bit.ly/3qGhDak, accessed on 4 January 2022.
91. Optimize, https://bit.ly/3JSG7p0, accessed on 28 February 2022.
92. Rob Newsom, 'Sleep Debt and Catching up on Sleep', *Sleep Foundation*, 20 September 2021, https://bit.ly/3qPGjgK, accessed on 4 January 2022; Shingo Kitamura et al., 'Estimating individual optimal sleep duration and potential sleep debt', *Scientific Reports*, Vol. 6, article no. 35812 (October 2016), https://go.nature.com/3znE08B, accessed on 4 January 2022.
93. Emma Seppälä, 'Social Connection Boosts Health, Even When You're Isolated', *Psychology Today*, 23 March 2020, https://bit.ly/3sV8KMR, accessed on 4 January 2022.
94. Emma Seppälä, 'Social Connection Boosts Health. Even When You're Isolated', *Emma Seppälä*, 23 March 2020, https://bit.ly/3r4QO03, accessed on 4 January 2022.
95. David Goggins, *Can't Hurt Me: Master Your Mind and Defy the Odds*, Lioncrest Publishing, 2021, p. 188.
96. Jack Canfield, *The Success Principles: How to Get from where You are to where You Want to be*, London: HarperCollins, 2005, p. 35.
97. Ibid. 81.
98. Ibid. 90.

99. Ibid. 98.
100. Gary Keller and Jay Papasan, *The ONE Thing: The Surprisingly Simple Truth Behind Extraordinary Results,* Hodder And Stoughton; 1st edition (2013), p. 149.
101. Phil Stutz and Barry Michels, *The Tools: Transform Your Problems into Courage, Confidence, and Creativity*, Spiegel & Grau, 2012.
102. Brian Tracy, *Eat That Frog!: 21 Great Ways to Stop Procrastinating and Get More Done in Less Time*, Berrett Koehler Publishers, 2018, p. 34
103. Jim Collins, *Good to Great: Why Some Companies Make the Leap... And Others Don't,* Harper Business, 2001.
104. James Clear, *Atomic Habits: Tiny Changes, Remarkable Results,* Penguin Random House, 2018, Chapter 2, p. 41.
105. Adl Jaffe, 'Why Is It So Hard to Change Bad Habits?' *Psychology Today*, 26 March 2019, https://bit.ly/3eUci9S, accessed on 4 January 2022.
106. B.J. Fogg, *Tiny Habits: The Small Things that Change Everything*, Harvest, 2019.
107. James Clear, *Atomic Habits,* Penguin Random House, 2018, Chapter 3, p. 53.
108. Hal Elrod, *The Miracle Morning: The Not-So-Obvious Secret Guaranteed to Transform Your Life Before 8AM,* Hal Elrod International, 2012, pp. 140–41.
109. Jayashri Kulkarni, 'Perimenopausal depression – an under-recognised entity', NCBI, 41(6): 183–85, 2018 December, https://bit.ly/3pmJs83, accessed on 28 February 2022.
110. Zeinab Samadi, Farzaneh Taghian and Mahboubeh Valiani, 'The effects of 8 weeks of regular aerobic exercise on the symptoms of premenstrual syndrome in non-athlete girls', NCBI, 18(1): 14–19, January–February 2013, https://bit.ly/3Htm3aU, accessed on 28 February 2022.